Utility Regulation in Competitive Markets

Utility Regulation in Competitive Markets

Problems and Progress

Edited by

Colin Robinson

Emeritus Professor of Economics, University of Surrey, UK

In Association with the Institute of Economic Affairs and the London Business School

Edward Elgar

Cheltenham, UK • Northampton, MA, USA

Published by
Edward Elgar Publishing Limited
Glensanda House
Montpellier Parade
Cheltenham
Glos GL50 1UA
UK

Edward Elgar Publishing, Inc.
William Pratt House
9 Dewey Court
Northampton
Massachusetts 01060
USA

A catalogue record for this book
is available from the British Library

Library of Congress Cataloguing in Publication Data

Utility regulation in competitive markets : problems and progress / edited by Colin Robinson
    p. cm.
  Papers from the 15th series of the Beesley lectures, held in 2005.
  "In association with the institute of Economic Affairs and the London Business School."
  Includes bibliographical references and index.
  1. Public utilities—Government policy—Congresses. 2. Competition—Government policy—Congresses. I. Robinson, Colin, 1932– II. Institute of Economic Affairs (Great Britain) III. London Business School.

  HD2763.U85 2007
  363.6—dc22

                2006024809

ISBN 978 1 84720 202 4

Printed and bound in Great Britain by MPG Books Ltd, Bodmin, Cornwall

Contents

Figures and tables

FIGURES

TABLES

Notes on the authors

Chris Bolt was appointed by the Secretary of State for Transport as the statutory arbiter for the London Underground public–private partnership agreements from 31 December 2002 for four years. He was appointed as Chairman of the Office of Rail Regulation (ORR) from 5 July 2004, for a five-year term. An economist by training, his career has included senior roles in both the public and private sectors. From 1988 to 1989, he was part of the Department of the Environment (DoE) team responsible for privatising the water industry and establishing its initial regulatory regime. He then joined Ofwat on its establishment, as Head of Economic Regulation. He moved to ORR in a similar role in 1994 and was appointed as Rail Regulator in December 1998. In July 1999, he joined Transco plc, and became Regulation and Corporate Affairs Director. He was appointed to a new role of Group Director, Regulation and Public Policy in Transco's parent company, Lattice Group plc, in November 2001. He left Lattice in October 2002 on completion of its merger with National Grid Group plc.

Richard Feasey is the Public Policy Director for the Vodafone Group, coordinating global public policy and regulatory affairs throughout Vodafone's 28 operating companies including Europe, Africa, the Americas and the Asia-Pacific. Richard has over 10 years experience in international telecommunications in fixed, internet and wireless sectors.

Philip Fletcher was appointed as Chairman of the Water Services Regulation Authority (Ofwat) from its establishment on 1 April 2006. His previous career was based mainly in central government public service, with an emphasis on financial issues. Ofwat is responsible for the economic regulation of the water industry. Its duties are prescribed by statute, and include the setting of price limits to enable a well-managed company to deliver the required services in a sustainable and efficient way, and the protection of consumers, wherever appropriate by promoting competition.

Julian Franks BA (Sheffield) MBA (Columbia) PhD (London) is Professor of Finance and former Director of the Institute of Finance and Accounting at the London Business School. He is widely published and his research focuses on bankruptcy and financial distress, corporate ownership and control, cost of capital and regulation. Recently his work on ownership and control (with Colin Mayer and Stefano Rossi) has won two international prizes. He is associate editor of five finance journals, a member of various advisory boards and consults widely. He served as a member of the DTI–Treasury committee for reviewing the UK's insolvency code and was a member of one of the Company Law Review's committees on corporate governance. He is an advisor to both Ofcom and BAA on regulatory matters and is on a committee of experts advising the education minister on a PFI investment programme for schools. He was an expert witness for the UK government at the World Court at The Hague on an intergovernmental dispute on the matter of landing rights at Heathrow. Recently, he advised (with Professor Brealey) the Office of Constitutional Affairs on the issue of outside equity for law firms and provided advice to a Treasury committee chaired by Paul Myners on a review of the governance of mutuals. He is a non-executive director of OXERA (Oxford Economic Research Associates) and is on the international advisory board of Stern Stewart. He has been visiting professor at the University of California at both Berkeley and Los Angeles.

Dermot Glynn is Chairman of Europe Economics, a specialist microeconomics consultancy. He read politics, philosophy and economics at Balliol. He was a member of the Department of Applied Economics at Cambridge. He served as economic director of the CBI, chief economist at KPMG, and UK managing director of NERA, before founding Europe Economics in 1998.

Thomas W. Hazlett is Professor of Law and Economics at George Mason University, and directs the Information Economy Project at the National Center for Law and Technology. An internationally recognised authority in regulation and public policy, he has published widely in academic journals such as the *Journal of Law and Economics*, the *Journal of Legal Studies*, the *Journal of Financial Economics*, the *Columbia Law Review* and the *University of Pennsylvania Law Review*. He has also written for many popular publications, including the *Wall Street Journal*, *New York Times*, *Barron's*, the *New Republic*, *Forbes* and the *Weekly Standard*. He is currently a columnist in the New Technology Policy Forum of the *Financial Times*. He frequently provides expert testimony to the courts, government agencies, and the US Congress, and has served as a consultant to numerous public and private organisations throughout the world. His book, *Public Policy Toward Cable Television*, written with Matthew L. Spitzer, was published by the MIT Press in 1997. Professor Hazlett has previously held faculty positions at the University of California, Davis, Columbia University, and the Wharton School of the University of Pennsylvania. In 1991–92, he served as Chief Economist of the Federal Communications Commission in Washington, DC.

Paul L. Joskow is Elizabeth and James Killian Professor of Economics and Management at Massachusetts Institute of Technology (MIT) and Director of the MIT Center for Energy and Environmental Policy Research. He received his PhD in economics from Yale University in 1972 and has been on the MIT faculty since then. At MIT he is engaged in teaching and research in the areas of industrial organisation, energy and environmental economics, and government regulation of industry. Professor Joskow has published six books and over 120 papers on topics in these areas. He began doing research and writing on competitive electricity markets over 25 years ago and was co-author (with Richard Schmalensee) of *Markets for Power* published by MIT Press in 1983. He has served on several government advisory committees and on five corporate boards. He is a Fellow of the Econometric Society and a Fellow of the American Academy of Arts and Sciences.

Stephen Littlechild was UK Director General of Electricity Supply from 1989 to 1998. Previously he advised ministers on the regulatory regime for British Telecom and the water industry. In 1983, he proposed the RPI-X approach to price controls which has since been widely adopted. He is now Emeritus Professor, University of Birmingham and Senior Research Associate, Judge Business School, University of Cambridge. Professor Littlechild is also an international consultant on privatisation, competition and regulation.

Philip Lowe was born in Leeds in 1947 and attended schools there and in Reading before going to St. John's College, Oxford where he read politics, philosophy and economics. In 1968, he started his professional career in the manufacturing industry. He also followed the two-year MSc Programme at London Business School. At the end of 1973, he joined the European Commission where he worked in the fields of loans and borrowings, steel restructuring and regional development before becoming Chef de Cabinet of Bruce Millan, European Commissioner for Regional Policies in 1989. In 1991, he was appointed Director of Rural Development in the Directorate General for Agriculture. From 1993 to 1995, he was Director of the Merger Task Force in the Directorate General for Competition. In January 1995, he was seconded to be Chef de Cabinet of Neil Kinnock, European Commissioner for Transport and Transeuropean Networks. In December

1997, he was appointed Director General for Development; he was responsible in particular for the negotiation of the EU–ACP Cotonou Partnership Agreement and the EU–South Africa Trade, Development and Cooperation Agreement. In June 2000, he was appointed Chef de Cabinet to Vice-President Neil Kinnock, who is responsible for the administrative reform of the Commission. From 1 February 2002, he was seconded to the Secretariat General and appointed acting Deputy Secretary General responsible for relations with the Council, until taking up his appointment as Director General of Competition on 1 September 2002. He is fluent in French and German.

John Mogg was appointed the non-executive Chair of Ofgem from 1 October 2003. Sir John was the Director General, Internal Market and Financial Services at the European Commission for the previous 10 years, following a period as the Deputy Director General, Industry, again at the Commission, from 1990 to 1993. He previously held posts in the UK as deputy head, European Secretariat, at the Cabinet Office and principal private secretary to three secretaries of state together with other senior posts at the Department of Trade and Industry. After university he spent 8 years in the private sector.

Chris Nash is Professor of Transport Economics in the Institute for Transport Studies, University of Leeds (ITS), which is one of the leading transport research groups in Great Britain, with the top (5*) rating for the quality of its research. He leads research in the fields of rail economics and transport infrastructure charges, in which fields he has led many projects for both the British government and the European Commission. He was coordinator for the PETS, CAPRI, UNITE and IMPRINT-EUROPE projects, which sought to advance the theory and implementation of marginal social cost-based pricing in transport, including the quantification and valuation of transport externalities, and now leads a further European project in this area, GRACE. Professor Nash has acted as expert advisor to many groups, including the High Level Group on Transport Infrastructure Charges of the EC, the Railways group of European Conference of Ministers of Transport (ECMT), and the Transport and European Union Select Committees of the British Parliament. He was a founder member of Rail Research UK, the British universities' rail research group. His publications number more than a hundred books, contributions to books and journal articles.

Ed Richards was appointed Ofcom Chief Executive in October 2006. He was previously Chief Operating Officer where his responsibilities included strategy, research, consumer policy, business planning, finance, human resources and Ofcom's functions in the Nations and Regions. Prior to Ofcom Ed was senior policy advisor to the prime minister for media, telecoms, the internet and e-govt. Before that he was Controller of Corporate Strategy at the BBC. He also worked in consulting at London Economics Ltd, as an advisor to Gordon Brown MP and began his career as a researcher with Diverse Production Ltd, where he worked on programmes for Channel 4.

Colin Robinson was educated at the University of Manchester, and then worked for 11 years as a business economist, mainly in the oil industry, before being appointed in 1968 to the Chair of Economics at the University of Surrey, where he founded the Department of Economics and is now Emeritus Professor. His research is principally in the energy industries and the regulated utilities. He is the author of 23 books and monographs and over 150 journal papers. He is a Fellow of the Royal Statistical Society, of the Society of Business Economists and of the Institute of Energy. He was named British Institute of Energy Economics 'Economist of the Year' in 1992 and in 1998 received from the International Association for Energy Economics its 'Outstanding Contribution to the Profession and its Literature' award. From 1992 to 2002 he was editorial director of the Institute of Economic Affairs.

Nigel Stapleton was appointed, by the Secretary of State for Trade and Industry, as chairman of the Postal Services Commission (Postcomm) for an initial three-year term in January 2004. He works three days a week for Postcomm. He is also chairman of UNIQ plc, a pan-European convenience food company, and a non-executive director of the London Stock Exchange plc and Reliance Security Group plc. His earlier business career was with Unilever for 18 years and with Reed International, as chairman and chief executive of the leading publishing and information company, Reed Elsevier, for 13 years. Born in 1946, he is a Fellow of the Chartered Institute of Management Accountants, and has a degree in economics from Cambridge University.

David Stubbs is an established postal sector expert. He worked on postal regulation and deregulation in the UK for the postal regulator, Postcomm, where he was a member of the founding interdisciplinary team that devised the agenda for opening the UK postal market. He was then a member of the European Commission's postal unit, where he managed key economic and regulatory studies, and where he represented the EC, as the postal expert in the GATS negotiations and in European and international postal policy matters.

Jorge Vasconcelos is Chairman of ERSE, the regulatory authority of the Portuguese electricity and natural gas industries. He was born in Porto, Portugal in 1959. He graduated from the State University in Porto and holds a degree in power systems engineering. He also holds the degree Doktor-Ingenieur from the Erlangen-Nuremburg University, Germany, where he was a research assistant from 1982 to 1985. He was invited to set up the Portuguese Electricity Regulatory Commission in 1996 and joined ERSE as chairman of the board in 1997. Following his appointment to a second term, the scope of ERSE was enlarged to natural gas. Prior to joining ERSE, Mr Vasconcelos was in charge of programme development for the dynamic simulation of power systems in the electrical networks department of AEG, in Frankfurt, Germany (1986–89). From 1989 to 1996 he was Deputy Secretary-General of EURELECTRIC (European Association of Electricity Industry). He was guest professor at the University of Pavia, Italy (1990–91) and has also lectured at the University of Coimbra since 2001. He is co-founder and has been the first chairman of the council of European Energy Regulators since 2000. He also chairs the European Regulators Group for Electricity and Gas, set up by the European Commission in 2003. He is co-founder and member of the executive committee of the Florence School of Regulation.

Leonard Waverman is Professor and Chair of Economics, as well as Director of the Regulation Initiative and the Global Communications Consortium at the London Business School. Current research is on the growth and productivity impacts of the rollout of telecommunications and computers and was the subject of the 'Economic Focus' section of the *Economist*, March 12, 2005. He is a non-executive Board member of GEMA – the UK's Electricity and Gas Market Authority. He is a member of the Scientific Advisory Board of the German Institute for Economic Research in Berlin (DIW) and a Fellow of Columbia University's Center for Tele-Information. He has recently been appointed to Vodafone's Advisory Board on the Social Importance of Mobile. He was on the advisory committee introducing competition in Ontario's electricity system (1995–96), a part-time board member of the Ontario Energy Board, as well as of the Ontario Telephone Service Commission, and a member of the US National Association of Regulatory Utility Commissioners (NARUC) for 6 years. He has edited the major journal in energy economics – *The Energy Journal* – for 6 years. He is a citizen of Canada and of France and has received the honour of *Chevalier dans l'Ordre des Palmes Academiques* from the French government.

Introduction

Colin Robinson

The fifteenth series of the annual Beesley Lectures, organised by Leonard Waverman of the London Business School and Colin Robinson on behalf of the Institute of Economic Affairs, took place in the autumn of 2005. The chapters in this book are revised versions of the papers given in the series and the comments made by the chairmen. Books based on the series, of which this is the latest, provide a unique insight into the development of utility regulation since its early days.

When the late Professor Michael Beesley founded the series in 1991, the British utilities had only recently been privatised, privatisation was beginning to spread around the world and utility regulators were trying to discover how best to supervise the industries for which they were responsible. Michael saw the series as a forum for discussing the many issues that arise from privatisation and regulation. In particular, he was aware of the dangers of over-regulation and inefficiency in the regulated industries. He was keen to see utility markets liberalised, with 'light touch' regulation confined to cases where there was no alternative. Fifteen years on, we can see that the results of privatisation and regulation have been mixed. In Britain, some utility markets have been liberalised but others are still virtually untouched by competitive forces, being governed instead by comprehensive regulation; a degree of politicisation has returned as, for example, social and environmental obligations have been imposed by government and industry 'policies' have reappeared; regulatory offices have grown in terms of staff and budgets; boards have replaced individual regulators; and regulators and regulated companies have learned how to play the regulatory game. But the underlying issues with which Michael was concerned – how to introduce competition, how to limit the scope of regulation and how to avoid the inefficiencies of traditional regulation – remain the same.

The chapters in this book discuss some specific topics in the context of particular utilities – energy, telecoms, broadcasting, the railways and postal services – and two more general topics – the proper scope of regulation and the cost of capital. They deal with regulatory issues in the United Kingdom, the European Union (EU) and the United States.

Chapter 1 is by Professor Stephen Littlechild who considers recent changes in the British system of utility regulation and also ways of going beyond conventional regulation. He concentrates on electricity markets, though he argues that there are wider lessons. He begins by pointing out the increasing influence of government in the UK electricity market, as demonstrated by the various requirements of the Utilities Act 2000 (including the replacement of individual regulators by commissions) and, particularly, by the government's energy and environmental policy measures. Littlechild then discusses the costs and benefits of electricity liberalisation in different countries, considering both wholesale and retail markets. In general, he argues that the introduction of competition has been a success. In several retail markets, customers are 'now determining for themselves the nature and duration of their contracts for electricity supply'. He concludes the chapter by examining some alternatives to traditional regulation for natural monopolies, such as merchant transmission lines in Australia, user-pays transmission in Argentina and negotiated settlements in North America.

Commenting on Littlechild's chapter, Professor Colin Robinson agrees that there are disadvantages in some of the recent changes to the UK regulatory regime, such as the introduction of authorities in place of individual regulators. He agrees also that government is becoming more intrusive, giving the example of the government's attempts to 'pick winners' in the energy sector, whether renewables, nuclear power or other energy sources, thereby encroaching on the energy regulator's territory. As regards overseas experience of innovative regulatory schemes for networks, Robinson argues that regulation is such an unsatisfactory business, risking arbitrary decision making, that every effort should be made to minimise it. It is therefore well worthwhile to examine ways of avoiding traditional regulation.

In Chapter 2, Professor Thomas Hazlett contends that Ronald Coase, in a 1959 article that preceded his famous paper on social cost and at a time when 'information age' technologies were unknown, discovered a 'simple model of human action' that deals with the spectrum allocation question. Governments should auction licences to the highest bidders, with well-defined rights, thereafter allowing market forces to work. 'Without any knowledge of the innovative advances to come, Coase got the public policy right.' It is time, says Hazlett, to rediscover 'the Coasean vision of property rights to spectrum question'. The state needs to be only a 'judicial back stop', defining rules and acting as referee: the actions of market participants will solve what appear to be intricate coordination problems. Moreover, empirical evidence shows that Coase was correct: bureaucratic allocation of spectrum has led to coordination failures whereas liberalisation has led to Coasean-type efficiencies.

Professor Leonard Waverman comments that Hazlett makes essentially two points. The first is that private property rights in spectrum are a long way from being established. The second is that there is confusion between the ownership of the property and the revenue-generating applications, the access regime: comments about 'commons' are frequently not about what the regime should be but about what the price should be. Scarcity of spectrum may often be a consequence of regulation, as in the case of cell phones in the United States. Suggestions that all voice calls will one day be free are a result of the ownership/access confusion pointed out by Hazlett: revenues have to recoup costs in a competitive market.

For many years, there have been attempts to liberalise energy markets in the EU. In Chapter 3, Jorge Vasconcelos examines to what extent the latest attempts to liberalise have succeeded and analyses the obstacles to progress. Vasconcelos says that EU liberalisation was initially inspired by experience of electricity liberalisation in the United Kingdom but went on to develop its own solutions, most recently under the 'Lisbon Agenda', followed by energy directives approved in 2003. The EU competition authorities have now stepped in to clarify the application of competition law to the energy sector. Proper implementation of the EU legal framework for energy is now urgent: some member states have only recently introduced the necessary amendments to their legislation and in some cases 'transposition of EU directives seems not to be in line at least with the spirit of these directives'.

Philip Lowe, commenting on the paper by Vasconcelos, argues that there are still barriers to entry which prevent there being a single market in energy. He sees many problems in moving to that single market. For example, increased interconnection capacity is required to make markets more competitive and to enhance security of supply. Market concentration is a key issue, especially in gas where the scope for competition is very small: the four major sources of gas imports are 'not competing in any serious sense'. Transparency about access to networks is a 'huge problem'. Moreover, the 'notorious links between gas and oil prices' do not create the right signals for investment and, in electricity, where wholesale markets are marginal, there is little confidence in pricing. The Commission's energy sector enquiry is expected to produce conclusions and remedies that will provide a 'political impetus for change'.

Chapter 4, by Professor Paul Joskow, is a comprehensive discussion of security of supply issues in liberalised electricity and gas markets, taking examples both from the United States and the United Kingdom. The UK's regulatory framework for liberalised electricity and gas networks in his view sets the 'international gold standard'. Joskow sees no inherent conflict between liberalisation and security where liberalisation has followed the right path. However, he sees challenges ahead for the UK's energy regulator in dealing with only partly liberalised European gas markets at a time when expansion of import capability has to be facilitated. He argues also that 'the jury is still out' on the question of whether UK electricity generation capacity will continue to be adequate now that the conditions that led to a big expansion of capacity in the 1990s no longer exist. In the US, the main challenge is to find a speedier and cheaper process for expanding liquefied natural gas (LNG) import capacity.

Commenting on Joskow's chapter, Sir John Mogg agrees that there is no inherent conflict between having liberalised markets and secure supplies, provided there are appropriate market rules, industry structure and regulatory institutions. Political intervention is to be distrusted but in a European context it is difficult to believe that governments will not be involved in electricity generation. Sir John sees some problems in energy trading between the UK and non-liberalised EU markets and fears flows of natural gas through the interconnector might in some circumstances be restricted. He is concerned also about uncertainties caused by the UK planning system.

In Chapter 5, Dermot Glynn and David Stubbs argue that reform in the European postal sector has lagged behind other network industries and that there should now be a move to end these delays. They describe the history of postal regulation in Europe, leading up to the 2002 EU Amended Postal Directive which sets out a timetable for full accomplishment of the internal market in postal services by end 2009. Some member states have been reluctant to introduce reforms and, unusually, reform has been 'primarily driven at European level'. After reviewing the development of European postal markets and some key trends, Glynn and Stubbs examine the case for the 'postal exception', based in the past on the need to maintain a universal postal service. They find the case wanting since the exception is costly in terms of its poor efficiency and innovation incentives and the market distortions it creates. In the UK, Postcomm should reduce the present degree of regulation, which is disproportionate to its objectives, relying on regulation of third-party access prices as the main instrument of price control.

Nigel Stapleton begins by pointing out that postal services regulation varies considerably across the EU. In particular, in the UK Postcomm is independent of government but, in some other EU countries, postal services are regulated by government departments. Stapleton challenges the argument of Glynn and Stubbs that the universal service obligation (USO) in the UK is financed by cross-subsidies. That is only partially true, he says: economies of scale also help to finance the USO and it is important to ensure that they are fully exploited. Stapleton also argues, contrary to Glynn and Stubbs, that the USO is still necessary for people to keep in touch. Retail price control may continue to be required so as to challenge the Royal Mail to improve its efficiency.

Chapter 6, by Chris Bolt, assesses the future of rail regulation, following the rail review and the 2005 Railways Act which, *inter alia*, abolished the Strategic Rail Authority and expanded the responsibilities of the Office of Rail Regulation (ORR). Bolt supports the government's view that there have been real benefits to rail consumers from the partnership between public and private sectors, and that maintaining that partnership is crucial to future success: the government provides strategic direction, the single regulator ensures safety and protects investors and the private sector supplies innovation and customer focus. Bolt sees a key role for ORR in making sure that the government's strategic objectives are achieved. ORR has some short-term challenges – such as integrating economic and safety regulation and monitoring Network Rail's performance – but it also needs to provide a regulatory framework in which rail investment decisions are taken using a long time horizon.

Professor Chris Nash says that the division of responsibilities under the new arrangements is rather puzzling. He would like to see the government declare objectives and set the appraisal framework, leaving specialist agencies to turn this framework into services. However, the Department for Transport (DfT) is going into considerable detail about individual routes and its new responsibility for franchising will also involve it in the detail of what services are to be run. Network Rail's lead responsibility for timetabling also looks odd, given its lack of any direct relationship with passengers or any contractual relationship with the DfT. Another area where Nash foresees problems is in the responsibility given to ORR, if there is a funding shortfall, to determine which services give poor value and where money should be saved.

Professor Julian Franks discusses, in Chapter 7, some issues in estimating the cost of capital. First, he asks whether regulators should worry about leverage. High leverage increases the probability of default, but the risk of default *per se* should not concern a regulator who should worry only if the costs of default are significant. High leverage, combined with a large investment programme, can produce a 'debt overhang problem' which makes raising new equity difficult. Regulators should, *inter alia*, promote low-cost means of transferring licences in the event of failures. Second, Franks questions whether it is wise to rely solely on the capital asset pricing model (CAPM) when estimating the cost of capital: most finance scholars would want to use another method, at least as a cross-check. Third, Franks sets out the case for using different costs of capital for different parts of a company's business. Finally, he makes a proposal for approaching a consensus on cost of capital estimation by forming a committee of economists that would review the evidence and produce regular estimates.

Philip Fletcher agrees that regulators should not rely on the CAPM, or any single approach, to estimating the cost of capital. Faced with the need to finance a large water investment programme, Fletcher says that Ofwat used a pragmatic approach, providing the companies with a 'financeability element', based on a basket of financial ratios, in addition to the estimated costs of capital. Ofwat's aim was to avoid a deterioration in balance sheets. The financeability element may become unnecessary in future as confidence grows in the companies' performance and the regulator's approach. Also, if the current pattern of low-cost debt becomes firmly established, that too will help to hold down the cost of capital. Fletcher points out also that provision exists for dealing with company failures.

The final chapter, by Ed Richards, is about Ofcom's strategic approach to regulation, covering a wide range of its economic regulatory activities. Richards begins with Ofcom's general approach to regulation in a fast-changing industry where it is important to weigh the prospective benefits of regulation against the options of doing nothing or doing less. In fixed link telecommunications, where there is a vertically integrated incumbent, Ofcom is attempting to establish equality of access for competitors, *inter alia*, by a new ring-fenced division of BT which controls the bottleneck asset. In broadcasting, Richards argues that there is still a case for public service broadcasting though it rests more on 'broader citizenship benefits' than on traditional market failures. As regards spectrum, Ofcom will be putting market-based measures at the centre of the allocation process. Richards summarises Ofcom's approach in all these areas as making markets more competitive, reducing barriers to entry and focusing regulation on the 'root causes' of bottleneck power.

In his comments, Richard Feasey says that Ofcom has high-quality management and that there is now a welcome degree of distance between regulator and regulatees. He is uncertain, however, about whether Ofcom's approach to regulating BT's copper assets is correct and he raises the question of whether sufficient prominence is given to the role that cable companies could play in competitive broadband. Ofcom, he suggests, has to consider to what extent it should act to promote entry and to what extent market concentration is necessary to permit infrastructure investments to be made. Ofcom should do more to make its thoughts known internationally and it should also be concerned with making the consumer's voice heard.

1. Beyond regulation

Stephen Littlechild

INTRODUCTION

This is a welcome opportunity to revisit and then extend some of the themes that I explored in my Beesley lecture in October 2001.[1] I start with competition and regulation but then I want to go beyond that, to look at some possible new ways of reducing regulation of the monopoly sectors of the utility industries.

The first part of this chapter looks briefly at the evolution of what the previous lecture called 'the standard model' of electricity reform, and in particular the role of government. The second part looks at the development of competitive markets in the electricity sector, both wholesale and retail, and the role of regulation there. The third and final part of the chapter looks at alternatives or complements to traditional regulation of electricity transmission and distribution networks. My title 'Beyond regulation' is not intended to suggest that in future there is no need for regulation, but rather to suggest that we should look beyond its presently accepted role.

I shall illustrate the chapter with empirical material, initially from the UK but also from the US including California and Florida, the Nordic countries, Australia and Argentina. The arguments and illustrations are taken mainly from my own research over the last few years.[2] Although the examples are limited to the electricity sector, there is scope for applying several of the suggested regulatory initiatives to the utility sector generally.

PART I: THE EVOLUTION OF THE STANDARD MODEL

COMPETITION AND REGULATION

The UK approach to regulating the privatised utilities – perhaps I should say the original UK approach – might be summed up in the phrases: competition where possible, regulation where not. Competition was seen as responding to the wishes of customers themselves, as encouraging efficient production and investment, as stimulating product differentiation and innovation, and as passing on these benefits to customers.

Regulation was more problematic. Conventionally, regulation was held to protect customers from monopoly. But economists had increasingly come to see it as protecting utilities rather than customers, as costly and intrusive, as reducing the incentives to efficiency and providing the opportunity to 'gold-plate', as distorting outputs away from what customers themselves wanted towards what regulators wanted, and as likely to discourage or delay change and innovation. The UK therefore sought to provide a new kind of regulation, one that would improve the incentives to efficiency in the monopoly sectors and encourage innovation. Regulation was none the less seen as a last resort, appropriate only where the other and better method of competition was unlikely to be applicable.

Previously, I suggested the concept of a 'standard model'. Broadly speaking, this acknowledged that networks would continue to be monopolies that would need regulation. In contrast, goods and services supplied over those networks could be subject to competition and would not need the same degree of intensive sector regulation. Some restructuring was typically required to separate these monopoly and competitive elements of an industry, and to secure sufficiently competitive markets from the beginning.

I suggested that this standard model had increasingly been adopted worldwide, but that two separate trends were then identifiable. There were moves to extend and refine the standard model where it was in course of implementation. At the same time, however, there was some reaction against it, especially following the events in California. There were now more proposals for government to supplement and influence regulation, or even to replace market and regulatory outcomes by its own decisions.

Moves to extend the model to additional countries have since largely come to a halt. For example, I noted that the model was then under active consideration in several countries including Mexico, the Philippines, India and Thailand. There have been few if any subsequent developments there, at least on privatisation and competition. Regulatory bodies have indeed been set up, but they do not yet have much of a private or competitive market to regulate. The World Bank, too, is now more cautious about privatisation and is rethinking its stance.

However, in those countries that had substantially accepted the standard model there has been continued implementation and refinement. Examples here would include the various separation and retail market directives in the EU, although there has been disappointingly little appetite for dealing with market power in national energy markets. Residential retail markets have opened in Texas and some states of Australia. I noted previously that two countries – Germany and New Zealand – had resisted sector regulation as being unnecessary and inappropriate, but that both countries were running into difficulties.[3] Since then, they have both established sector regulators.

To some extent, the view that competitive sectors of the industry did not need regulation was an oversimplification. We now see more clearly than before that introducing and monitoring competition can itself require substantial regulatory effort. That must be at least part of the explanation for the fivefold increase in the cost of UK electricity and gas regulation in the period up until 2001. Admittedly the cost has reduced somewhat since then and Ofgem has recently imposed an RPI-X price cap on itself.

THE INCREASING ROLE OF GOVERNMENT

There is also further evidence of government supplementing or replacing the role of regulation. Governments do not always want the outcome of a competitive or regulated market, and sometimes prefer to take their own decisions. UK policy illustrates this.

The Utilities Act 2000 replaced the individual gas and electricity regulators by a commission (the Gas and Electricity Markets Authority: GEMA), which at present has 12 members (of which seven are non-executives). The authority must publish its forward work programme, and before that its draft forward work programme, and consider representations and objections to it. These steps might be expected to reduce the speed of regulatory decision making and to discourage innovation.

The act also increased the influence of government. For example, it provided that the secretary of state shall issue guidance on social and environmental issues in relation to electricity, to which the authority must have regard. It abolished the electricity consumer committees appointed by the director general, and substituted a new council with members appointed by the secretary of state. The secretary of state was given extensive new powers: to impose energy efficiency and renewable energy obligations on suppliers, to modify licences where he considers it expedient to implement new trading arrangements, and to require transmission and distribution companies and suppliers to adjust their charges to help disadvantaged groups of electricity customers.[4]

These powers have been exercised and they have not been negligible. Energy efficiency obligations on suppliers imposed by the regulator originally cost £1 per year per electricity customer. The latest proposals by the government will cost about £8 per energy customer per year.

The government is also increasing the requirements on suppliers to source a specified percentage of their electricity from renewable sources.

The cost per customer of the renewables obligation has been calculated at over £400 million in 2003/04.[5] It is likely to increase significantly over time, as the severity of the obligation increases.[6] The National Audit Office has estimated that the cost of these subsidies will rise to £6.5 billion (cumulative) by 2010 and to £12.5 billion by 2015.[7]

A recent seminar invitation began as follows:

> Energy policy is one of the most important challenges facing Labour in its third term – with major issues including meeting the ambitious targets in the energy white paper to reduce carbon dioxide emissions, with important implications for the public debates and policy agenda around both renewables and the future of nuclear power; the security of the energy supply; affordability and social justice concerns with rising prices; and how to effectively improve energy efficiency among both business and domestic consumers.
>
> The new Energy Minister will lead this high-level seminar discussion and address how the government will deal with these policy and political challenges: of environmental sustainability, security and affordability.[8]

Energy policy, emissions, renewables, nuclear power, security of supply, affordability and social justice, rising prices and energy efficiency – is it not remarkable that all these important issues concerning the future of the industry are now the responsibility of the government rather than the market or the regulator? And also remarkable that responsibility for these important long-term issues is best discharged by appointing seven different energy ministers in eight years – including four in the last 18 months?

This is not quite what I had in mind in arguing for reducing the role of regulation. I am interested in ways of reducing regulation that transfer important decisions to customers and other market participants rather than to government.

PART II: THE DEVELOPMENT OF COMPETITIVE ELECTRICITY MARKETS

WHOLESALE MARKETS: THE GAINS FROM PRIVATISATION

The introduction of privatisation, deregulation and competition into electricity markets seems to have produced both gains and pains worldwide. I shall look in turn at the wholesale and retail sectors.

Increasingly, economists are documenting and quantifying the productivity gains in the wholesale markets.[9] An important and innovative early calculation, which has been much copied, was by David Newbery and

Michael Pollitt at Cambridge.[10] They calculated that privatising the Central Electricity Generating Board (CEGB) led to operating cost savings and reduced costs of capital expenditure with a net present value of about £9 billion.

Geoff Horton and I have been looking again at this calculation. We make two modifications. First, we note that generation costs have continued to reduce since the time of their study. Second, we argue that, in the absence of privatisation, the CEGB would have engaged in a more extensive and costly programme of building coal and nuclear plant than the study assumed. Our preliminary calculations, which are still in progress, suggest that the benefits of privatisation were of the order of twice what Newbery and Pollitt calculate. This confirms their conclusion that privatisation was beneficial in aggregate.

But who gets these benefits? Have prices to consumers gone down to reflect these cost savings, or have they gone up? There have been concerns about such issues in newly liberalised electricity markets all around the world. Newbery and Pollitt concluded that such concerns were well founded: they found that nearly all the benefits had gone to producers, and virtually none to customers.

Again, we have made two modifications. First, we note that generation prices as well as generation costs have come down since the time of their study. Second, we argue that, in the absence of privatisation, prices to customers would not have stayed constant or reduced, but would have increased in line with evolving Treasury policy on the required rate of return in nationalised industries. In consequence, our preliminary estimate is that, relative to this revised counterfactual, the gains were shared about equally between producers and consumers. So there is reason to be confident about the distribution, as well as the magnitude, of the benefits of restructuring, privatising and liberalising the UK generation market.[11]

GENERATION MARKET POWER IN THE US

There have been concerns about price levels in several US wholesale electricity markets, not least in California but not only there. Previously I mentioned the debate between economists as to whether market power had been exercised, and questioned how far it was possible for a regulator or market monitor to give a definitive view on this, particularly in a short timescale. I also expressed concern about using a benchmark based on marginal cost.

Some economists sought to quantify the extent of market power in terms of the Lerner index, that is, by measuring the extent to which price exceeds marginal system cost in each hour.[12] They found significant departures from competitive pricing in California during the summer months from 1998 to 2000, including prices nearly 50 per cent above this benchmark for most of 2000. New England had prices about 17 per cent above the benchmark during most of 1999 and 2000. The PJM (Pennsylvania–New Jersey–Maryland) was 'virtually perfectly competitive' during the early part of 2000 but had prices averaging about 33 per cent above the benchmark in the later part of 1999. On this basis the authors concluded that market power was being exercised to some extent most of the time. The question was whether it was worth doing anything about it.

If market power is claimed to exist, consumers and the media are not likely to be satisfied with an argument that it is not worth doing anything about it. Not surprisingly, concerns about generation market power have led to a variety of bidding price caps in these markets, of varying degrees of severity.

There is, however, a longstanding question as to whether marginal cost is the right benchmark to use.[13] Generators with existing plant need to do more than simply cover their marginal operating costs. If they are not to close plant and exit the industry, they need to cover also their additional costs of staying on the system (for example, the costs of rent, rates and maintenance). If generators are to enter with new plant to meet increasing demand, then over a period of time, at least, they need to cover the capital cost of building new plant. Arguably, only if generators persistently secure prices that exceed this long-run new entry cost should there be a significant concern about market power.

Seabron Adamson, Richard Green and I have recently tried to calculate how prices in the US wholesale markets compare against these exit and entry criteria. Our results are again still preliminary. However, they suggest that wholesale prices received by thermal plants barely covered their costs of staying on the system, at least at the margin. These prices made only very modest contributions to covering the capital costs of building new plant, and at the margin were not sufficient to do so.

It is true that, if the prices obtaining in California in summer 2000 had continued over the lifetime of a plant, they would have been higher than needed to reward that plant for entering the system. But those prices did not obtain for more than a few months. At other times prices have been very much lower. Over the whole period for which we have data, covering nearly five years, prices in California were no more than the average needed to remunerate new entry. Once again, this suggests that wholesale markets and generator market power are not the problems that some have feared. In fact, a more serious concern is that regulation may be holding wholesale prices at an unreasonably low level.[14]

RETAIL COMPETITION IN THE UK

Competition at the retail level has had a mixed reception. Competition for industrial and commercial customers has been eminently successful, and is now taken for granted. I therefore want to focus on retail competition at the residential level, where the policy has often been questioned.

The EU has decided to require all member countries to open their residential markets by 2007, but several other countries or jurisdictions have decided against it. Several US states tried it, but many without success. As I noted previously, California even granted customers the right to choose a supplier then withdrew that right, not because retail competition had failed, but because the Public Utility Commission decided to impose on all customers the cost of expensive contracts entered into by the state government.

There is no doubt that UK residential customers have taken advantage of the opportunity to switch supplier. The net switching rate from incumbent to non-incumbent suppliers was a remarkably stable 1 per cent of customers per month (11 per cent per year) for the first three years after the market opened during 1998/99. By 2002 some 34 per cent of residential customers were with a supplier other than their local incumbent.

Not surprisingly, the switching has increasingly been between entrants themselves, and in some cases back to the incumbents, as well as away from incumbents. But remarkably, switching still continues at a significant rate. In 2004/05 about 16 per cent of all electricity customers switched supplier. This led to a shift of nearly 3 per cent of customers away from incumbents, which actually represents about 5 per cent of the customers remaining with incumbent suppliers. The proportion of customers with a non-incumbent supplier has now risen to 43 per cent, and continues to increase over time. At this rate, by about the end of next year (2006) non-incumbents will supply more residential customers than incumbents will.

There has been a concern that artificially high switching rates can be induced by setting artificially high price caps on incumbents that provide an excessive margin for competitors. However, an implication of the above figures is that during 2004/05 a net 13 per cent of UK customers moved between non-incumbents, representing nearly 23 per cent of their customers. These customers were evidently attracted by better offers *within* the competitive non-incumbent market, quite independently of the level of the previous price cap on incumbents (which has anyway now been abolished).

RETAIL COMPETITION WORLDWIDE

Many other countries have now opened their residential markets. Table 1.1 shows that some of them exhibit significant switching, but others do not.[15]

Of those residential markets that opened about six years ago, in the period from 1998 to 2000, the proportions of residential customers with non-incumbent suppliers are now 43 per cent in UK, 29 per cent in Sweden and 24 per cent in Norway, but only about 11 per cent in Finland[16] and 5 per cent in Germany; 26 per cent in New Zealand[17] but seldom over 7 per cent in North America. In a few US states some high proportions were observed initially,[18] but the territories where switching occurred contained less than 40 per cent of the total residential customers in the state.[19]

Of those residential markets that opened in January 2002, the proportions are already 24 per cent in Texas and 33 per cent in Victoria[20] though only 11 per cent in New South Wales.[21] In Ontario, which opened in May 2002, 20 per cent of customers had signed with another supplier by the day the market opened, but within a few months the market had disappeared.[22]

With the exception of most North American markets, the proportions of customers switching are growing steadily over time; in North America (apart from Texas) they are generally static or declining.

POSSIBLE OBSTACLES TO RETAIL COMPETITION

It is evidently not impossible for a substantial proportion of residential customers to switch supplier within a short period: nearly a quarter within a few months in Ohio and up to 40 per cent within a couple of years in a few other areas of the US. But these seem to have been exceptional. It is now apparent that it generally takes time for residential customers (and their suppliers) to adapt to new markets. For the first few years, at least, a net switching rate in the range 5 to 10 per cent per year might be considered successful. A rate less than 2 or 3 per cent a year suggests that certain obstacles must be preventing the development of a competitive retail market.

What might these obstacles be? What distinguishes the more successful markets from others? Many factors no doubt have some adverse impact. These include regulatory failures to distinguish clearly between distribution, wholesale and retail activities; to allocate regulated costs appropriately; and to make adequate provision for non-discriminatory access to transmission and distribution networks. In some countries there has been lagged response by public and municipal enterprises to increasing wholesale market prices; and unwillingness of municipal enterprises to compete

Table 1.1 *Residential customer switching in international electricity markets*

Market	Proportion (%) of residential customers served by non-incumbent supplier	
	After approx. 3 years	After 5–6 years
Markets opened 1998–2000		
UK	34	43
Sweden	18	29
Norway	15	24
Finland	5	11
Germany	4	5
New Zealand	18?	26
Alberta	2	7
California	2	1
Maine		
MPS	36	7
BHE & CMP	0	0
Maryland		
Potomac Electric	15	6
Other utilities (3)	0	0
Massachusetts	3	3
New Jersey	0	0
New York	4	6
Ohio		
First Energy (3)	40	45
Cincinnati	2	3
Other utilities (4)	0	0
Pennsylvania		
Duquesne Light	35	23
PECO Energy	18	2
Other utilities (4)	1–7	1
Markets opened January 2002		
Texas	19 (now 24)	
Ontario (May 2002)	23 (in September 2002, but now 0)	
New South Wales	9 (now 11)	
Victoria	24 (now 33)	

Sources: Data or estimates mainly based on publications of regulatory offices in these countries, plus some correspondence with these offices and references below.

for customers outside their areas. There may be some obstacles to new entry, particularly of smaller new entrant suppliers.[23]

In a few cases, US commissions have made novel and effective use of retail market opening. Ohio has established a process of 'governmental aggregation'.[24] Under this process, 'more than 170 counties, cities, villages and townships passed ballot issues and were certified by the Public Utility Commission of Ohio to allow local units of government to represent communities' interests in the competitive electricity market'. The largest of these governmental aggregators 'represents more than 350,000 residential customers in eight counties and 112 communities in North East Ohio'. The municipal aggregation programme now accounts for 95 per cent of the residential customer switching in Ohio (2005 report, p. 5).

A few other US jurisdictions have required incumbents to put their requirements out to competitive tender. Switching has been negligible because the prices achieved have in some ways been difficult for retail competitors to beat. I return to this method shortly.

An important and widespread limiting factor on retail competition has been the actions of governments and/or regulators in demanding initial price cuts and/or imposing unrealistically tight price controls. Their aim may have been to protect customers, but their actions have had the effect of distorting or restricting the development of retail competition.

In the Nordic countries and New Zealand there never were retail price controls in the first place. In the UK and Texas the price caps consciously allowed scope for competition, and in the UK they were removed after four years. Victoria has maintained price controls, but they are evidently not unduly severe. In New South Wales, by contrast, the regulator has consciously kept many prices to small customers below cost, recognising that this will discourage competition.[25] The paucity, decline or even absence of retail competition in many US states, where often-unrealistic price controls still apply, is apparent from the table.[26]

Transitional price caps seemed a sensible means of protecting UK residential customers when the market first opened. They ensured that the incumbent suppliers (the Regional Electricity Companies (RECs)) passed on to customers the significant reductions in wholesale prices deriving from the reductions in coal purchasing costs as the monopoly franchise period came to an end. They also precluded any undesirable price increase following the opening of the market by incorporating provision for the RECs to buy wholesale hedging contracts for the next two years. Some other jurisdictions seem to have imposed price reductions when the market opened without a corresponding cost justification, or seem not to have made allowance for wholesale contracts in setting retail price controls.

However, even in the UK it proved more difficult to remove the price caps than might have been expected. Other countries have so far found it impossible. This raises the question whether the price caps were necessary and desirable in the UK. On reflection, I suspect that the RECs would have publicly committed to pass on the initial cost reductions and not to increase their prices for a specified period of time. Formal price caps embodied in the licences were not really needed. In retrospect it would probably have been preferable not to introduce them in the first place.

NON-PRICE COMPETITION

It has rightly been said that customer switching is not the only measure of retail competition or of benefits to customers. Price cuts are another manifestation. However, some have questioned the price cuts offered as merely reflecting the level of prices embodied in the price caps. It is therefore worth noting that other evidence of competition is available.

New products and services are constantly emerging. In the UK this includes bundled offers notably dual fuel, credits in the form of airmiles, loyalty points with specific retailers or shopping cards (Nectar), contributions to charities and deserving customer groups, green tariffs, energy efficiency packages, insurance cover, discounts for self-reading meters, the Staywarm scheme offering unmetered electricity for a fixed monthly fee, discounts for various prepayment meter schemes, discounts for a range of home services and financial products, tariffs with no standing charges, single billing for up to six utility and other services, and no doubt many others.[27]

COMPETITION AND CONTRACTS IN THE NORDIC ELECTRICITY MARKETS[28]

One of the most interesting forms of competition is in the types of contract offered to customers. This is best illustrated in the Nordic electricity markets. The residential sectors of these markets were effectively opened to competition in 1998/99.[29] There has been active switching of suppliers in these markets, particularly in Norway and Sweden, as noted above. But arguably more important than this has been the extent to which customers have been able to choose between a variety of different contract types, whether or not they have changed supplier.

In the Nordic countries, as in the UK and elsewhere, incumbent suppliers have traditionally set a tariff that they can change at a few weeks' notice. In the past they typically reviewed and perhaps changed that tariff annually.

Nowadays, as the market has become more competitive, Nordic suppliers have begun to change their standard tariff more than once a year. The largest supplier in Sweden has changed its tariffs twice a year on average since the market opened, and four times in 2004/05. In Norway the main suppliers have been changing their standard tariffs on average at least once a month since 2001.

However, the tariff is not the only or even the most important means of competition nowadays. All suppliers including incumbents now offer fixed-price contracts for fixed periods of time. This period is generally for one to three years, although contracts as short as three months and as long as five years have been offered. At any time, many such contracts are available in the market. In Sweden in June 2005, the consumer website listed about 250 fixed-price offers from about 70 suppliers. In Norway and Finland about 20 per cent of residential customers have chosen such contracts, and in Sweden about 46 per cent.

Another form of contract is one directly linked to the spot price (on a daily basis rather than hourly), with an agreed fixed fee for administrative expenses. In Sweden over 40 spot-price contracts are on offer. About 4 per cent of Swedish residential customers have chosen such a contract; in Norway the proportion is about 16 per cent.

In total, then, over a third of residential customers in Norway have actively chosen contractual alternatives – fixed or spot prices – in preference to the standard tariffs. In Sweden the proportion is about half.

The Australian markets are also moving rapidly to contracts. In Victoria, 44 per cent of small customers have chosen contractual terms (with incumbents or new suppliers) and in South Australia, open for less than three years, the proportion is already 42 per cent. Even in New South Wales, where below-cost-price controls have severely limited competition, 16 per cent of customers have chosen a new contract. Typically, the contracts are for 2–3 years and involve a specified discount off the regulated price.[30] Admittedly, contracts in Australian markets do not seem to be associated with fixed- or spot-price offers. In Ontario, by contrast, 23 per cent of customers signed up for fixed-price contracts (some up to five years' duration) within four months of market opening. The competitive contracts in Alberta also seem to be for a fixed price.

COMPETITION AND CONTRACTS IN THE UK MARKET

All this is in contrast to the UK, where there has been relatively little development of contracts other than the standard variable tariff. Two major

suppliers, accounting for about 30 per cent of the market, have given voluntary undertakings not to increase their prices until January 2006. But
their existing customers, while perhaps welcoming these undertakings, did
not actively choose them. The other four major UK suppliers have offered
fixed-price fixed-term contracts from time to time, but only sporadically
and not more than one at any time. I estimate that under 10 per cent of UK
residential customers have actively chosen such an arrangement.

The situation is still evolving.[31] Some fixed-price contracts are gradually
emerging. But the UK has nothing like the Nordic range of alternative contract forms available at different prices.

In the UK, the so-called '28 day rule', which I plead guilty to having introduced when the market first opened, requires that all residential customers
must be able to change supplier at 28 days' notice. I have argued elsewhere
that this has discouraged innovation in the UK.[32] The rule was originally
intended to protect inexperienced customers, possibly faced with little choice
when the market first opened, from entering into a long-term contract that
they might subsequently regret. But customers are evidently now experienced and have a range of choices available, and the rule seems to be limiting the emergence of more such choices. In retrospect, the rule seems to have
distorted and restricted retail competition for UK domestic customers.

This may not have been so serious during a period when energy prices
were generally falling. But prices have now risen considerably and most customers were not protected against this. It is evident that many customers
would now like to freeze their energy prices for a period of time of their
choice. The 28 day rule has not precluded fixed-price contracts entirely, but
it prohibits termination fees for contracts of under one year and introduces
regulatory uncertainty about allowable fees for longer ones. If the rule dis-
courages suppliers from exploring and offering the kinds of contracts that
customers generally prefer, then abolishing it would make a useful contribution to promoting retail competition and the welfare of customers.

IS RETAIL COMPETITION WORTHWHILE? WHAT IS THE ALTERNATIVE?

Some commentators question whether retail competition is worthwhile at
the domestic (residential) level.[33] Others implicitly assume that retail competition is not feasible for economic or political reasons, and agonise over
the problems caused by its absence.[34] As with all such policy choices, before
rejecting retail competition it is necessary to identify the alternatives and
consider how they would work in practice. I dealt with some of these
possibilities previously, but let me briefly look at them again.[35]

   The regulator might be required to approve the purchases of the incumbent monopoly suppliers. That was the situation in the UK for eight years, where the RECs had an economic purchasing obligation. It was very unsatisfactory. The regulator faces an actual or proposed portfolio of wholesale energy purchases, perhaps covering a year or several years, perhaps with tens or hundreds of components. No one has yet explained satisfactorily how the regulator should go about evaluating these and ensuring that this is the most economic portfolio of purchases that could reasonably be expected.

   One suggestion is that contract costs of one utility should be benchmarked against those of other utilities. Comparison is always useful, but this seems to underestimate the difficulty of making proper comparisons between utilities with different customer bases and load shapes, subject to different climates and other factors. It also glosses over the problems of cost allocation between different customer groups, and the possible incentives to collusion. These difficulties and problems are particularly acute where one or a few vertically integrated suppliers dominate the market. For example, what is the appropriate benchmark comparator for Electricité de France (EdF) in France or Enel in Italy?

   Another suggestion is that each distribution company's supply (or default supply) requirements should be put out to tender. As noted, this has in fact been done in some states in the US. It has been rather successful in some respects. There is now evidence from New Jersey, Maine and elsewhere that this process can yield a very competitive price for the specified tender.[36]

   However, the regulator still has to administer or at least approve the tendering process. The regulator has to decide what quantities of wholesale supply should be purchased and when and for what period ahead. The regulator has to decide how the outcome is to be translated into prices for customers. (Should customers be given a fixed price for a fixed period, and if so how long, or should the price vary over time, or should customers be offered a choice of terms?) The regulator may also have to consider whether the results of an auction are less attractive than some alternative process. There is also the question of possible impact on the wholesale market and the development of competition in generation.

   It is interesting to see how the US regulators have dealt with these issues. In New Jersey, the decision was to tender for one year's requirements in the initial auction. This raised a concern about buying the power all at once.[37] It was also noted that more products would increase complexity, raise barriers to entry and reduce the number of bidders. Multi-year tranches would have slowed down the auction and increased risk.[38] In Maine's 2004 purchase programme, the Commission debated the merits of a 6-month versus 1-year tranche: the former would better reflect wholesale spot-market prices but the latter would give better protection to suppliers and customers. For the first two tenders in 2004, the Public Utilities Commission decided on 6-month tranches. For the next year, however, it called for bids on a wide range of bases (including up to five years ahead), then decided on a one-year tranche plus a proportion of the requirements for the second and third years.[39] In Ohio the Public Utilities Commission rejected the bids from the auction held in December 2004 and instead agreed to let the incumbent implement its proposed rate plan for the next three years, 'drawing a rebuke from the state's utility watchdog'.[40]

It is apparent that the regulator has to make many judgements here, especially about customer preferences and future market conditions. Is the regulator better placed than consumers to say what they prefer, or more adept than suppliers at judging when to buy short or long term in the market? Economists generally regard the market process as an important device for discovering the preferences of customers and identifying those organisations and individuals who can best judge market conditions. It encourages those suppliers that are good at this and weeds out those that are not. Is this not true in the electricity sector too?

Will regulatory decisions on purchasing and supply have an impact on industry structure and on wholesale competition? There was concern about this in New Jersey. Looking further ahead, will a concentration on short-term contracts have an impact on new entry in generation, where long-term contracts are often said to be helpful? More generally, if the competitive retail market is not part of the process of discovering and bringing about whatever market structure is most conducive to efficiency, competition and responsiveness to change, then the regulator will need to perform this task. Are the regulators ready for this?

This leads to the final question, whether a regulatory body in charge of a utility's purchasing policy will conscientiously follow the kind of policy that the proponents advocate. Public choice theory and international experience suggest that there may be some overoptimism here. Regulators are typically required to have regard to many considerations apart from the lowest price for consumers. And it would be surprising if federal and state governments did not have an influence on the process.

There is in fact considerable evidence worldwide as to how regulatory bodies and governments have operated in such situations. The California state government and regulators substituted their own views on purchasing, prohibited retail competition, and imposed tens of billions of dollars of excess costs on California residential consumers and taxpayers. This was not the first time that residential customers in California had had to pay a high price for regulatory policies on purchasing.[41] In the UK, retail competition brought savings to residential customers of some £400 million a year, by freeing these customers from the obligation to support the UK coal industry. These are perhaps dramatic examples, but many others could no doubt be cited.[42]

Some fundamental questions thus need to be answered if regulation is to be a credible long-term alternative to retail competition. For the most part, these questions have not yet been addressed. Meanwhile, several markets have shown that retail competition does not need ongoing regulation. These markets are characterised by active competition between suppliers, by an increasing variety of services and terms available, and by greater flexibility than in the regulated markets. Customers in these markets, with differing hopes and fears about future energy prices, no longer have to accept the terms decided by governments, regulators or monopoly incumbents. These customers are now determining for themselves the nature and duration of their contracts for electricity supply.

PART III: BEYOND TRADITIONAL REGULATION

MERCHANT TRANSMISSION VERSUS REGULATED TRANSMISSION

Let us now go beyond competitive markets to sectors that have hitherto been held to be monopolies needing regulation. The first example is high voltage electricity transmission.

It was conventionally assumed that transmission companies could not economically compete with each other to build transmission lines. Hence, the regulator would either approve or determine what new lines are built or what reinforcements are made, and similarly would approve or determine the prices to be charged for the use of such investments.

There have been suggestions that it would, instead, be possible to leave the building of transmission lines to private investors competing with each other. They would derive their revenues from the differences in value of the electricity at either end of the line. Under certain conditions the outcome would be efficient or optimal. That is, so-called 'merchant transmission lines' would be built when and where expansion or reinforcement was needed, and built at least cost, without the need for traditional regulation.

Against this, it was argued that the specified conditions for such an efficient outcome were in practice unlikely to be met. Key requirements were some form of nodal pricing together with an adequate set of transmission property rights. But this type of pricing often did not exist or the property rights would be difficult or costly to define and enforce. Merchant transmission companies would have market power, or at least would not find it profitable to invest as much or as early as would be optimal. The implication seemed to be that merchant investment was vulnerable to market failure – it would build 'too little, too late' – and that regulated transmission was necessary after all.

If the case for merchant transmission depended on meeting these various theoretical assumptions, and if the case for regulated transmission depended on identifying a market failure with merchant investment, then regulated transmission would be superior to merchant transmission. But neither of these initial postulates is true. There is a possibility – indeed probability – of regulatory failure just as much as of market failure. A substantial economic literature has documented the likelihood of various inefficiencies due to regulation, notably 'gold-plating'.[43] This could take the form of excessive and premature investment in capacity. Consequently, the relevant question is whether in practice, and under what circumstances, merchant transmission or regulated transmission is less vulnerable to these various inefficiencies. Put simply, which is less serious: market failure or regulatory failure?

MERCHANT AND REGULATED INTERCONNECTORS IN AUSTRALIA

Experience in Australia provides an opportunity to explore some of these ideas.[44] During the 1990s, two transmission lines were built on a merchant basis, one to Queensland and one to South Australia. At about the same time, two other transmission lines were proposed on a regulated basis over similar routes, and one was actually built. All these lines were interconnectors between neighbouring electricity regions.

In retrospect it seems that all the lines overestimated the size of the future price differentials between the regions that they connected. Primarily, they underestimated the speed and extent to which other merchant investors built new generation plant in the hitherto high-priced regions (Queensland and South Australia), and thereby reduced the differentials that previously obtained.

This meant that, far from having significant power over the market, the merchant lines were very vulnerable to the market. Far from merchant transmission capacity being too little and too late, it was too much and too soon. But the merchant investors soon recognised the market realities and cut their losses.

The regulated interconnectors were no more immune to such misjudgements of future market conditions. In fact their record was worse. The regulatory line to Queensland was more than five times the capacity of the

merchant line, and was correspondingly more uneconomic. The proponents of the regulated line to South Australia pressed on regardless of the
accumulating evidence that the already-built merchant line made the additional and duplicate capacity entirely superfluous. This second regulated
line was eventually halted only by an adverse judgment of the Victoria
Supreme Court.

What are the lessons to draw from this experience? In this particular
instance, regulated transmission comes out somewhat worse than merchant transmission. The property rights and market power problems
conventionally associated with merchant transmission turned out to be
negligible or non-existent. In contrast, the gold-plating and overexpan-
sion problems conventionally associated with regulated investment
turned out to be very significant. And while both groups made forecasting errors, investors picked up the excess cost of the two merchant lines
but consumers are still paying the excess cost of the regulated line to
Queensland.

Whether these experiences of interconnectors between neighbouring
regions would be equally applicable to transmission investment within electricity regions is for further consideration. However, analyses of transmission policy need to incorporate explicitly both market and regulatory
failure, to evaluate the likely extent of each, and to take steps to minimise
the extent of this. Analyses also need to recognise that a significant part of
transmission investment seems to be driven by considerations other than
economic efficiency. It would seem more sensible to recognise and quantify
any 'non-economic' considerations, and to enable both merchant and regulated investments to qualify for any associated remuneration. This seems
to have been an early aim of the Australian regulatory framework but it has
remained undeveloped.

USER-PAYS TRANSMISSION ARRANGEMENTS IN ARGENTINA

The next example is an alternative to both regulated and merchant transmission. In 1992 Argentina reformed its electricity sector along similar
lines to the UK, with considerable restructuring and privatisation. This
was generally deemed a success.[45] However, one rather novel aspect of
Argentine reform has attracted particular and critical attention, namely
the arrangements for transmission expansion. Major transmission expansions were no longer to be decided by the transmission owner or the
regulator, but were henceforth the responsibility of the users of the transmission system. A new so-called 'public contest' method required users to

propose and vote on major expansions. Approved expansions were then put out to competitive tender. All users within a defined area of influence of the expansion – the so-called beneficiaries of the expansion – would then share the cost on the basis of their actual usage over an agreed amortisation period.

The public contest method was adopted in order to avoid the inefficiencies and overexpansions of the previous state-owned era, for which inadequate regulation was partly to blame. In economic language, it was to overcome the incentive to gold-plating associated with regulated transmission. The users (or beneficiaries) of an expansion would be best-placed to decide whether the benefits of an expansion were worth the costs. The public contest arrangements were designed to maximise the role for market participants and competition, and to minimise the role for regulation.

Critics soon found a reason to attack the method. In the mid-1990s, a major transmission expansion known as the Fourth Line was proposed to convey electricity to meet expanding demand in Buenos Aires. The Fourth Line had been long expected and the regulator described it as 'much needed'. But at the first vote the line was rejected, though a subsequent proposal was accepted. Many held the rejection and delay to be an indication of the lack of success of the transmission expansion policy.[46] Some said that a voting method involving users would be unworkable because of transactions costs.

Carlos Skerk and I have examined the history of transmission and its regulation in Argentina.[47] On closer inspection, we find that the Fourth Line was an uneconomic project. The increased value of the electricity transmitted was less than the cost. Over time, the economic situation had changed. It was now more economic to build gas pipelines to Buenos Aires and to generate electricity there, than it was to build a new powerline to Buenos Aires.

In our view, the Argentine public contest method enabled economic expansions to take place, and generally avoided uneconomic expansions. It was characterised by mostly harmonious relationships between the parties rather than discord. There was competition to build the expansions that were put out to tender, and the cost per kilometre of major lines was roughly halved. Criticism of the public contest method was largely misplaced.

Argentine experience shows that it is feasible to transfer decision-making power from transmission companies and regulatory bodies to transmission users, and to put proposed investments out to competitive tender. This approach brought about greater efficiency in Argentina by disciplining decisions about whether and how to make transmission expansions, and securing their construction and operation at lower cost. This suggests that there may be scope for enabling market participants rather than regulators to make decisions about an even wider range of network investments that are presently subject to regulation, in a wide range of industries.

NEGOTIATED SETTLEMENTS IN NORTH AMERICA

My final example is taken from North America, where in some jurisdictions market participants effectively make decisions about a wide range of matters that have traditionally been thought to be the province of regulation alone. Typically there is an initial process during which the company is required to provide relevant information. Then interested parties including user and consumer groups negotiate a settlement or 'stipulation' with the regulated company, and put this proposal to the regulatory authority for confirmation. Although the practice is apparently widespread, there has been virtually no economic analysis of it. It appears to have been encouraged by the Federal Power Commission during the early 1960s as a way of working off a backlog of regulatory decisions. Several state utility commissions followed suit. It has since been seen primarily as a way of economising on time and cost, or reducing uncertainty, compared to traditional regulation which proceeds by litigation. The implication is that the outcome is unlikely to be significantly different from the outcome of litigated regulation.

Recent research on Federal Energy Regulatory Commission (FERC) practice suggests that, on the contrary, the outcomes are quite different.[48] The most innovative settlement outcome was the rate moratorium, a simple price cap, which FERC could not impose in a regulated (litigated) case. And in general the main purpose of substituting a negotiated settlement for a regulated one was to achieve a different outcome, not to reduce the cost or uncertainty of a similar one.

These conclusions mirror those that I found when examining the role of the Office of Public Counsel (OPC) in negotiating settlements (stipulations) of rate cases before the Florida Public Services Commission (PSC).[49] The OPC was set up to represent the citizens of Florida in utility matters. It often worked in tandem with representatives of larger consumers.

For the gas, electricity and telephone sectors in total, stipulations were agreed in 31 per cent of earnings reviews. These stipulations brought tangible benefits. From 1976 to 2002 stipulations accounted for 77 per cent of rate reductions, but only 0.7 per cent of allowed rate increases.

There is evidence that these settlements secured a much better deal for customers than regulation would have done. Across these three sectors, the average value of a rate reduction was $49.6 million with a stipulation and

$6.7 million without. In the electricity sector, nine stipulations accounted for $3.8 billion worth of rate reductions. Detailed examination suggested that most of these reductions were attributable to the stipulations. They would not otherwise have been achieved. At the very least they were achieved earlier than they otherwise might have been.

What did the utilities gain from settlements in return for these very significant rate reductions? They saved some costs, but these savings were relatively small, estimated at under 0.5 per cent of the amounts involved in the settlements. Perhaps companies avoided some uncertainty or embarrassment of public hearings. But mainly they achieved innovative modifications to the traditional PSC procedures, often in the face of opposing advice by commission staff.

One example of such a modification was more flexible accounting procedures (including deferring accounting provisions, and either not increasing depreciation or even reversing it). More importantly, companies and users were often able to agree on the adoption of revenue-sharing incentive arrangements lasting several years instead of traditional rate-of-return regulation or earnings-sharing schemes. That is, they were able to get rid of a cap on profits in return for accepting a cap on prices or revenues. In effect, they managed to achieve a UK-type approach to regulation, which the traditional US framework of regulation via litigation was unable to deliver.[50]

Whether Florida's experience is unique, associated with the person appointed as public counsel during this whole 25-year period, remains to be seen. Whether it would generally be helpful to introduce or increase the role of consumer advocates elsewhere is a matter for further research. But the idea of negotiated settlements deserves further consideration.

The consumer committees at the Office of Electricity Regulation (Offer) would probably have rather enjoyed hammering out distribution price control settlements with their regional electricity companies. They might not all have come to the same conclusions as Offer and Ofgem (Office of Gas and Electricity Markets) did, but we should have learned much from the diversity and innovation. I would not rule out the possibility of such an approach even now. There might need to be provisions for users to obtain relevant information from the companies, perhaps via the regulator, and to commission expert advice as required. There might need to be a regulatory backstop in the event of the companies and users failing to agree on certain aspects. The regulator might need to price the capita expenditure items on the menu. But user and consumer groups should be able to specify the items that should appear on the menu, and choose which items to accept. Unfortunately, working out the details of such a possible approach is beyond the scope of this chapter.

CONCLUSIONS

I hope to have shown in this chapter:

- that competition has developed in both generation and retail supply, and has done so more effectively than many have feared;
- that some further steps could be taken to facilitate such competition, not least by reducing some governmental and regulatory interventions in these markets;
- that mechanisms are presently in use whereby market participants themselves can determine transmission expansions, and which have proved more economic than regulated transmission;
- that there are also mechanisms by which market participants including consumer representatives do in practice negotiate settlements with utilities over a wide range of monopoly sector issues that are conventionally thought to require regulation; and
- that these mechanisms have turned out to be better for consumers and also rather more innovative than conventional regulation.

All this is not to say that some form of regulation is unnecessary. Rather, it is possible to look beyond the present role of regulation. Competition and the market can play a yet greater role than they presently do. It would seem desirable to explore such possibilities further.

NOTES

1. 'Electricity: Regulatory Developments from Around the World', IEA/LBS Beesley lectures on regulation series XI, 9 October 2001, reprinted in Colin Robinson (ed.), *Competition and Regulation in Utility Markets*, London: Institute of Economic Affairs and London Business School, 2003, pp. 61–87. Some similar themes to those explored in the present chapter are set out in my Foreword 'The market versus regulation' to F. Perry Sioshansi and Wolfgang Pfaffenburger (eds), *Electricity Market Reform: An International Perspective*, London: Elsevier, 2006, pp. xvii–xxix.
2. Some of this research has been undertaken with colleagues mentioned in the text, to whom I am extremely grateful for assistance. None the less, to avoid implicating them in what follows, I should emphasise that this chapter represents a strictly personal view. With the same disclaimer, I should like to thank many colleagues and officials worldwide for helpful assistance in obtaining and clarifying data, including Gert Brunekreeft, Bill Heaps, Roy Hrab, Paul Joskow, Greg Mathews, Alan Moran, Susan Pelmore, Mike Renfro, Jessica Studdert, Calvin Timmerman, Claire Tyler and Lisa White.
3. Other have documented problems in these countries. For example, it has been estimated that New Zealand distribution network revenues have been about NZ \$200 million per year higher than they might otherwise have been. Geoff Bertram and Dan Twaddle, 'Price–cost margins and profit rates in New Zealand electricity distribution networks since 1994: the cost of light handed regulation', *Journal of Regulatory Economics*, **27**(3), May 2005, 281–308.

4. The Energy Act 2004 further increased the role of government. For example, s 134 gives the secretary of state power to modify licence conditions if he considers it necessary or expedient for the purpose of implementing new trading and transmission arrangements; s 172 requires the secretary of state to publish an annual report to parliament on security of supply (covering short- and long-term availability of electricity and gas for meeting the reasonable demands of consumers, including assessments of generating, transmission and distribution capacity, to prepared jointly with GEMA); ss 184–5 empower the secretary of state to order transmission licensees to reduce transmission charges in areas of high distribution cost and to order distribution companies to pass on such reductions to suppliers, and to limit transmission charges to renewable generators in high-cost areas (presumably remote locations); and ss 154–69 empower the secretary of state to apply for energy administration orders for companies in financial difficulties, to give indemnities and guarantees and to modify licences. The act also further circumscribes the regulator's powers. For example, s 173 gives interested parties the right to appeal to the Competition Commission GEMA's decisions on all industry codes; and s 178 imposes an additional duty (on the secretary of state and GEMA) to have regard to best regulatory practice (regulatory activities should be transparent, accountable, proportionate, consistent and targeted only at cases in which action is needed).

5. In 2003/04 the total renewables obligation in Great Britain was 13.6 MWh. Multiplying this by the buyout price of £30.51/MWh gives a total cost to consumers of £416 million. *The Renewables Obligation, Ofgem's second annual report*, Ofgem, February 2005, 44/05, para 1.20.

6. The present obligation rises from 4.3 per cent renewable in 2003/04 to 10.4 per cent renewable by 2010/11 and thereafter increases by 1 per cent per year until it reaches 15.4 per cent in 2015/16, at which level it remains until 2027. Renewables Obligation Order (ROO) 2005, Statutory Instrument number 926, at www.opsi.gov.uk.

7. *The Times*, 15 September 2005, p. 54. The total cost over the period 2003/04 to 2026/27 was estimated at £21 billion. This implied a support cost of £50–£140/tonne of CO_2 avoided, noted as high in relation to current valuations of carbon of well under £10/tonne CO_2 avoided. OXERA, *Economic Analysis of the Design, Cost and Performance of the UK Renewables Obligation and Capital Grants Scheme*, Report prepared for the National Audit Office, January 2005. National Audit Office, *Department of Trade and Industry: Renewable Energy*, Report by the Comptroller and Auditor General, HC 210 Session 2004–05, London: The Stationery Office, 11 February 2005. House of Commons Committee of Public Accounts, *Department of Trade and Industry: Renewable Energy*, Sixth Report of Session 2005–06, HC 413, 15 September 2005, London: The Stationery Office.

8. Fabian Society, Environmental Policy Network Seminar, 30 June 2005.

9. For example, Catherine Wolfram, 'The efficiency of electricity generation in the US after restructuring', in James Griffin and Steve Puller (eds), *Electricity Deregulation: Choices and Challenges*, Chicago and London: University of Chicago Press, 2005, and subsequent papers by the same author.

10. David M. Newbery and Michael G. Pollitt, 'The restructuring and privatisation of Britain's CEGB – was it worth it?', *Journal of Industrial Economics*, **45**(3), September 1997, 269–303. Later work applied similar methods to the rest of the UK electricity sector. For example, Preetum Domah and Michael G. Pollitt, 'The Restructuring and privatisation of electricity distribution and supply businesses in England and Wales: a social cost–benefit analysis', *Fiscal Studies*, **22**(1), 2001, 107–46.

11. We have also begun to review the work of Domah and Pollitt. The significant reduction in distribution prices in 2000, following the second distribution price control review, yields further benefit to customers in that sector too.

12. For example, S. Borenstein, J. Bushnell and F. Wolak, 'Measuring market inefficiencies in California's deregulated electricity industry', *American Economic Review*, **92**(5) December 2002, 1376–95. J. Bushnell and C. Saravia, 'An empirical assessment of the competitiveness of the New England electricity market', Center for the Study of Energy Markets (CSEM) Working Paper No. 101, University of California Energy Institute, May

2002, revised November (mimeo). E. T. Mansur, 'Pricing behavior in the initial summer of the restructured PJM wholesale electricity market', POWER Working Paper PWP-083, University of California Energy Institute, April 2001. Available at www.ucei.org.

13. Ronald H. Coase, 'The marginal cost controversy', *Economica*, n.s. **13**, 1946. Reprinted in Coase, *The Firm, the Market and the Law*, London and Chicago: Chicago University Press, 1988. Also Coase, 'The theory of public utility pricing and its application', *Bell Journal of Economics and Management Science*, **1**(1), Spring 1970, 113–28.

14. See also Paul L. Joskow, 'The difficult transition to competitive electricity markets', in James M. Griffin and Steven L. Puller (eds), *Electricity Deregulation: Choices and Challenges*, Chicago and London: University of Chicago Press, 2005; and W. W. Hogan, 'On an "energy-only" electricity market design for resource adequacy', mimeo, Harvard University, 23 September 2005.

15. In yet other markets that are open, relevant data do not seem to be available. For example, the South Australia residential market has been open since January 2003. One commercial study (*Utility Customer Switching, Research Project, World Retail Energy Market Rankings*, University of Vaasa, Finland: Peace Vaasaemg, June 2005) has reportedly characterised Great Britain, Victoria and South Australia as 'by a clear margin the world's "hottest" energy retail markets'. *Monitoring the Development of Energy Retail Competition in South Australia, Statistical Report*, Essential Services Commission of South Australia, September 2005, p. 12. Surprisingly, however, the South Australia regulator takes the view that it should not publish figures on the level of switching to non-incumbents in order to protect the commercial position of the single incumbent retailer. For other Australian jurisdictions, NEMMCO publishes relevant switching data for each day within a few days of the end of each month. The data do not distinguish between residential and other small consumers, but residential customers account for most (around 95 per cent) of the small consumers. See www.nemmco.com.au/data/ret_transfer_datafiles/700-0323.pdf and www.nemmco.com.au/data/ret_transfer_data.htm.

16. Littlechild, 'Competition and contracts in the Nordic residential electricity markets', *Utilities Policy*, **14**(3), August 2006, 135–47.

17. There seem to be no official figures in New Zealand, although the new Electricity Commission provides a graph of present customer numbers by distribution network and another graph of gross switching rates over time. The present figure is believed to be accurate but the 3-year figure is my rough estimate.

18. The Pennsylvania figures for three years refer to the maximum observed levels, which occurred within about one year of market opening. Joskow, op. cit. and Paul L. Joskow, 'Electricity sector liberalization: lessons learned from cross-country studies', in Sioshansi and Pfaffenburger op. cit. For present figures see *Pennsylvania Electric Shopping Statistics*, July 1, 2005, PA Office of Consumer Advocate at www.oca.state.pa.us/cinfo/instat.htm. In Ohio, First Energy Corporation's figures are an average of three areas (Cleveland 60, 69; Ohio 26, 33; and Toledo 41, 48) and are after two and four years, respectively.

19. In the US states where Table 1.1 lists more than one company, the estimated proportions of total residential customers living in the areas with switching are as follows: Maine: MPS about 5%; Maryland: Potomac 26%; Pennsylvania: Duquesne 10%, Peco 27%; Ohio: First Energy 24%; Cincinnati: 14%.

20. By April 2004, 13 per cent of residential customers had switched supplier. Essential Services Commission, Special Investigation: *Review of Effectiveness of Retail Competition and Consumer Safety Net in Gas and Electricity*, Final Report to Minister, 22 June 2004, section 2.4. Updated to December 2004 and September 2005 using NEMMCO website data.

21. The proportion was 7 per cent in February 2004. *NSW Electricity Regulated Retail Tariffs 2004/05 to 2006/07*, Final Report and Determination, Independent Pricing and Regulatory Tribunal of New South Wales (IPART), June 2004, p. 33. Updated to December 2004 and September 2005 using NEMMCO website data.

22. The proportion reached 23 per cent by September 2002, but in November 2002 the state government announced a price freeze on all suppliers that essentially eliminated the competitive retail market. Michael J. Trebilcock and Roy Hrab, 'Electricity restructuring

in Canada', in Sioshansi and Pfaffenburger op. cit. Reportedly, a few retailers may now be returning.

23. Stephen C. Littlechild, *Smaller Suppliers in the UK Domestic Electricity Market: Experience, Concerns and Policy Recommendation*, published 5 July 2005, www.electricity policy.org.uk/pubs/misc.html.

24. *The Ohio Retail Electric Choice Programs, Reports of Market Activity, 2001–2002* and *January 2003–July 2005*, Public Utilities Commission of Ohio, May 2003 and August 2005, respectively. Another factor in Ohio seems to have been a particularly high regulated price for the incumbent First Energy companies in order to facilitate recovery of stranded costs.

25. 'In recent years, these prices [for small retail customers in NSW] have in many cases been *lower* than the full costs of supply' (original emphasis, p. 1). 'The Tribunal is aware that the presence of under-recovering tariffs may undermine the development of a competitive retail market. Customers who are charged less than the costs to supply them are unlikely to move from regulated tariffs. Potential competitors may be discouraged from entering the market' (p. 16), IPART op. cit. The regulator IPART decided to increase prices to cost-covering levels by June 2007 for two retailers but not for two others. The document does not explain who pays for the under-recovering tariffs. A subsequent review embodies a different approach, reflecting the Council of Australian Government (COAG) endorsement of the ministerial Council on Energy's agenda to phase out retail price regulation. 'Review of regulated retail tariffs and charges for electricity 2007 to 2010', Issues Paper, IPART, July 2006.

26. See also especially Paul L. Joskow (2005) op. cit. and Taff Tschamler, 'Competitive retail power markets and default service', in Sioshansi and Pfaffenburger op. cit. The price controls apply to various concepts including default service, provider of last resort, standard offer, price to beat and so on.

27. See successive Ofgem reviews, for example, *Review of Domestic Gas and Electricity Competition and Supply Price Regulation: Conclusions and Final Proposals*, 16/02 February 2002; *Electricity Supply Competition*, 83/02, December 2002; *Domestic Gas and Electricity Supply Competition: Recent Developments*, June 2003; *Domestic Competitive Market Review: A Review Document*, 78/04, April 2004.

28. This section draws on my paper 'Competition and contracts in the Nordic residential electricity markets', op. cit.

29. Strictly speaking they opened earlier but only at that time was load profiling accepted instead of requiring installation of a new hourly meter.

30. In February 2004, 12 per cent of small customers were on contract in NSW and the discounts were 2–5 per cent for electricity-only offers and up to 10 per cent for combined electricity and gas offers. IPART op. cit., pp. 33, 35. In Victoria and no doubt elsewhere there are discounts for direct debit billing and often a one-off bonus (commonly A$50).

31. In September 2005, British Gas announced a 14.2 per cent price increase but also offered an agreement that would freeze electricity prices for an unprecedented five years, until 2010, at a discount of 4.8 per cent on the new standard price. On 5 October 2005 Scottish Power too raised its prices and announced a new two-year capped price offer.

32. 'Residential energy contracts and the 28 day rule', *Utilities Policy*, **14**(1), March 2006, 44–62.

33. For example, E. Salies and C. Waddams Price, 'Charges, costs and market power: the deregulated UK electricity retail market', *Energy Journal*, **25**(3), 2004, 19–37; Joskow op. cit.; David Newbery 'Electricity liberalisation in Britain and the evolution of market design', in Sioshansi and Pfaffenburger op. cit. For earlier discussion, see R. Green and T. McDaniel, 'Competition in electricity supply: will "1998" be worth it?', *Fiscal Studies*, **19**(3), 1998, 273–93.

34. For example, Beatriz Arizu, Luis Maurer and Bernard Tenenbaum, 'Pass-through of power purchase costs: regulatory challenges and international practices', World Bank Energy and Mining Sector Board Discussion Paper No. 10, February 2004. This gives a good assessment of alternative forms of regulation but makes virtually no mention of retail competition.

35. For more extensive discussion, see Tschamler op. cit.
36. Arizu et al. op. cit. pp. 21–2; Colin Loxley and David Salant, 'Default service auctions', *Journal of Regulatory Economics*, **26**(2), September 2004, 201–29; Jeanne M. Fox, 'New Jersey's BGS auction: a model for the nation', *Public Utilities Fortnightly*, September 2005, 16–19. Ken Silverstein, 'Maine uses innovative approaches to deregulation', Reason Public Policy Institute, 19 February 2003.
37. 'The Ratepayer Advocate expressed concern that a single auction for obtaining all 17,000 MWh of load at one time exposed the New Jersey ratepayers to significant risk of high prices, mainly due to the impact a single purchase of that amount at one time could have on the market', Loxley and Salant op. cit., p. 224.
38. Ibid., p. 227.
39. *2004 Annual Report on Electric Restructuring*, Maine Public Utilities Commission, 31 December 2004, at www.maine.gov/mpuc/doing_business/docmuments_services/reports/electric_reports.html.
40. The office of the Ohio Consumers' Counsel filed an appeal to overturn the rate plan. 'We believe this plan violates Ohio's electric choice law, fails to protect residential customers, and will result in the continuation of high rates', 'Ohio Retail Electricity Competition: auction fizzles; Toledo, Ohio Edison rates prevail', *The Blade*, Toledo, Ohio, 10 December 2004, per Public Utility Law Project at www.pulpny.org/html/ohio_retail_electricity_compet.html.
41. 'In the 1980s the California Public Utility Commission required California utilities to sign multi-year contracts with qualifying independent power producers at prices that were based on the Commission's expectation that world oil prices would remain at above $30 a barrel for many years. Shortly after the mandatory contracts were signed, world oil prices collapsed. . . . it is estimated that California consumers ended up paying several billion dollars above actual market prices', Arizu et al., op. cit., p. 15.
42. See, for example, Trebilcock and Hrab, op. cit., on Ontario.
43. For example, Louis De Alessi, 'An economic analysis of government ownership and regulation: theory and the evidence from the electric power industry', *Public Choice*, **19**, Fall 1974, 526–38.
44. This section draws on my papers 'Transmission regulation, merchant investment, and the experience of SNI and Murraylink in the Australian National Electricity Market', 12 June 2003, and 'Regulated and merchant interconnectors in Australia: SNI and Murraylink revisited', 13 January 2004. Both are available at www.electricitypolicy.org.uk/pubs/wp.html and on the Harvard Electricity Policy Group website.
45. For example, Michael Pollitt, 'Electricity reform in Argentina: lessons for developing countries', Cambridge–MIT Institute Electricity Project, CMI Working Paper 52, September 2004.
46. Most commentators cite the important study by O.O. Chisari, P. Dal-B and C.A. Romero, 'High-tension electricity network expansion in Argentina: decision mechanisms and willingness-to-pay revelation', *Energy Economics*, **23**, 2001, 697–715.
47. Stephen C. Littlechild and Carlos J. Skerk, 'Regulation of transmission expansion in Argentina: Part I, state ownership, reform and the Fourth Line' and 'Regulation of transmission expansion in Argentina: Part II, Developments since the Fourth Line', Cambridge–MIT Institute Electricity Project, CMI Working Papers 61 and 62, Cambridge–MIT Institute, 15 November 2004, available at www.electricitypolicy.org.uk/pubs/wp.html. Revised versions are in the course of a journal review process.
48. Zhongmin Wang, 'Settling utility rate cases: an alternative ratemaking procedure', *Journal of Regulatory Economics*, **26**(2), September 2004, 141–64.
49. 'The bird in hand: stipulations, the consumer advocate and utility regulation in Florida', unpublished manuscript, 7 April 2003. Some initial results were published in 'Consumer participation in regulation: stipulated settlements, the consumer advocate and utility regulation in Florida', Market Design 2003 Conference, Stockholm, 17 June 2003, Slide presentation and conference paper (called Report) are in *Proceedings* at www.elforsk-marketdesign.net/archives/2003/conference/conferencemain_en.htm. See also S.C. Littlechild, 'Stipulations, the consumer advocate and utility regulation in Florida',

EPRG Working Paper 06/15, Cambridge University, 25 February 2006, and 'The bird in hand: stipulated settlements in the Florida electricity sector', EPRG Working Paper, Cambridge University, January 2007 (forthcoming), both available at www.electricity-policy.org.uk/pubs/wp.html.

50. Some research presently under way with Joseph Doucet suggests that similar findings apply in Canada too. Negotiated settlements have enabled participants to introduce incentive regulation that would otherwise have been beyond the scope of the National Energy Board. See: J. Doucet and S.C. Littlechild, 'Negotiated settlements: The Development of Economic and Legal Thinking', Electricity Policy Research Group Working Paper EPRG 06/04, Cambridge University, 17 February 2006, available at www.electricitypolicy.org.uk/pubs/wp.html, in *Utilities Policy*, (14) December 2006, 266–77; J. Doucet and S.C. Littlechild, 'Negotiated settlements and the National Energy Board in Canada', Electricity Policy Research Group Working Papers, No. EPRG 06/29, Cambridge: University of Cambridge, at www.electricitypolicy.org.uk/pubs/index.html; J. Doucet and S.C. Littlechild, 'Negotiated settlements: The Alberta Energy and Utilities Board', (research in progress).

CHAIRMAN'S COMMENTS

Colin Robinson

Stephen's chapter, like the last one he produced in this series, is both wide ranging and stimulating. Moreover, it draws on his international experience. My comments are on a few selected issues.

The first one is a matter that he mentioned almost in passing, but is probably quite important, which is the replacement of individual regulators in this country by authorities. I agree with him that this substitution may not be the step forward that people generally seem to think it is. There is surely scope for entrepreneurship in regulation as elsewhere, and I find it quite difficult to believe that the kind of authorities we have now, subject to the constraints under which they operate, would have liberalised the gas and electricity markets in this country as early and as wholeheartedly as the regulators did in the 1990s.

My second point is something I shall make some longer remarks about and that is the increasing role of government, to which Stephen drew attention. The original intent in the British regulatory system to have light touch regulation does seem rather a distant memory now. The costs of the regulatory bodies have soared, as Stephen said, and rather more importantly, the government is back on the scene. Even in the energy sector, where there has been the most determined and successful attempt to liberalise markets, the government is interfering extensively, and inevitably it is encroaching on the territory of the so-called 'independent regulator'. One of the reasons for preferring independent regulatory bodies to direct intervention by government is that the experience of nationalisation taught us that there are huge inefficiencies in backdoor government action. The rules of the game constantly change, whereas under independent regulation, rules do have to be specified and the regulatory body can be challenged if it does not abide by them. Yet we are apparently now moving back to government action that bypasses the regulators.

If we look specifically at energy policy, Nigel Lawson, in his brief tenure at the old Department of Energy, more or less killed off the old form of interventionist energy policy, in which the civil service used to draw up blueprints for the future and particular forms of energy were favoured by the government, but that type of policy has crept back in the last few years. We have an extensive programme of subsidising renewables, and energy efficiency measures and Combined Heat and Power (CHP), all undertaken ostensibly to avoid damage from climate change. The government is not willing to rely on market-based measures like emission trading schemes for instance, but seems to think that direct intervention is necessary. This kind of policy invites advocates of support for other forms of energy to join the queue for handouts, and on consistency grounds, it becomes difficult for government to resist.

Not surprisingly, Britain's powerful nuclear lobby now seems to be getting to the head of the queue, and appears to have persuaded the government that it should look more seriously at more support for nuclear power. Now of course, if there were a revival of nuclear investment, because investors had decided that they should risk their own money, because, for instance, they thought fossil fuel prices were going to remain high for a very long time, or they were worried about security, that would be unobjectionable, but that is not what most of the nuclear lobbyists want, as I understand it. They are looking for another government-promoted nuclear programme. We have had three of those, in the mid-1950s, mid-1960s, and a one-reactor 'programme' in the 1980s. Anybody who is aware of the history of nuclear power in this country – the inflated expectations, the poor construction record and inadequate operating performance – should be sceptical of the case now being made for another government-sponsored programme.

More generally, the return of energy policy involves a reversion to the discredited approach of governments trying to 'pick winners'. Government efforts to select activities that are worthy of taxpayer support risk huge and expensive errors: past experience does not offer much hope that support will go to the 'right' activities. Moreover, rent seeking is stimulated. Lobbying and corruption emerge as market participants concentrate on seeking government favours, rather than trying to be efficient and innovative. So I agree very much with what Stephen said about the return of an interventionist energy policy. It is a retrograde step, and it will encroach on independent regulation of the energy market.

Stephen said some very interesting things about going beyond regulation, particularly merchant transmission in Australia, public contest arrangements in Argentina and these American-negotiated settlements. I do not know to what extent these experiences can be generalised, but it is surely right to point out that in looking at policy towards so-called 'network monopolies', we should take into account likely regulatory failure as well as apparent market failure.

The problem with regulation is that it is always and everywhere very unsatisfactory for a fundamental reason, which is regulatory ignorance, which is virtually impossible to correct. I do not mean information asymmetry, which is a relatively minor issue; I mean that regulators, by definition, cannot obtain the information they require to allow them to act to improve welfare. If there is a market, regulation is unnecessary. If there is no market, it is only a slight exaggeration to say that regulators do not know what to do, and so they tend to act arbitrarily because of the absence of information. So there is a very powerful case for minimising regulation.

Many of us have argued of course that all potentially competitive markets should be liberalised and that natural monopoly networks should be regulated by price caps or otherwise, but the problem with this is that in practice the split is rarely clean, and in addition, as I have just been trying to explain, government is often not prepared to keep out of the market. In Britain, for example, the original privatisations caused a lot of confusion by failing to separate out the networks. Some of the regulators, notably in energy, have done the government's job for it, but where there is no separation, regulators effectively rule the industry with a price cap, which is a long way from the original aim of light touch regulation, and it risks arbitrary decision making across a great part of the industry.

Even where separation has occurred, government intervention is confusing regulatory issues. Given all this confusion about regulatory aims and the problem of regulatory ignorance, there seems to me a serious danger, in this country and abroad, of empire building in regulation and bureaucratisation. The rising costs of regulation in Britain, to which Steve drew attention, may just be early symptoms of these kinds of problems. So it is very wise to try to find ways of avoiding traditional regulation, which really does carry some very serious problems and unfortunately is likely to increase in scale as time passes.

2. Ronald Coase and the spectrum question

Thomas W. Hazlett[1]

COASE'S QUERY

On his way to discovering the 'Coase theorem' and picking up a Nobel Prize in Economics, Ronald Coase was put to the task of understanding the US government's arguments for allocating radio spectrum according to 'public convenience, interest, or necessity' (Federal Radio Act, 1927).[2] In the First Amendment to the US Constitution, the state is specifically enjoined from regulating a particular industry: 'Congress shall make no law abridging freedom of speech . . . or of the press;' Yet, American radio and television broadcasters were licensed by a federal regulatory commission, and no entry – no airwave speech – could occur absent a government finding that the new competition was in the public interest.

The conflict was seemingly resolved in a 1943 US Supreme Court decision, *NBC v. the United States*.[3] The case formed a crucial legal precedent, determining the contours of constitutional protections in the era of the electronic press. What caught Coase's attention, however, was the economic rationale for regulation that constituted the basis of the court's decision. While licensing a newspaper would violate the First Amendment, the high court granted the Federal Communications Commission (FCC) wide latitude to license radio and TV stations and to mandate rules governing content.[4]

The Court's justification was that broadcast frequencies were unique economic resources. Whereas anyone could purchase a printing press and newsprint, jumping into the newspaper market, airwaves were subject to 'physical scarcity'. Given that there were many more potential broadcasters than there were available frequencies, it was inevitable that free speech could not be extended to all. It was therefore permissible for government to do in broadcasting what it could not do in print publishing: ration the right to speak, and regulate what was communicated.

The Court further argued that licensing avoided what would later become called a 'tragedy of the commons'. Without some selection process, the entire possibility of broadcast communications would be squandered. Indeed, the Court pointed to the historical development of the broadcast radio market in the United States as proof positive that, prior to the 'public interest' spectrum allocation scheme legislated in the Radio Act of 1927, chaos reigned:

> Before 1927, the allocation of frequencies was left entirely to the private sector, and the result was chaos. It quickly became apparent that broadcast frequencies constituted a scarce resource whose use could be regulated and rationalized only by the Government. Without government control, the medium would be of little use because of the cacaphony [sic] of competing voices, none of which could be clearly and predictably heard.[5]

Coase critiqued the logic from two directions.[6] First, excess demand for zero-priced broadcast frequencies was precisely the condition affecting economic resources generally – it is *scarcity*, the scourge of undergraduates struggling to focus in Week 1 of Introduction to Microeconomics. Government assignments are one mechanism for awarding valuable rights, but alternative use of 'the price system' was not only possible, it was the standard approach. Instead of relying on bureaucrats to divine the best, most socially productive broadcasting solutions, government might simply auction licences to high bidders, allowing market forces to make assignments.

Second, once such awards were made, whether administratively or through the market, private owners of spectrum could then determine radio interference levels. Coase discovered that what prevented chaotic outcomes was not centralised control, but well-defined rights that allowed users to coordinate their activities. Spillovers from one frequency space to another were not eliminated by government assignment of licences, in any event, but by rules limiting what licensees could do: 'the real cause of the trouble was that no property rights were created in these scarce frequencies'.[7] Rather than relying on regulators to apply the proper constraints, a more efficient system – thoroughly tested as an allocation mechanism throughout the rest of the market economy – could be employed. Private ownership of frequencies would allow competitive markets to determine the most productive use of radio waves.

With extreme clarity of thought, Coase elucidated that property rights could prevent chaos in a sophisticated, balanced way. He began with the insight that interference was not a categorical problem, as regulators posed the dilemma of spillovers. It was an incremental problem. The social objective is not to eliminate all interference between radio users, but to experience the optimal level: 'It is sometimes implied that the aim of regulation in the radio industry should be to minimize interference. But this would be wrong. The aim should be to maximize output'.[8]

This occurs when the gains from additional spillovers (the benefits enjoying by those spewing interfering signals) just equal the additional costs imposed on radio users elsewhere. It is socially beneficial to allow radio interference that enables valuable communications while damaging (through emission spillovers) only relatively low-valued radio traffic.

This process involves complex trade-offs among rival spectrum users. Giving those users incentives to cooperate in adjusting their activities yields information about possible efficiencies no government regulator is privy to. Decentralised owners would better discover efficient arrangements, because they possessed monetary incentives to do so and because they possessed, collectively, far more knowledge about where potential gains from trade were available than did disinterested bureaucrats.

Professor Coase, critiquing US radio law, stumbled upon one of the great advances in modern economics. Calling it a 'Eureka moment', George Stigler dubbed the proposition 'the Coase theorem'. While the theory was famously elaborated in Coase's 1960 paper, 'The problem of social cost',[9] it was first published in his 1959 FCC article:

> The reduction of interference on adjacent frequencies may require costly improvements in equipment, and operators on one frequency could hardly be expected to incur such costs for the benefit of others if the rights of those operating on adjacent frequencies have not been determined. The institution of private property plus the pricing system would resolve these conflicts.[10]

This understanding, which Chicago economists unanimously considered incorrect when first advanced, was to have profound implications in economics, public policy analysis, and environmental law. Here, however, we return to the roots of the Coase theorem, and explore the path of its theoretical logic in radio spectrum.

That is a most interesting pursuit. While the Coasean analysis of property rights has won wide influence among economists, it is today under attack. Critics of the 'property rights' approach believe that advanced wireless technologies have fundamentally altered the efficient regime for governing airwave use.

FROM RADICAL HERESY TO PASSÉ ORTHODOXY

The Economist magazine recently selected five august individuals to receive its 'Innovator Award'. This prestigious honour is typically awarded to technology gurus or entrepreneurs who, in devising a faster chip or writing a better programme, shake markets. In December 2003, however, an elderly academic from the University of Chicago was selected. He held no patents, and was not a billionaire. The magazine described his contribution this way:

> In papers published in 1959 and 1960, Dr Coase asked why valuable radio spectrum was going to waste. He suggested that the problem was the lack of *private property rights over spectrum*, which prevented the formation of a market to allocate spectrum efficiently. The answer, he proposed, was to open the allocation of radio spectrum to market forces.[11]

Coase's radio spectrum policy ideas were seminal, and had influenced every economist working in the area. His policy recommendations were compelling, as well. In February 2001, a petition signed by '37 Concerned Economists' (prominent US scholars, including Coase) was submitted to the FCC. The proposal urged implementation of the property rights approach outlined by Coase. Policy makers listened, as well, and many spectrum regimes moved towards liberalisation. The most apparent example is the introduction of competitive bidding to assign wireless licences. First used in 1990 in New Zealand, auctions are now employed in over 30 countries, including the United States, India, Germany and the United Kingdom.

The consensus formed that permitting licensees to have broad flexibility in the use of radio waves would empower market forces to efficiently configure technologies, services and business models. This would signal a sea change from the traditional approach, where a government licence dictates the precise use of frequencies. By delegating choices to competitive licensees – de facto spectrum *owners* – the efficiencies of the 'price system' would replace the rigidities and politicisation of administrative allocation.

Yet, as formulated, the policy has been adopted only in limited circumstances. A handful of nations have legislated reforms that fundamentally alter spectrum regulations, moving decisively towards private property rights.[12] More commonly, the licensing of mobile phone carriers has led to a relaxation of spectrum use restrictions specifically for these wireless operators. In other words, mobile phone licensees generally enjoy far more extensive 'spectrum property rights' than do radio or broadcast licensees.

This limited liberalisation has occurred because the political costs to regulating are higher, while the benefits lower. The first outcome stems from the additional complexity of cellular systems (versus broadcast transmitters); it would involve far more administrative micro management were only limited frequency use rights to be issued to operators. Second, the regulation of common carriers does not directly implicate politically charged content issues. To regulators, this lowers the gains from regulation. The original interests that combined to form spectrum allocation regimes in the United States and elsewhere were most pointedly concerned with the control of radio broadcasting, a medium seen to possess profound social and political influence.[13]

Expanding options for licensees offering mobile phone service brought demonstrable efficiencies into the marketplace. Wireless networks more rationally evaluated economic trade-offs than did broadcasters. When building new capacity to satisfy customer demands, they weighed the gains from incremental investments in technology or infrastructure (such as base stations or more sophisticated handsets) against the expense of additional bandwidth. Costs and benefits accruing to individual users were internalised, as wireless carriers coordinated, literally, millions of spectrum access transactions. This used the 'price system', but not primarily (if ever) by auctioning minutes to subscribers. Markets devised far more complex forms of organisation. Consumers were linked to networks, myriad equipment suppliers and application vendors by contracts and various pricing menus. The outcome was a cooperative effort between users, service suppliers and network investors.

The ability of unregulated spectrum markets to select technical standards has also been proven in those regimes where such choices are allowed. In the US, as opposed to the European Union and most other countries, mobile phone operators are free to select their wireless phone system. Multiple standards have emerged, and some have come and gone (or are going[14]) – a vivid illustration of the process of creative destruction. The marketplace exhibits the fruits of rivalry between technological foes. The emergence of the CDMA (code division multiple access) platform, which forms the basis for all third generation (3G) wireless systems, stems from this liberal policy.[15]

Thus, the development of mobile telephony exhibits the precise social gains that Coase forecast, while following his Hayekian intuition that competitive resource owners would discover opportunities unknown to regulators. Political institutions have been slow to embrace the overarching opportunity from the property rights approach, given the 'tyranny of the status quo' (to use Milton Friedman's apt phrase) and strong institutional support for traditional spectrum regulation.

Indeed, when Coase's ideas first appeared, he was asked to appear before the FCC in Washington DC to explain his theory for pro-consumer reform. Commissioner Philip S. Cross began the questioning with: 'Are you spoofing us? Is this all a big joke?'. A stunned witness responded, 'Is it a joke to believe in the American economic system?'.[16] And when the Rand Corporation funded Coase, with fellow economist Jora Minasian, and William Meckling, to produce a study of how to actually implement a spectrum property regime, Rand refused to publish their paper. A referee warned about damaging 'Rand's "public relations" in Government quarters and in Congress' by an inquiry 'asking for trouble in the Washington–Big Business maelstrom'. Rand, dependent on public and private sector grants, elected not to incur the wrath of 'CBS, FCC, Justice and – most of all – Congress'.[17]

Incumbent firms often lobby in favour of rules that raise entry barriers, and the support of major commercial broadcasters was central to the creation of 'public interest' spectrum regime. Legislative leaders and executive branch policy makers joined the broadcasters; both parties saw that a licensing regime could create entry barriers and thereby rents. The rents could then be distributed politically, and incumbency – in the market or in office – would be rewarded.[18] While Coase's analysis did not reflect the strategic self-interest of the parties that supported the 1927 Radio Act, the public choice analysis fully supports his policy conclusions.[19] Moving spectrum out of administrative allocation and into the market would eliminate the entry barriers that wreaked havoc on competition in the wireless sector, impediments actively erected to create rents.

But a funny thing happened between the Coasean economic consensus and free market reforms. In recent years, just as the rise of the information economy was pointing to a meltdown of the political forces that supported the *ancien régime*, including a decisive move away from the traditional broadcasting model in radio and television,[20] a theoretical attack was launched against Coase. A new paradigm was hailed that rendered the property rights approach at best irrelevant, at worst, dangerous. This view gained cache in academia and the media, and quickly. Within months of awarding him its prestigious 'Innovator's Award', *The Economist* all but revoked the prize, reporting on a paradigm shift that swept his model away:

> The old mindset, supported by over a century of technological experience and 70 years of regulatory habit, views spectrum . . . as a scarce resource that must be allocated by governments or bought and sold like property. The new school, pointing to cutting-edge technologies, says that spectrum is by nature abundant and that allocating, buying or selling parts of it will one day seem as illogical as, say, apportioning or selling sound waves to people who would like to have a conversation.[21]

This was perhaps the first time in human history that an important idea has gone from radical heresy to passé orthodoxy, all without ever having been implemented.

The counter argument to property rights in spectrum has been labelled the 'commons' view, and it sees modern wireless systems as reducing the importance of exclusivity. 'The property approach made sense in 1960, but is now questionable',[22] precisely because advanced technologies allow multiple users, perhaps unlimited users, to productively share radio frequencies. The conclusion is that developments in the marketplace have rendered the

Coasean vision moot. 'Although we will not attempt here to entirely dismiss Coase's theory . . . Coasian spectrum markets might be an outmoded relic of the era in which they were conceived'.[23]

Private property in spectrum relegated to the dustbin of economic theory? Larry Lessig, the provocative legal scholar at Stanford University, is the most persuasive proponent of the announced 'counter-revolution'. He places its motivation firmly on the empirical observation that wireless markets lacking exclusive rights are now eclipsing those that do have them: 'The passion behind this counter-revolution . . . comes from the success of the most important spectrum commons so far – the "unlicensed" spectrum bands that have given us Wi-Fi networks'.[24]

The rise of Wi-Fi, the marketing term given to radios known to the Institute of Electrical and Electronic Engineers (IEEE) as 802.11x devices, is hailed as a paradigmatic shift. Using spectrum allocated for low-power use by governments around the world, most commonly the 902–928 MHz and 2.4–2.4835 GHz bands, Wi-Fi links provide high-speed data links for millions of users enjoying non-exclusive spectrum access rights. As put forth by Yochai Benkler:

> The most immediate debate-forcing fact is the breathtaking growth of the equip-ment market in high-speed wireless communications devices, in particular the rapidly proliferating 802.11x family of standards (best known for the 802.11b or 'Wi-Fi' standard), all of which rely on utilizing frequencies that no one controls.[25]

The smartness of the radio units substitutes for the lack of a private property right. If each user can easily navigate around the potential inter-ference of rival spectrum users, then the creation of exclusive rights merely obstructs traffic. Better to let the low-cost engineering solutions to airwave congestion crank out increasingly less expensive, increasingly more sophis-ticated devices whose transmissions roam freely across the electromagnetic dial. Lessig explains the architecture of this market by analogising to the protocols of the Ethernet, deemed to be 'spectrum in a tube':

> When a machine on an Ethernet network wants to talk with another machine . . . [it] requests from the network the right to transmit. It asks, in other words, to reserve a period of time on the network when it can transmit. It makes this reser-vation only if it hears that the network at that moment is quiet. It behaves like a (good) neighbor sharing a telephone party line: first the neighbor listens to make sure no one is on the line, and only then does she proceed to call.[26]

As smart radios adeptly share spectrum, the coordination offered by tra-ditional licensing regime – with broadcasters given operating permits to conduct just the specific wireless operations authorised – is no longer needed, even if it were efficient during a previous epoch.[27] Moreover, spectrum owners are no longer helpful. Polite protocols – proper etiquette – allow all to use 'spectrum commons' more efficiently than markets organised by private property rights.

THE EVOLUTION OF PROPERTY RIGHTS

In the pioneering treatment by Harold Demsetz, private ownership tends to occur where the net benefits of creating and enforcing rights are positive.[28] Hence, native North American tribes refrained by enforcing ownership of beaver habitat until the New World arrival of European traders. With this large increase in the demand for furs, customs changed. Ownership of productive fur trapping grounds was claimed, and rights were respected. The increase in the value of productive assets had rendered the cost of property rights enforcement affordable. And, conversely, the increasing security of investment afforded by exclusive control (barring free riders from reaping what others had sown) led to improving stocks. A virtuous circle: productivity increases led to more property, and then more property led to greater productivity.

Many other historical examples were found. The 'evolution of property rights' became a popular topic of analysis. One of the most important contributions was made in a 1975 paper by Terry Anderson and P.J. Hill, which demonstrated that barbed wire, introduced into the American West in the 1880s, had a profound impact. In lowering the cost of fencing vast tracts of land, it altered the economics of private rights enforcement. This not only triggered a movement away from open range grazing, but fundamentally altered the course of agriculture. With exclusivity, farms sprang up, and crops increasingly took the place of cattle. Productivity increased and society was made wealthier.[29]

The current argument in favour of moving towards greater reliance on spectrum commons flows in this vein, but in the opposite direction. With the costs of non-exclusive use of radio spectrum declining, the net benefit of private property falls. This is what I have called the 'barbed wireless' hypothesis.[30]

A STROLL THROUGH CENTRAL PARK

It is distinctly ill-mannered to offer a Central Park analogy while in London, a city boasting an abundance of spectacular public parks. But I am an American, and I strive to live up to a reputation for brash egocentrism earned so dutifully over so many years.

Central Park is a commons, writes Lessig, that produces great social benefit. It serves as a useful metaphor for the commons he and others would like to see extended in spectrum. What is its defining feature?

> By a commons I mean a resource that is free. *Not necessarily zero cost, but if there is a cost, it is a neutrally imposed, or equally imposed cost.* Central Park is a commons: an extraordinary resource of peacefulness in the center of a city that is anything but; an escape and refuge, that anyone can take and use without the permission of anyone else . . . The point is not that no control is present; but rather that the kind of control is different from the control we grant to property.[31]

The models offered by Lessig to illustrate the structure of a spectrum commons – the Ethernet and a public park – are highly instructive.[32] The Ethernet is described by Lessig as 'spectrum in a tube', which is a good way to think of the high-capacity data conduits that link our office computers to the internet via local area networks (LANs). The 'good neighbour' manners that allow disparate users to cooperate is not a product of a commons or an open access regime. Quite the reverse: the Ethernet imposes the 'listen before talk' protocol on users, coordinating spectrum access. Control is exercised by the private LAN owner. The Ethernet is spectrum in a tube, and exclusive ownership of the tube enables efficient creation and utilisation of this communications technology.

The Ethernet's friendly *access regime*, rules determining terms and conditions of resource use, is distinct from the *property regime* that governs its component parts. To identify a particular access regime as useful, and to then propose that this access regime be imposed elsewhere, is one approach to spectrum policy. In fact, it is the traditional approach of administrative allocation. This is the regime that has produced demonstrably inefficient and anti-competitive outcomes, and which Coase sought to improve upon by the use of decentralised markets. Moreover, the argument that the Ethernet's access regime is successful and should be widely imposed by the allocation of additional unlicensed bands exhibits a break in logic. The Ethernet's *property* regime – which produced the admired outcome – would be rejected. In its place would be a radio spectrum regime with distinct property rules, incentives and efficiencies. The analogy is stood on its head.

As seen in the Central Park 'commons': accept precisely the conclusion that Lessig reaches: that a given public park is socially valuable; accept, further, that no private entity has the economic incentive or ability to construct such an institution. Under these 'pro-commons' assumptions, the existence of Central Park demonstrates that a private property regime produces such socially valuable outcomes, because the land that comprises Central Park is allocated by the rules of private property.

That a state agency (in this case, the City of New York) has acquired these private land rights is itself an outcome (or integral feature) of the market process. It is the rich assortment of innovative solutions created under decentralised property rights that yields such an impressive array of pro-consumer solutions, as compared with the alternative of centralised control. The argument for moving away from exclusive radio spectrum rights to an all-encompassing spectrum commons imposed by policy makers fails to gain sustenance from the public park. Quite the reverse.

If New York City real estate was *not* governed by private property, but was instead administered by an FCC-type administrative agency, it is clear that the social amenities of Central Park would be far more difficult to supply.

First, the system of property rights allows competitive markets to productively utilise land for myriad developments and opportunities, and many of these productive outcomes are complementary to the provision of a public park. Were political barriers to entry to result in massive under-utilisation of New York City land, as have 'public interest' allocations in frequencies, the value of Central Park would be far reduced. A vibrant private marketplace, perched upon the efficiencies of private property rights in land, creates the opportunity for a lush 'commons' as an oasis in the City.

Second, without active and fully operational land markets, the true opportunity cost of land would be unknown. Hence, the choices facing the City in creating, expanding, or contracting Central Park would be made blindly, without information as to what values are associated with alternative uses.

In short, there is no conflict between a 'commons', as defined by Central Park, and private property rights in land. Indeed, the advantages of private ownership rights are manifest, even when private rights migrate to public agencies. So long as the overarching property regime empowers a process of competition in the use of the resource, public enterprises gain just as do private bidders in the rationalisation of asset deployments.

THE IRONY OF THE COMMONS

While spectrum commons are said to, increasingly, productively dominate exclusively controlled spectrum, the evidence from the wireless marketplace suggests otherwise. The causative and much heralded technological advances in radio do render increased social value, but gains accrue under rival property regimes. The spread spectrum radios cited as the most common example of how smart devices are changing the optimal regulatory paradigm, have been most profitably developed by Qualcomm, a CDMA technology provider to the cellular and PCS market. Similar success stories are seen with Nokia, Siemens and Ericsson, large wireless technology suppliers for mobile carriers using TDMA, the basis of GSM cellphone systems and a sophisticated way to multiply wireless connections transmitted in a given frequency space by alternating links over tiny increments of time. Similar deployments of advanced wireless systems are taking place with smart antennae, orthogonal frequency division multiplexing, mesh networks and software defined radios.

The argument that such wireless technologies make it easier to share radio frequencies is correct, but irrelevant to the question of property rights. That question is answered by evidence suggesting that additional bandwidth would be most profitably deployed under one regime or another, given the full panoply of opportunities available. Such evidence should be garnered from observation of markets, where consumer usage and network formation under alternative rights regimes will tend to tilt in response to paradigmatic changes that alter optimal property rules. Indeed, this is precisely the appeal made in arguments citing the 'breathtaking growth' of Wi-Fi as the driver of optimal policy regime switch.

Calibrating the magnitude of alternative levels helps formalise the test, however. The breathtaking growth of any one market is not, in itself, evidence of a rights-altering efficiency change, because only relative shifts in rights productivity yield evidence. And in fleshing out the relative value changes, one must focus on the proper policy margins. This is now a source of great confusion in spectrum's 'property versus commons' debate.

For instance, the 'commons' argument offers, as its primary empirical exhibit, the aforementioned 'breathtaking growth' of Wi-Fi. But even if every household in every country in the world were to buy and use a Wi-Fi router, it would not establish that the proffered shift in spectrum rights would be warranted. The success of a given application – as suggested by the widespread popularity of Wi-Fi – is consistent with the interpretation that the current regime accommodates its use. Whether additional spectrum made available for unlicensed frequencies would result in substantially greater consumer surplus is what we desire to understand.

In addressing the marginal valuations, we must explore what incremental gains accrue not only from one proposed change – say, an increase in unlicensed spectrum – but also from alternative policies – say, an increase in liberal property rights. In comparative evaluations of marginal benefits we expect to observe the patterns that reveal how the social value of spectrum is to be maximised.

It is not necessary to contrive laboratory experiments, or to wait for dramatic new reforms (although such reforms could yield useful information), as the international marketplace today boasts abundant information about the nature, value and functionality of property rights to radio spectrum.

One thing we learn is that unlicensed spectrum bands are not commons, in the technical sense of being commonly owned. Unlicensed (or licence-exempt) frequency allocations are the product of administrative allocations – the product of a state property regime.[33] These bands can be used according to rules crafted by regulators, agents that are subject to bureaucratic and political constraints distinct from those of collective owners (as in a commons).

Another thing we learn is that unlicensed bands are not subject to 'open access'. There are sharp limitations on unlicensed radio operations, most notably maximum power rules and technology restrictions. Regulators impose these constraints in lieu of licensing, an alternative way to reduce the scope of conflict between users. In unlicensed bands, governments regulate the radios rather than the users; in traditionally licensed bands, government regulates both radios and users; and in liberally licensed bands, government regulates neither, but delegates control to a de facto spectrum owner.

It is important to note the exclusivity of unlicensed applications. While some radios are permitted, others are not. The limitations are costly. They eliminate the economic viability of a good many advanced wireless technologies, including the CDMA and TDMA networks so spectacularly successful in cellular. These costs are high, but may be worth the price, if great value is generated in their absence. Yet lacking the information generated by bidding for spectrum, a process truncated by the state property regime, there will be little information available to reveal the relevant trade-offs.

The precise access regime utilised for unlicensed devices could be implemented by owners of private property, including Intel, Microsoft, Cisco or Apple – firms with a long record of lobbying for unlicensed spectrum allocations. With liberal spectrum rights, private owners would have the option of employing their own commons, with various payment mechanisms – including royalties from devices[34] – possible. Of course, public agencies (including regulatory agencies) could also enter the market and acquire spectrum rights, as in the Central Park commons supplied by New York City. This offers an efficient remedy for any asserted market failure, not the extension of administrative allocations lacking information about relative spectrum values.

Private property rights in spectrum play a key role in the development of Wi-Fi routers and other unlicensed devices. The use of the unlicensed band, with power limits, allows short-range applications. Hence, the links

provided by Wi-Fi chips and cordless phones, the two dominant applications using licence-exempt airspace, extend wide area networks – networks
built by owners with exclusively controlled spectrum. The cable modem and
digital subscriber line (DSL) platforms are known to drive Wi-Fi adoption
in home networks. And vice versa, as broadband service providers often
bundle their high-speed services with a free Wi-Fi router.

It is often thought that the cost of using the unlicensed bands is that there
is potential interference; indeed, this is a key business consideration, and a
prime reason why some applications or networks prefer to pursue licensed
solutions where they have greater control over the radio frequency environment. Proponents of spectrum commons also devote time and energy
to disproving allegations that interference is rampant between unlicensed
users. The general problem is summarised as the 'tragedy of the commons'
problem, made famous in Garrett Hardin's 1968 *Science* article by this
name.[35]

But incidents of conflict, while interesting, provoke as many questions as
answers. That is because conflicts can always be eliminated by regulators
(or owners, in the case of exclusively assigned rights) by adjusting the access
regime. Were unlicensed bands to be protected with stricter technology
standards and lower power limits, any given level of user interference could
be reduced. Pushing this envelope far enough can eliminate all use, of
course, overprotecting radio waves and produced a suboptimal level of
interference. This is a very standard outcome in administratively allocated
spectrum, which is traditionally overconservative.

It is also the observed outcome in the unlicensed PCS band (U-PCS) in
the United States. While allocated in 1993, largely at the behest of Apple,
for licence-exempt, low-power devices using a 'listen before talk' format for
data services, the 1910–1920 MHz has not seen a single device approved for
use by the FCC. This decade-plus of absolute silence represents a social
waste of considerable magnitude. A nationwide PCS licence allocated 10
MHz has recently been valued at $4.8 billion by the FCC, and this estimate
considers only the present value of producers' surplus (profits). Evidence
in cellular markets suggests that consumers' surplus is likely to be at least
10 times as much.[36]

A lack of static can be much too quiet. As Coase discovered, we ought
to embrace the *optimal* level of interference. Ultimately, the social advantages of a spectrum property regime must be gleaned from the magnitude
of the total benefits produced, net of costs. Those costs entail the opportunity to utilise the spectrum resource under alternative property rules. The
empirical evidence is simply overwhelming that the competitive spectrum
market model advanced by Coase was, and is, the regime allowing for more
socially advantageous organisation of wireless.

SHARING EXCLUSIVITY

Just as there is much excluded from the spectrum commons, there is a vast amount of sharing in what some have called 'exclusive use' spectrum.[37] Step back, focus on the cellular market, and observe the Big Picture. With relatively broad rights to determine the use of radio spectrum and to exclude unauthorised users, wireless carriers build vast networks that serve millions of customers. In the US, four national carriers have cumulatively invested well over $25 billion, each, in infrastructure – base stations, network transport and other fixed assets – to make the spectrum they control more valuable.

The business proposition, of course, is to profit by selling access to air-waves in tiny increments – phone calls and data connections. There are now some 200 million US subscribers, who consume more than 1 trillion minutes of use per year, roaming around the vast geography of America. These networks are not so different from those in the UK, Europe, Africa, Asia or Latin America, where the scale and scope of mobile phone networks is similarly impressive.

These networks coordinate extremely intense and complex spectrum sharing, and they do so using precisely the advanced digital technologies which are argued to render property rights moot. The assertion is often made by 'commons' proponents that transactions costs make access to exclusive spectrum too cumbersome or expensive, but one trillion minutes a year argues persuasively the other way. Airwave access is made convenient by de facto spectrum owners who internalise the gains from eliminating transactional barriers.

Wireless networks sell customers 'spectrum in a box', bundling handsets set to transmit and receive on authorised bands. These include a wide range of national or international roaming partners, far-flung networks where pre-negotiated access terms are seamlessly incorporated into the customer's opportunity set, just by making a phone call. Handsets used are commonly multi-mode, encompassing multiple technological standards, and multi-band, tuned to work on different frequencies depending on location or cost. Competition between carriers continuously drives a broadening and widening of these transactional efficiencies, bringing new services and applications within the subscriber's zone of convenience.

The mobile phone user shares radio waves with many other subscribers, according to coordination provided by the network. A range of sophisticated wireless innovations are enlisted in this effort, as the carrier seeks to carefully manage interference – blocked calls, dropped calls – and quality of service, while maintaining prices that simultaneously appeal to a large number of users while recouping infrastructure costs. Resource ownership produces a vector of optimising choices, evaluating trade-offs between quality and cost, bandwidth and interference, speed and functionality, reliability and ease of use. For instance, a CDMA cellphone chip dynamically adjusts its power level some eight times per second, searching for the lowest transmit levels it can use while maintaining its link to the base station. Not only does this prolong the battery life of the handset, a plus for the customer which increases demand and hence operator profit, it also makes the allocated radio waves quieter. This environmental impact frees up bandwidth for other traffic, gains that the spectrum owner internalises.

Precisely the same economic trade-offs exist in the use of unlicensed bandwidth, yet the structure of property rights yields weaker incentives for spectrum conservation. Actions to make more bandwidth available for others are less likely to be compensated and will therefore be supplied less than the optimal amount. Government regulators could mandate these actions, promoting efficient sharing. They could call it a 'good neighbour policy'. But regulators do not know the value of the options. All they can know are what rival petitioners claim to want the regulators to do. This is a political rent-seeking process, not a reliable mechanism for determining which economic innovations create the optimal level of spectrum use or conservation. The trial and error of the market's quest for profits yields greater, and more trustworthy, information. Herein lies the weakness of the state property regime.

The ingenuity of market solutions is most vividly on display in managing the inordinately complex interactions between *investors* and *network users*. The investments sunk by network owners must anticipate future users, yet unknown. The networks built today will compete – or be augmented by – technologies invented tomorrow, yet unknown. None the less, enormous capital expenditures creating vast opportunities for wireless service are undertaken, with network carriers then striving to recoup outlays by enticing customers to pay for service.

Pricing schemes extended to subscribers are themselves complex, with multi-part tariffs and widespread use of zero-priced minutes. This is the marginal price (up to a capacity limit) of access in a 'bucket' plan offering 500 or 1000 minutes of use for a flat monthly fee; unlimited, free off-peak minutes or on-net minutes are now familiar, as well. Small increments of access are also sold. Pre-paid subscribers in US markets typically pay several times the price per minute as post-paid subscribers, but the latter commit to a much higher level of usage. Network operators strive to efficiently lower prices for marginal usage, increasing value for large users who help support network investments.

The development of wireless networks utilising exclusively assigned spectrum rights stands in sharp contrast to the evolution of unlicensed bands. The latter are, in some cases – not U-PCS – hosts to valuable activity. But there is relatively little network development. Applications are short-range, cordless phones and cordless PCs that complement wide area communications systems, which are themselves the product of private spectrum owners. All manner of services can be supplied via 900 MHz, 2.4 GHz, or 5 GHz unlicensed spectrum in the US and many other countries, but applications are sharply truncated. It is not an advantage that users self-provide in the unlicensed band, but a limitation produced by the very expensive manner in which coordination of spectrum usage occurs. Given the power limits and technology constraints imposed by regulators, and options available with exclusive rights, it proves uneconomic to invest in the creation of wide area wireless networks.

MARKET TESTS

The marginal value of radio spectrum rights assigned exclusively is, in general, extremely high. Estimates produced by Thomas Hazlett and Roberto Muñoz, two economists I am happy to recommend, is that another 20 MHz of mobile telephone spectrum in the US would produce nearly $300 billion in consumer welfare; another 200 MHz would generate some $1.6 trillion.[38]

The marginal valuation of unlicensed spectrum appears far lower. Thirty MHz of U-PCS spectrum (the total allocation) has produced only sparse economic activity since being allocated in 1993, with 10 MHz of this band completely idle (as discussed above). While an additional 200 MHz of unlicensed spectrum was allocated for spread spectrum devices in the 5 GHz band in 1997, bringing the total available to 300 MHz, the bandwidth has generated virtually no service revenue and only about $200 million per year in equipment sales.[39]

Data from beyond the US market point in the same direction. Ofcom, the British regulatory authority, has recently investigated the utilisation of 5 GHz licence-exempt spectrum and has determined that no significant demand exists for additional bandwidth. South Korea, meanwhile, is thought to feature more Wi-Fi hotspots per capita than any other country. A 2003 *Business Week* article (28 April 2003) was entitled: 'Half the world's hotspots'. Seoul has just been named the city with more hotspots than any other. Yet, South Koreans use only the 2.4 GHz band for Wi-Fi; in fact, the government has yet to allocate the additional 200 MHz of 5 GHz spectrum for unlicensed use that was allocated in the US, the UK and elsewhere in the 1990s. Lack of additional spectrum has not deterred Wi-Fi. If the 'breathtaking growth' of Wi-Fi is the driver of regime shift, the market data do not support the shift. Rather, they suggest that the marginal value of unlicensed spectrum for more Wi-Fi is low.

Relative orders of magnitude in spectrum regime valuations are suggested by infra-marginal data, which measure existing (as opposed to prospective) activities. In the US, 2004 service revenues for mobile services totalled about $100 billion. Service revenues for hotspots offering Wi-Fi connectivity generated sales of about $28 million. While the primary usage model for Wi-Fi was as a wireless LAN at the home or the office, most households with broadband connections did not use a Wi-Fi router with it, and as many households used a fixed line connection (such as an Ethernet) to route their broadband connection around their house.[40] Enterprises, while widely adopting Wi-Fi nodes to distribute network access through their factories, campuses or buildings, also relied heavily on wired LANs. And network connections stretching over a few hundred feet were achieved almost entirely via fixed line connections – privately owned 'spectrum in a tube'.

Worldwide, total *equipment* expenditures for mobile telephony in 2005 were projected to be a little over $200 billion. This includes both network infrastructure and spending on radio handsets. (Service revenues are excluded from this accounting.) In contrast, total expenditures for all wireless LANs, including Wi-Fi, was estimated at just about $3 billion. This sum was divided roughly evenly between home and enterprise deployments. Mobile network equipment spending exceeds in one week the investments made in unlicensed bands over the entire year.

These comparisons exclude sales of wide area wireless network equipment utilised in licence-exempt bands. In fact, however, there are only tiny sales of wireless broadband equipment deployed outside of the cellular bands. In 2005, global sales for all non-cellular wireless broadband equipment (base stations and customer-premises equipment) totalled only $1 billion. The emergence of WiMAX has exciting potential, and expenditures may increase dramatically. Yet, currently the largest spending in wide area networks (outside of the cellular bands) occurs in the 3.5 GHz band. Not only is this a licensed band internationally, but it has also been withheld from the market in the United States, where regulators are spending some number of years to consider an unlicensed allocation in the nearby 3.65 GHz band. Even while the state property model in the US blocks utilisation of this spectrum, it is projected to host the most active WiMAX activity for years to come.

The 'spectrum commons' argument is that smart radios are increasingly able to use spectrum where no central control is exercised. Networks are therefore increasingly superfluous, and exclusively assigned spectrum rights a needless barrier to entry. But actual choices made in the marketplace reveal a different reality. Mass market applications are being provided via exclusively assigned rights, and difficult cooperative arrangements are robustly supplied with de facto spectrum ownership. These involve wide area networks, where investors must coordinate with users over multi-year (or multi-decade) time horizons.

Unlicensed applications may compete directly with the network applications provided by spectrum owners.[41] Commercial services are offered via unlicensed bands in the United States, for example. Wi-Fi can, and in some instances does, compete with wireless carriers using liberal licences. A hotspot at Starbuck's coffee house offers internet access via a Wi-Fi link (which quickly hands off to a DSL or T1 pipe offered by a 'spectrum in a tube' owner), and that broadband connection is fully capable of delivering voice service through a VoIP (voice-over-internet protocol) service such as Skype or Vonage.

But fully capable of competing *in a technical sense* does not decide the issue. The market reveals relatively little substitution. Wi-Fi, cheap to use for short-range links, is expensive to use for wide area coverage – the essential driver of mobile phone demand. A wireless phone with short-range coverage is easy to understand: it is called a cordless phone. And it does not appear that households with cordless phones are less likely to use mobile phones; the two devices serve different purposes.

The 'barbed wireless' thesis is that property rights to spectrum are becoming eclipsed by more efficient structures emerging in unlicensed bands. This is testable. The empirical implication is that consumers will increasingly use devices accessing unlicensed bands, migrating away from services using exclusively assigned frequency rights. Equipment manufacturers and service vendors, alert to profit opportunities available from this shift, compete to offer increasingly appealing substitutes to applications provided by exclusive rights. The prediction applies across wireline, as well as wireless, markets.

It is observed that while many services and devices are offered that rely on unlicensed airwaves, it is simultaneously observed that an array of alternatives are available via exclusively assigned spectrum rights. In valuations offered by consumers, revenues or industry profits, the exclusively assigned spectrum space dominates. Of course, we are specifically interested in forward-looking trends that may, as yet, be invisible in operating markets. Evidence from capital markets offers better information.

As investors value wireless licences, permits allowing liberal use of radio spectrum to an exclusive owner, they reveal their opinion as to the utility of property rights. They are willing to pay for cellular licences to the degree they anticipate that they will generate future profits exceeding, in present value, their outlays. And bidders, investing real resources, have strong incentives to undertake due diligence in determining the long-term viability of the anticipated business proposition. Predictably, paradigm shift rendering exclusive rights obsolete in the face of more efficient 'spectrum commons' leads investors not only to pursue profit opportunities in unlicensed bands, but to reduce bids for licences. Sharply declining licence values is a predictable outcome.

It should instantly be noted that asset prices are known to follow a 'random walk', meaning that securities prices incorporate publicly available information and that price movements over time are not easily predictable. Price changes resulting from a paradigm shift in favour of unlicensed bands, then, are most carefully interpreted as incremental changes not explained by other factors – say, interest rates, business cycles, tax policy switches, or changes in the supply of wireless licences. This has been oddly misinterpreted in the prediction, from spectrum commons proponents, that wireless licence prices will crash: 'Incumbent mobile operators and broadcasters will almost certainly face greater competitive pressures from both licensed and unlicensed alternatives. The spectrum portfolios of incumbent operators, especially the large cellular phone companies, may be the first to be devalued'.[42]

It would *not* be evidence for the barbed wireless thesis were licences to decline in value due to an increase in the quantity of such licences. That outcome would be attributed to the existence of a downward-sloping demand curve, the standard assumption in economic markets.

It turns out that such caveats are not much needed, however. In examining the data over the past decade in the United States – and recalling that the 'breathtaking growth' of Wi-Fi began in the late 1990s – it appears that prices (adjusted for population and MHz allocated to the licence) have risen substantially. In 1995, PCS licences sold for about $0.51 per MHz per capita, while in 2004 the FCC determined that a nationwide 10 MHz PCS licence had a value of $4.8 billion, or $1.71 per MHz per capita.[43]

These valuations are further endorsed by two recent US mega-mergers. In 2004, Cingular successfully bid $41 billion to acquire AT&T Wireless; in 2005, Sprint paid $35 billion to purchase Nextel. The deals placed a value of approximately $2000 to $3000 per subscriber on wireless networks operating (almost entirely) via licensed spectrum. While licence costs were a relatively small part of this (Robert Crandall estimates that carriers invest about $375 per subscriber in spectrum[44]), the entire network infrastructure is created as a complement to the exclusive spectrum rights held. The empirical evidence is that investors are betting heavily that exclusive ownership of spectrum resources will yield competitive superiority for decades to come, technological paradigm shifts notwithstanding.

DIGITAL COASE

It is not time to bury the Coasean vision of property rights to radio spectrum, but to rediscover it. The march of science has delivered a host of pretty amazing new stuff, and consumers of wireless service are reaping its rewards. But the limitations of centralised spectrum allocations still bite, and for precisely the reasons elucidated by Ronald Coase in the era before Wi-Fi or digital cell phones.

Without any knowledge of the exciting opportunities to come in the information age, Coase discovered a simple model of human action. By assigning exclusive ownership to scarce resources, natural economic activity would solve many intricate coordination problems. Individuals would negotiate and contract, plan and invest, innovate and deploy, buy and sell. In myriad self-interested activities, they would be led to discover the most productive ways to coordinate the use of their assets and abilities. The state was most helpful not as a system designer, but as a judicial backstop, defining rules and refereeing the economic agents actually on the field of play.

The results of decades of bureaucratic spectrum allocation have led to precisely the coordination failures associated with centralised economic systems, while the liberalisation of exclusive rights within the mobile phone sector has led to just those efficiencies anticipated by Coase. The argument that empirical realities of the modern marketplace render exclusive frequency rights costly or difficult relative to sharing regimes arranging by government 'protocol' setters is, in fact, rejected by the evidence. The 'killer app' of mobile telephony, as well as a realistic evaluation of the gains produced by unlicensed bands, reveal that property rights to radio spectrum give life to impressive social efficiencies, and most intelligently accommodate a wide variety of access regimes.

This is a powerful conclusion. Ronald Coase, pondering the nature of property rights in the 1950s, was blissfully unaware of the marvellous wireless applications to come. He reasoned within the logic of economic theory, fortified by some knowledge of the actual workings of the Federal Communications Commission. This was sufficient to discover the optimal policy regime for radio spectrum – not only in 1959, but also today.

This discovery was 'technology neutral'. Without any knowledge of the innovative advances to come, Coase got the public policy right. That is why *The Economist*'s 'Innovator's Award' was justifiably bestowed in December

2003, why it continued to be deserved in August 2004, and why it will continue to be a rational allocation of scarce prize resources for centuries to come.

NOTES

1. The author is indebted to Professor Len Waverman of the London Business School and Professor Colin Robinson of the Institute for Economic Affairs for their kind invitation to deliver a Beesley Lecture.
2. 1927 Federal Radio Act is still prevailing US Policy; Thomas W. Hazlett, 'The Wireless Craze, the Unlimited Bandwith myth, the Spectrum Auction Faux Pas, and the Punchline to Ronald Coase's "Big Joke": An Essay on Airwave Allocation Policy', *Harvard Journal of Law & Technology*, 15(335), Spring 2001, pp. 350–357.
3. 319 US 190 (1943).
4. The NBC case directly concerned the legality of FCC rules governing the operation of radio networks. A later case, which the government also won, established the legality of the 'fairness doctrine' and other rules yielding regulators power to coerce certain types of programming. *Red Lion Broadcasting Co. v. FCC*, 395 US 367 (1969).
5. *Red Lion*, 395 US 367, at 375–6.
6. Ronald H. Coase, 'The Federal Communications Commission', 2 *Journal of Law and Economics* 1 (1959).
7. Ibid., p. 14.
8. Ibid., p. 27.
9. R.H. Coase, 'The problem of social cost', 3 *Journal of Law and Economics* 1 (1960).
10. Coase (1959), p. 29.
11. 'Innovator's award', *The Economist* (December 6, 2003) (emphasis in original), p. 15.
12. Four countries that have substantially liberalised their spectrum regimes are New Zealand, Australia, Guatemala and El Salvador. These regimes are described in Thomas W. Hazlett, 'Property rights and wireless license values', AEI–Brookings Joint Center for Regulatory Studies Working Paper (April 2004).
13. See Thomas W. Hazlett, 'The rationality of US regulation of the broadcast spectrum', 33 *Journal of Law and Economics* 133 (April 1990); Thomas W. Hazlett, 'Assigning property rights to radio spectrum users: why did FCC license auctions take 67 years?', 41 *Journal of Law and Economics* 529 (October 1998).
14. The TDMA (time division multiple access) standard was adopted by some US carriers as an early digital standard in the 1990s, but carriers are now migrating these networks to GSM (the Global System for Mobile Communications). In addition, the AMPS (Advanced Mobile Phone Standard) analog standard was used by all cellular carriers in the US during the 1980s, given that the US then mandated this standard. In 1988, the FCC relaxed this rule, allowing cellular carriers to select their own digital standard without constraint. This policy was extended to PCS licences, which were awarded beginning in 1995. The AMPS standard is still used by a few US subscribers, but the transition to digital systems is nearly complete.
15. The social value of standards competition in mobile telephony is nicely evaluated in Neil Gandal, David Salant and Leonard Waverman, 'Standards in wireless telephone networks', 27 *Telecommunications Policy* 325 (2003).
16. Ronald H. Coase, 'Assigning property rights to radio spectrum users: comment on Thomas W. Hazlett', 41 *Journal of Law and Economics* 577 (October 1998), p. 579.
17. Ibid., p. 580. 'CBS' is a reference to the Columbia Broadcasting System, one of the (then) three television broadcasting networks and owner of many valuable TV and radio station licences. 'Justice' is a reference to the US Department of Justice, the federal law enforcement agency.

18. Hazlett (1990). See also, Thomas W. Hazlett, 'The wireless craze, the spectrum auctions faux pas, the unlimited bandwidth myth, and the punchline to Ronald Coase's "big joke": an essay on airwave allocation policy', 14 *Harvard Journal on Law and Public Policy* 335 (Spring 2001).

19. Ronald Coase, I might note, has dissented from the public choice analysis. He has remained committed to the view that the adoption of the 'public interest' regime was a policy error. See Coase (1998). Coase's view actually lessens the persuasiveness of his policy argument. It is, in my view, incorrect.

20. Hazlett (2001).

21. *The Economist* (August 14, 2004), p. 61.

22. Kevin Werbach, 'Supercommons: toward a unified theory of wireless communication', 82 *Texas Law Review* 863 (March 2004), p. 867.

23. Patrick S. Ryan, 'Wireless communications and computing at a crossroads', 3 *Journal on Telecommunications and High Technology* 239 (2005), p. 260.

24. Lawrence Lessig, 'Spectrum for all', *CIO Insight* (March 14, 2003) available online at www.eweek.com/article2/0,1895,123875,00.asp.

25. Yochai Benkler, 'Some economics of wireless communications', 16 *Harvard Journal of Law and Technology* 25 (2002), p. 30.

26. Lawrence Lessig, *The Future of Ideas* (New York: Random House, 2001), p. 78.

27. There is some disagreement among 'commons' advocates as to whether the existing spectrum regime was originally a necessary regulatory construct. Economists, following Coase, are virtually unanimous in their appraisal that the existing regime has always misallocated radio spectrum.

28. Harold Demsetz, 'Toward a theory of property rights', 57 *American Economic Review* 347 (May 1967).

29. Terry Anderson and P.J. Hill, 'The evolution of property rights: a study of the American West', 18 *Journal of Law and Economics* 163 (1975).

30. Thomas W. Hazlett, 'Barbed wireless and the vertical structure of property rights', paper delivered to the Mont Pelerin Society, Reykjavik, Iceland (August 21, 2005).

31. Larry Lessig, 'The architecture of innovation', 51 *Duke Law Journal* 1783 (2002), p. 1788 (emphasis in original, footnotes omitted).

32. I note that the passage quoted above gives Lessig's general view of the value of commons. The use of the public park example as directly analogous to unlicensed spectrum has been made elsewhere, both by Lessig and others.

33. Dean Lueck and Thomas J. Miceli, 'Property rights and property law', in A.M. Polinsky and S. Shavell (eds), *Handbook of Law and Economics* (North Holland, forthcoming 2007).

34. Two FCC spectrum experts have offered this idea, and suggested expansively increasing exclusively assigned, flexible use spectrum to enable such market possibilities. Evan Kwerel and John Williams, 'A proposal for a rapid transition to market allocation of spectrum', Federal Communications Commission, Office of Plans and Policy Working Paper No. 38 (November 2002), p. 7.

35. Garrett Hardin, 'Tragedy of the commons', *Science*, 34(162) (December 13, 1968) 1243–8. It has often been noted that the correct title for Hardin's essay would have been, 'The tragedy of open access'.

36. Thomas W. Hazlett and Roberto Muñoz, 'What really matters in spectrum allocation design', AEI–Brookings Joint Center for Regulatory Studies (August 2004).

37. See, for example, Federal Communications Commission, *Spectrum Policy Task Force Report* (2002).

38. Hazlett and Muñoz (2004).

39. Thomas W. Hazlett and Matthew L. Spitzer, 'Advanced wireless technologies and public policy', *Southern California Law Review* 79, (March 2006), 595–665.

40. And, of course, virtually no household used a Wi-Fi router without also subscribing to a spectrum-owning broadband provider.

41. In some cases, regulations bar unlicensed spectrum users from providing commercial services, a policy followed in the United Kingdom until 2002, and a policy still in effect in

Mexico. It is important to note that this constraint is not exogenous; government rules police government-allocated spectrum, and unless spectrum ownership is delegated to private owners, the resulting limitations are properly seen as a product of the unlicensed regime.

42. Kevin Werbach and Gregory Staple, 'The end of spectrum scarcity', *IEEE Spectrum* (2004), p. 52.
43. The FCC valuation was based on comparable licence sales in the marketplace.
44. Robert Crandall, *Competition and Chaos: US Telecommunications Since the 1996 Telecom Act* (Washington DC: Brookings Institution Press, 2005), p. 105.

CHAIRMAN'S COMMENTS

Leonard Waverman

I am really a poor choice to comment on this because I agree with the analysis: you should never have a neo-classical economist following another neo-classical economist. We should thank Tom for what he has done. He has really made two essential points. One is that we have not established private property rights in spectrum; we are still a long way from that. The second main point is the crucial confusion between on one end, the ownership of the property and, on the other, the access regime. A lot of the comments on 'commons' are really about what the price should be, and not what the regime should be.

I searched for the definition of scarcity in Wikipedia: it says 'scarcity is the central concept in economics'. In fact, neo-classical economics is about the allocation of scarce goods. Scarcity means not having sufficient resources to produce enough to fulfil unlimited subjective wants. But there are many meanings, unfortunately, and a lot of loose talk at the moment.

For example, recently (Spring 2005) a Saudi oil minister was quoted as saying that there is no scarcity of oil. Does he mean that oil is available at a zero price? No. He says the world has sufficient oil resources, that the problem is not one of availability, but rather one of deliverability: 'There will be no scarcity of petroleum in the foreseeable future. Prices are under pressure because the petroleum infrastructure is stretched'. So he says, 'The fears of oil scarcity, which surfaced in the 1970s, have not been realised. The resource base is more than sufficient to meet demand'. So oil is not scarce, even though the price is \$60, and spectrum is scarce, even though it is free – odd. So, we have got to put a price in there at some point to define what scarcity means.

Some academics argue, for example, David P. Reed, MIT Media Laboratory, June 2005, powerpoint presentation, argues that physics proves that spectrum is essentially vast – that is, at a zero price, we can have as much as we want with smart radios. The fact that we perceive the spectrum as full, is simply because we regulate it. So, we have extreme views on the scarcity of spectrum and the essence is that scarcity is an empirical question, as well as scarcity imposed by poor economic regulation.

We would all agree that the spectrum could be full. Data show that in the US, cell phone use is near capacity but the problem is that there is so little capacity that is allowed for that kind of device, and so scarcity is the fault of the present system. It is not the fault of neo-classical economics but of regulation.

The Economist magazine, September 17th 2005, has on the cover page: 'How the Internet killed the Phone Business'. The quote is: 'People in the industry are already talking about the day, perhaps only five years away, when telephony will be a free service'. Does that mean that *The Economist* believes that voice calls will be free? That is, will there be so much available capacity that the demand will not exceed capacity at a zero price? They do not mean that, since voice revenue is now 85 per cent of telecom revenue. What they are confusing is exactly Tom Hazlett's point, which is the confusion between the network, that is the infrastructure or the property regime, and the revenue-generating applications, that is the access regime. Maybe what *The Economist* means is that in five years from now, the bundle will be such that networks will offer free voice calls along with the other things so that they get sufficient revenue to pay for the networks that are being built, because we all know that the internet is not free. There may be free access for some services, but ultimately, there are billions invested and revenues have to equal costs in a competitive market.

3. European energy liberalisation: progress and problems

Jorge Vasconcelos

INTRODUCTION

Energy liberalisation in the European Union was strongly influenced by the UK electricity liberalisation process. On the other hand, UK electricity liberalisation and privatisation, started in 1989, had been preceded by the liberalisation and privatisation of the gas (1986) and telecommunications (1984) industries. Stephen Littlechild and Michael Beesley were among the most influential leaders of regulatory developments arising from the liberalisation and privatisation of the telecommunications and energy industries in the UK.

Chairing the Portuguese energy regulatory authority, which I helped set up in 1996, as well as the Council of European Energy Regulators (CEER), which I co-founded with some other colleagues in 2000, I felt obliged to trace this path of affiliation for two reasons:

- first, to highlight the logical and historical nexus between the subject of this chapter and its patron; and
- second, to emphasise the debt of the European regulatory community towards the UK pioneers of the 1980s.

The UK experience of electricity liberalisation was one of the major sources of inspiration for the political decision makers who launched the European internal energy market.[1] It provided the necessary initial momentum and one of the most influential paradigms shaping energy restructuring in Europe. However, later on this process got its own dynamics and, inevitably, the shortcomings of a model designed for a self-sufficient island became apparent. New solutions better suited for a large, interconnected and energy-dependent continental system were designed and implemented. Subsequently, these new EU rules influenced the development of energy markets within the UK (for example, in Scotland and in Northern Ireland) and elsewhere.

'European energy liberalisation: progress and problems' is the subject that I was invited to address. I shall be very brief as regards assessment of progress, for two reasons:

1. Several recent books (Henry et al., 2001; Cameron, 2002, 2005; Chevalier, 2004; Jones, 2004, 2005) and papers (Glachant and Lévêque, 2005; Green et al., 2005; Vasconcelos, 2005) have been published that describe in detail the history and the main characteristics of EU energy legal and regulatory frameworks. Because as a regulator I am familiar with the problem of asymmetric information, I am sure that those at the London Business School know more than me about the scientific literature.
2. In November 2005 the European Commission published its annual report to the European Parliament and the Council concerning the application of the internal energy market directives,[2] as well as a detailed report outlining progress in creating the internal electricity and gas markets. Again, because I am familiar with the problem of asymmetric information, I am sure that the Commission's views will be wider and deeper than the picture I would be able to paint here.

I shall focus my chapter on some problems related to the achievement of fully integrated and efficient, liberalised European electricity and gas markets. I shall approach these problems in an informal, unconventional way. The views I shall express are my own and do not commit the Council of European Energy Regulators or the Portuguese energy regulatory authority.

LIBERALISATION AND PRIVATISATION

In the UK, liberalisation of several sectors, including electricity and gas, was associated with the privatisation of the utilities acting in the respective sectors. Liberalisation and privatisation were two dependent variables in one single equation. Independent regulation was the third variable in that equation.

Following the right sequence, market rules and the role of regulators were established before privatisation took place. This was a well-coordinated process carried out within a coherent political and economic framework.

Privatisation was a clear trend in the late twentieth century, especially after 1985. Between 1977 and 1997 more than 1850 large privatisation processes occurred, providing governments with revenues in excess of $750 billion (Siniscalco et al., 1999, p. 9). Almost 60 per cent of these revenues correspond to privatisation of utilities (ibid., p. 18). About one-third of the

1850 privatisations and more than half of the total revenues were located in Western Europe. Within Western Europe, 27 per cent of the operations and 31 per cent of the revenues were generated in the UK (ibid., p. 18).

Between 1977 and 1997, 99 per cent of UK and 55 per cent of continental Western European energy utilities' capital was privatised (ibid., p. 22).

Although some continental European countries started privatisation of the energy sector before the entry into force of the first electricity directive, in February 1997, privatisation was not on the political agenda in many EU member states or was introduced only after liberalisation started.

The Nordic countries liberalised their electricity markets and built a regional Nordic market based on competition among a relatively large number of non-private-owned utilities (that is, owned by the state, by regional governments or by municipalities).

Until 2005, France discussed liberalisation and regulation of energy markets in the perspective of their compatibility with the 'public service' concept, without challenging state ownership (for example, Bergougnoux, 2000; Albert and Buisson, 2002; Chevalier et al., 2002; Glachant, 2002; Henry and Quinet, 2003). However, for political and financial reasons, privatisation of the giant state-owned monopolies GdF (Gaz de France) and EdF (Electricité de France) started recently.

The coexistence of public and private energy undertakings in the EU was seen by some governments as an obstacle to the development of a level playing field in Europe. A few member states went so far as to introduce national laws discriminating against foreign state-owned utilities. This type of discrimination was ruled illegal by the European Court of Justice.

The UK privatisation/liberalisation model inspired reform in many countries. Unfortunately, the right sequence was not always applied, particularly in developing countries and in post-Soviet Union transition to market-based economies. As stated by Stiglitz in his critical analysis of globalisation:

> [P]rivatizing a monopoly before an effective competition or regulatory authority was in place might simply replace a government monopoly with a private monopoly, even more ruthless in exploiting the consumer. (2002, p. 141)

> [O]f course it is easy to privatize quickly, if one does not pay any attention to how one privatizes: essentially give away valuable state property to one's friends. Indeed, it can be highly profitable for governments to do so – whether the kick-backs come back in the form of cash payments or in campaign contributions (or both). (Ibid., p. 144)

'Sequencing' mistakes led to unnecessary litigation and inefficiency and, in some cases, to disaster. Disorder in some non-EU energy markets had a negative impact on the balance sheet of many European energy undertakings.

Also the rise of 'private' monopolies in some non-EU energy exporting countries still has a negative impact on EU electricity and gas markets.

LIBERALISATION AND INTEGRATION

Privatisation is a decision of individual member states – nothing in EU law obliges member states to privatise any type of undertaking. Therefore, unlike in the UK, at EU level energy liberalisation was not associated with privatisation.

On the other hand, at EU level, liberalisation has always been considered as a necessary condition for integration of national markets into one single European market. 'Common rules' for liberalisation of electricity and gas markets were adopted in 1996 and 1998, respectively. The initial assumption was that if all member states adopted similar or equivalent rules construction of the single European market would be straightforward.

In the UK, full electricity liberalisation was introduced first in England and Wales; integration with Scotland followed many years later. In the EU, liberalisation and integration of national markets are parallel processes from the very beginning.

Reality proved less simple than initially assumed and more prescriptive directives and regulations were adopted in 2003 in order to facilitate integration of national markets. At the same time, the scope of liberalisation was enlarged – for example, full retail competition must be introduced by all member states not later than July 2007.

This link between liberalisation of national markets and integration of national markets into one supra-national market makes the EU approach to energy restructuring unique. The European model allows for the coexistence of different types of energy undertaking, from the tiny municipalities to the very large private and state-owned multi-utilities acting in several EU member states and even in several continents. The main features of the European model can be summarised as follows:

1. Freedom to invest and to trade energy in all member states, including cross-border trade.
2. Freedom of choice for all electricity and gas consumers.
3. Regulated access to all electricity and gas networks, as well as to liquefied natural gas (LNG) facilities.
4. Legal unbundling of transmission and distribution operation from all activities related to generation, import and supply.
5. Compatibility with specific missions of general economic interest and energy and environmental policies defined by each member state.

Although a clear, consistent and comprehensive legal framework for the European energy market was established in July 2003, some member states have not yet implemented it. Others have introduced the necessary amendments to national legislation only recently and in some cases transposition of EU directives seems not to be in line at least with the spirit of these directives. Proper implementation of the EU legal framework is therefore a crucial and urgent task.

In order to ensure convergence of national and regional developments it is also important to develop an appropriate EU regulatory framework. The CEER, together with the European Commission, through the European Regulators Group for Electricity and Gas (ERGEG), are building this regulatory framework which we shall discuss later. However, no legal or regulatory framework can deliver the expected results if transmission capacity, and in particular cross-border capacity, is missing.

LIBERALISATION, INTEGRATION AND TRANSMISSION CAPACITY

In liberalised markets, if network operators are fully independent from any interests in generation, trade or supply, networks will support efficient electricity trade. This means that enough transmission and distribution capacity will be made available at all nodes and branches of the network, bottlenecks will not exist or will be kept to a minimum and network losses should be as low as possible. However, the fulfilment of these objectives may increase network costs by an amount that could offset the benefits consumers would obtain from efficient electricity trade. Therefore, a trade-off is necessary between different, contradictory interests.

The need for increased transmission capacity is dictated not only by liberalisation but also by integration of national markets. Without enough cross-border capacity, cross-border trade cannot take place, price differentials will persist and integration of national markets into one single market will not be feasible.

Networks may also have to support the political choices of member states concerning the primary energy mix – for example, targets for decentralised, renewable generation. In this case, network planning must take into account not only market preferences, but also politically determined generation profiles and connecting capacities.

In liberalised markets, network planning must be a transparent, cooperative process. Network operators and network users should keep a permanent dialogue and the resulting outcome should be submitted to regulatory scrutiny and supervision in order to ensure a proper balance among all stakeholders' interests and to safeguard public interest. Network system operators should publish, on a regular basis, expansion plans indicating the expected available capacity at each node of the network and the time schedule of all major construction and reinforcement projects.

Within the new, competitive and unbundled EU legal framework, network operators must adopt a different approach to network reliability as they did in the old days of vertically integrated monopolies. Probabilistic methods play an increasingly important role and new mathematical tools are being introduced. Planning methodologies must be fully transparent to network users and regulators. The reliability standards of each network operator must be clearly identified and published.

In supra-national markets, the pressure upon network operators to reduce costs also increases as a result of 'yardstick competition'. However, blind cost reductions may affect reliability and quality of supply. Therefore, benchmarking of network operators under regulatory supervision is crucial for the development of a more-efficient and -reliable interconnected network. Network operators should monitor reliability of their respective networks and publish reports on their performance on a regular basis.

The layperson may think that network planning is an exact science. However, this is not true: different methods have been applied and can be applied, both to transmission and to distribution. Recent scientific and technical developments offer network planning engineers a wide spectrum of new tools. The choice of these planning tools is not an academic question: whatever the choice is – even if it is the choice not to choose new methods and new tools, keeping the old toolkit – it has costs and impacts upon reliability and the quality of service offered to market agents, namely as regards the amount of available capacity for commercial transactions, its stability and flexibility. Therefore, it is important that network operators publicise the planning methods they use – this is a basic way of ensuring accountability towards network users.

In fact, network planning has never been a consensual and easy issue. This can be confirmed by having a look at the *Standard Handbook for Electrical Engineers* published in New York, in 1908:

> The economics of transmission has formed the debatable ground upon which electrical engineers have fought many a wordy battle. The questions in controversy, however, are usually, on analysis, found to resolve themselves, like the old druid shield, into differences in point of view.
>
> When a system of conductors is to be designed there are at least *eight viewpoints* that must be considered:
>
> Conductors must be so proportioned as to be within safe heating limits; conductors must be so proportioned as to be mechanically strong; conductors may be designed for minimum first cost of line construction; conductors may be planned for minimum first cost of central station; conductors may be designed

for minimum first cost of operation and maintenance; conductors may be designed for minimum total installation cost; conductors may be designed to secure to the customer certain predetermined service conditions; conductors may be calculated to attain a maximum income with a minimum cost.

The foregoing conditions are in many respects incompatible and therefore cannot all be realized in any one plant. The designer must *select* such *conditions* as he wishes to realize in the plant in question, though the first two are usually essential in all installations. (Emphasis added)

The introduction of new planning methods and new investment on networks are essential steps towards well-functioning energy markets. These steps are even more important when networks must support efficient trade not only at national level, but also at supra-national level.

If transmission and distribution network operators are not effectively unbundled from the competitive parts of vertically integrated companies, it is unlikely that they will engage in the required investments. Instead, they have an interest in keeping the previous network topology which favours the incumbent and makes life difficult for newcomers. Hence, where ownership unbundling was not adopted, strict implementation of unbundling in terms of accounts and management under close regulatory supervision is essential.

THE REGULATORY FRAMEWORK: TECHNICAL SUBSTANCE

The first internal energy market directives defined some common rules to be applied by all member states in order to open up their energy markets. For instance, the directives defined minimum unbundling requirements applicable to vertically integrated undertakings, minimum eligibility thresholds, a menu of network access regimes and so on. However, these directives provided little guidance as regards cross-border energy trade, development of regional markets, interaction with non-EU markets, development of interconnectors and so on.

The European Commission recognised the difficulties arising from these omissions and decided to convene the so-called European Electricity Regulation Forum and the European Gas Regulatory Forum – the first in 1998 in Florence and the second followed one year later in Madrid. The main aim of these fora was to facilitate integration of national energy markets into one single European market. The method applied was voluntary cooperation: first of all, cooperation between national energy regulatory authorities and the European Commission; second, cooperation between the European Commission and national regulatory authorities on the one hand, and system operators and network users (producers, traders, suppliers, consumers and so on) on the other.

The first important result was delivered by the European Electricity Regulation Forum in Spring 2000, when the European Commission, regulators and network users succeeded in convincing transmission system operators to accept a mechanism for cross-border electricity trade. This very simple mechanism enables consumers located in any place in Europe to get access to any supplier connected to the interconnected network. The consumer – and the supplier – only have to inform the local transmission system operator to which they are physically connected; afterwards, transmission system operators communicate among themselves and enable the commercial transaction to take place from the physical point of view. Of course, if that transaction crosses any congested border it has to go through appropriate congestion management mechanisms. Implementation of this mechanism was delayed until 2003 due to the reluctance of some transmission system operators and to new political developments.

In March 2000 the European Council approved the 'Lisbon Agenda'. Energy was considered one of the critical fields to improve competitiveness of European undertakings and the European Council asked the European Commission, *inter alia*, to present new directives to accelerate liberalisation and integration of electricity and natural gas markets. These directives were presented by the Commission in 2001 and approved in June 2003.

Meanwhile, the number of independent regulators was growing and cooperation among them was increasing. Informal cooperation had started in March 1997 involving the regulatory authorities of Italy, Spain and Portugal. In March 2000, 10 energy regulatory authorities decided to sign a memorandum of understanding whereby the Council of European Energy Regulators was created. The main aim of the CEER was to increase cooperation – among regulators, on the one side, and between regulators and the European Commission, on the other – in order to contribute to a more efficient internal energy market.

The CEER provided support to the European Commission both within the framework of the Florence and Madrid fora and in preparation of the new internal energy market directives and regulations. Some further voluntary agreements were reached both in electricity and in gas, introducing more transparency (for example, regular publication of available transmission capacities) and facilitating cross-border trade (for example, access to gas storage facilities). However, voluntary agreements proved difficult to reach, to implement and to monitor because some transmission system operators were not properly separated from other interests (generation, trade, supply) and also because some countries, namely Germany and Switzerland, delayed the introduction of independent regulators – regulated network access does not yet exist in these two countries whose geographical position is critical for the development of the internal energy market.

In order to cope with a growing number of issues and improve coopera- tion at the operational level, regulators decided in 2003 to adopt a not-for- profit statute under Belgian law and to set up a small office in Brussels.

Directive 2003/54/EC concerning common rules for the internal market in electricity and Regulation (EC) No. 1228/2003 on conditions for access to the network for cross-border exchanges in electricity provide the legal framework for the development of the EU electricity market. They foresee several regulatory actions to be undertaken by the European Commission and by energy regulatory authorities, such as:

- Regulation (EC) No. 1228/2003 foresees that '[w]here appropriate, the Commission shall . . . adopt and amend guidelines', according to comitology procedures, on three issues:

    a. inter-transmission system operator compensation mechanism;
    b. principles for the setting of transmission network tariffs;
    c. management and allocation of available transfer capacity of interconnections.

- Regulation (EC) No. 1228/2003 also foresees that '[t]he safety, opera- tional and planning standards used by transmission system operators shall be made public [and] shall include a general scheme for the cal- culation of the total transfer capacity and the transmission reliability margin . . . subject to the approval of the regulatory authorities'.
- On the other hand, Directive 2003/54/EC assigns to national regula- tory authorities the responsibility for 'fixing or approving' transmis- sion tariffs and balancing service tariffs.

Clearly, all these issues – transmission tariffs, inter-transmission system operator compensations, balancing service tariffs, operational rules, relia- bility standards, calculation of available transmission capacities, manage- ment and allocation of available transmission capacities – are closely interrelated. Some 'operational' issues have a strong economic impact and some 'economic' issues raise complex technical questions. All issues have a significant impact upon the information and communication infrastruc- ture managed by transmission system operators, as well as upon the way they collect, process and disseminate data. Moreover, the way these issues can be handled depends on the way that energy markets are organ- ised, on a national or regional basis. Therefore, close cooperation between the European Commission and national regulatory authorities is essential to ensure consistency of the electricity regulatory framework. Similar conclusions can be reached for natural gas.

THE REGULATORY FRAMEWORK: PROCEDURES

Efficient regulation of the internal energy market requires not only a clear technical framework ensuring coherence of national, regional and EU regulatory developments, but also transparent procedures allowing all interested parties to participate in the regulatory process. The European Regulators Group for Electricity and Gas, a consultative body established by a Commission decision of 11 November 2003,[3] provides the appropriate platform to achieve these goals.

ERGEG's objective is to 'advise and assist the Commission in consolidating the internal energy market, in particular with respect to the preparation of draft implementing measures in the field of electricity and gas'.[4] It is ERGEG's mission to 'facilitate consultation, coordination and cooperation of national regulatory authorities, contributing to a consistent application, in all Member States, of the provisions set out in Directive 2003/54/EC, Directive 2003/55/EC and Regulation (EC) N° 1228/2003, as well as of possible future Community legislation in the field of electricity and gas'.[5] ERGEG Rules of Procedure and ERGEG Guidelines on Consultation Practices have been approved and are in the public domain.[6]

At the request of the European Commission, ERGEG has developed several guidelines related to cross-border energy trade. The first proposal, on congestion management at electricity interconnectors, should now go into the comitology process foreseen in Regulation 1228/2003.

When preparing the above-mentioned guidelines on congestion management, ERGEG ensured the highest degree of transparency, according to regulatory best practices:

- Consultation rules were adopted and published following public consultation and prior to the development of the guidelines.
- Draft guidelines were published and submitted to public consultation.
- All received written comments were published on ERGEG's website.
- Stakeholders had the opportunity to discuss the draft guidelines first at the so-called Florence Forum and subsequently at a public hearing in Brussels, in the presence of regulators and the European Commission.
- All comments received were analysed and reasons for their acceptance or rejection were given in written form.

Stakeholders have publicly indicated their positive evaluation of both contents and procedures adopted by ERGEG. Indeed, the best possible consideration was given to the technical and economic arguments submitted by all stakeholders.

The guidelines ERGEG was requested to develop, namely under Regulation (EC) No. 1228/2003, clearly belong to the category of non-legislative, implementation acts. They have exclusive regulatory purposes and are subject to a complete set of principles established in legislation. However, the distinctive character of this type of regulatory implementation acts is not recognised and, consequently, standard comitology procedures apply.

The present comitology decision-making process will not add any relevant value, either from the technical or from the procedural point of view, to the regulatory process carried out by regulators and the European Commission. On the contrary, it will unnecessarily delay implementation of much-needed measures to improve the efficiency of the internal electricity market.

In the same way that legislation requires national regulatory authorities to regulate their relevant national markets, legislation could enable regulatory authorities and the European Commission to jointly regulate the internal energy market. The scope and the limits of EU regulatory action are already clearly established in legislation; therefore, simplifying the regulatory decision-making process can only reduce the risk of jurisdictional conflicts. In any case, the Council and the Parliament could always 'blow the whistle' – for instance, requesting written or oral explanations – and might, if necessary, introduce appropriate legislative changes.

The provisions which govern comitology are extremely complex and result from a dynamic evolution of the balance of powers among European Institutions (Bergström, 2005) – therefore, any changes will probably take a long time to be adopted and will require considerable political and cultural developments. Nevertheless, streamlined decision-making procedures related to regulatory implementation acts would be an important contribution to the European Union goal of implementing 'better regulation'.

Regulation itself is not a self-evident concept in the European political and institutional context, as rightly pointed out by Helen Wallace and F. McGowan some 10 years ago (1996; see also La Spina and Majone (2000)):

> The UK has been, both historically and currently, the most prone to opt for regulation as a method of governance, while other European countries, with different traditions, have none the less increasingly resorted to regulation as a means of coming to terms with the predicaments of modern government. In many cases, this shift in policy is achieved as a consequence of collective

European policies. These new forms of regulation around and through a European level of governance have begun to give the EU as such the features of a regulatory state, with strong resemblances in important respects to the US model of regulation (Majone 1994). This interplay between levels of regulation is reflected in two developments: the creation of a kind of division of labour between national and Community regulation, and a tension between the residual national approaches to public policy and the emerging European techniques of regulation.

BEYOND THE REGULATORY FRAMEWORK: COMPETITION POLICY

The 'Europeanisation' of energy markets leads naturally to mergers and acquisitions among energy companies – mainly historical incumbents. Because construction of the internal energy market is a step-by-step process, application of competition law in general and merger control in particular, is a challenging task.

The big European energy companies became even bigger since the beginning of the internal energy market. Nowadays, most of them reach about 40 per cent of total turnover outside their original national borders.

Creating, managing and ultimately integrating regional energy markets into one single EU energy market is a complex process. This process may imply some short- or medium-term distortions of competition. Therefore, it is crucial to address these risks and to design the appropriate mechanisms to ensure a level playing field for all EU players, as well as the quick and smooth convergence of all regional markets into a single EU energy market.

The European Commission's Director General of Competition, Philip Lowe, has remarked: 'mergers can have pro-competitive effects when they allow new operators to enter national markets dominated by former legal monopolies. They can, however, have negative effects on competition when they strengthen the dominant position of a former monopoly' (Lowe, 2003). It is not always easy to assess the positive and negative effects of individual cases. Therefore, further analysis and some joint work by the European Commission, competition authorities and energy regulatory authorities is needed regarding the application of rules to the approval or refusal of mergers and acquisitions in the energy field, as well as definition of remedies.

The European Commission's inquiry into the energy sector, launched on 13 June 2005, represents a very important opportunity to clarify some key issues and to improve consistent application of competition law to the energy industry, both at national and at EU levels.

CONCLUSIONS

We live in the world's largest interconnected energy market under a clear, comprehensive and consistent legal framework built by EU legislators. The European Commission and energy regulators are implementing and fine-tuning a light, yet comprehensive, regulatory framework in order to speed up convergence of national and regional markets into one single, integrated market. The European Commission, competition authorities and energy regulators cooperate in order to enable, stimulate and sustain efficient competition in energy markets. Millions of energy consumers regularly select the best supply offers and switch supplier. The largest electricity undertakings all over the world, and some of the largest gas undertakings, are located in the EU.

For all old problems of the liberalisation process we have been able to find new legal and regulatory solutions. Of course, we are still busy implementing these solutions and making markets working properly.

Meanwhile, the combined effect of market forces, consumer power and sustainability policies leads us straight to a new set of problems – problems whose solution will require more than new legislation and innovative regulation, forcing real progress to be made. New problems for which an old answer is waiting: technology.

'No liberalisation without innovation' – this may sound like a prospective, revolutionary cry, but it might well become the title of a Beesley lecture in 2010.

SUMMARY

To sum up there are a few key messages:

- Liberalisation is considered as a necessary condition for integration of national markets into one single European market.
- Liberalisation and integration of national markets necessitate sufficient cross-border capacity in order for efficient cross-border trade to take place.
- Network system operators should publish the planning methods they use and, on a regular basis, publish expansion plans indicating the expected available capacity at each node of the network and the time schedule of all major construction and reinforcement projects.
- Benchmarking of network operators under regulatory supervision is crucial for the development of a more efficient and reliable interconnected network.

- Network operators should publish their reliability standards and they should monitor reliability and publish reports on their performance on a regular basis.
- Voluntary agreements do not always work. Instead an appropriate EU regulatory framework of the regulators working hand in hand with the Commission must be allowed to develop.
- ERGEG should continue to ensure the highest degree of transparency, according to regulatory best practices in providing advice to the Commission and the comitology procedure should not unnecessarily delay implementation of much-needed measures to improve the efficiency of the internal electricity market.
- There must be effective monitoring by relevant authorities and the European Commission and to this end the DG TREN Progress Report and the DG COMP sectoral enquiry are warmly welcomed.
- The combined effect of market forces, consumer power and sustainability policies leads us straight to a new set of problems whose solution will require a technological leap forward.

NOTES

1. The US gas deregulation process, implemented in the 1980s, was the other major source of inspiration for the European Commission in the early days of the internal energy market.
2. Directive 2003/54/EC of the European Parliament and of the Council of 26 June 2003 concerning common rules for the internal market in electricity and repealing Directive 96/92/EC and Directive 2003/55/EC of the European Parliament and of the Council of 26 June 2003 concerning common rules for the internal market in natural gas and repealing Directive 98/30/EC.
3. *Official Journal* L 296, 14 November 2003, 34–5.
4. Commission decision of 11 November 2003 establishing the European Regulators Group for Electricity and Gas, Article 1, No. 2.
5. Ibid.
6. See www.ergeg.org.

REFERENCES

Albert, S. and Buisson, C. (2002), *Entreprises publiques: le role de l'État actionnaire*, La documentation française, Paris.
Bergougnoux, J. (2000), *Services publiques en réseau: perspectives de concurrence et nouvelles régulations*, La documentation française, Paris.
Bergström, C.F. (2005), *Comitology: Delegation of Powers in the European Union and the Committee System*, Oxford University Press, Oxford.
Cameron, P. (2002), *Competition in Energy Markets: Law and Regulation in the European Union*, Oxford University Press, Oxford.

Cameron, P. (ed.) (2005), *Legal Aspects of EU Energy Regulation: Implementing the New Directives on Electricity and Gas across Europe*, Oxford University Press, Oxford.

Chevalier, J.-M. (2004), *Les grandes batailles de l'énergie*, Gallimard, Paris.

Chevalier, J.-M., Ekeland, I., Frison-Roche, M.-A. and Kalika, M. (eds) (2002), *Les stratégies d'entreprises dans les nouvelles regulations*, Presses Universitaires de France, Paris.

Glachant, J.-M. (2002), 'Construction européenne, enterprises publiques et industries de réseaux', in Ngo-Maï, S., Torre, D. and Tosi, É. (eds), *Intégration européenne et institutions économiques*, De Boeck & Larcier, Brussels.

Glachant, J.-M. and Lévêque, F. (2005), 'Electricity internal market in the European Union: what to do next?', www.sessa.eu.com, Draft version 31 August.

Green, R., Lorenzoni, A., Perez, Y. and Pollitt, M. (2005), 'Policy assessment and good practices', www.sessa.eu.com, 29 September.

Henry, C., Matheu, M. and Jeunemaître, A. (eds) (2001), *Regulation of Network Utilities: The European experience*, Oxford University Press, Oxford.

Henry, C. and Quinet, É. (eds) (2003), *Concurrence et service publique*, L'Hartmann, Paris.

Jones, C. (ed.) (2004), *EU Energy Law*, Vol. I: *The internal energy market*, Clayes & Casteels, Leuven.

Jones, C. (ed.) (2005), *EU Energy Law*, Vol. II: *EU Competition Law and Energy Markets*, Clayes & Casteels, Leuven.

La Spina, A. and Majone, G. (2000), *Lo stato regolatore*, Il Mulino, Bologna.

Lowe, P. (2003), 'Applying EU competition law to the new liberalised energy markets', Brussels, 13 May, http://europa.eu.int/comm/competition/speeches/text/sp 2003_012_en.pdf.

McGowan, F. and Wallace, H. (1996), 'Towards a European regulatory state', *Journal of European Public Policy*, **3**(4), December, 560–76.

Siniscalco, D., Bortolotti B., Fantini, M. and Vitaliniu, S. (1999), *Privatizzazioni difficili*, Il Mulino, Bologna.

Standard Handbook for Electrical Engineers (1908), McGraw, New York.

Stiglitz, J.E. (2002), *Globalization and Its Discontents*, W.W. Norton, New York.

Vasconcelos, J. (2005), 'Towards the internal energy market: how to bridge a regulatory gap and build a regulatory framework', *European Review of Energy Markets*, **1**(1), September.

CHAIRMAN'S COMMENTS

Philip Lowe

Jorge Vasconcelos indicated towards the end of his chapter that we are living in one of the largest interconnected energy markets in the world. But at the beginning, he quite clearly pointed to the lack of progress in creating that market. In reality, every single competition authority in the European Union at present bases its competition assessment on a national market definition, despite the existence of the energy directives going in the direction of a single market. Why? Because the barriers to entry are still there, because we do not see, for example, interconnection being created in a time period which allows agreements, mergers and other transactions to take place without potential exploitation of consumers.

Jorge emphasised very clearly that the liberalisation process in the EU is necessarily linked to market integration. If we do not get wider markets in the EU, then we will not get the vaunted benefits of liberalisation. He rightly pointed out that of course we are doing this in an environment of law and politics, in which there is no power or capacity to impose a privatisation process. The liberalisation process in the EU has been completed in legal terms, respecting the possibility of public ownership of firms on the market, at whichever stage of the vertical chain they are. This has posed challenges which have partly been met, such as the capacity to combat critics who said that liberalisation of these markets was incompatible with maintaining public service obligations. We have proved in Europe that you can write legislation and also respect universal service and other public services.

At the same time, there are other challenges which are ongoing and increasing, not least the reality that if you unbundle a publicly owned company from its previous environment, the question arises as to whether the costs which it has attributed to its balance sheet and profit and loss account are really the correct ones. Was the stranded cost calculation correct? If publicly owned companies are legally unbundled, but still have very close relationships with their sister public companies, is it credible to say that they are operating on a commercial basis and competing fairly? So there is a very strong obligation on the Commission, not just as a competition agency in an anti-trust and merger sense, but also in its role as controller of state aids to oversee the behaviour and structure of publicly owned energy companies. In this respect there has been some degree of clash between the Commission and several member states, which are very anxious to associate in the public eye public ownership of an energy concern with protection of the rights of individual consumers. That is the political presentation of it – not in the UK, not in perhaps Germany, but certainly in other countries.

Of course Jorge placed emphasis on the crucial link between a lack of progress in market integration in the energy sector across Europe with the competitiveness of the European economies. If we do not make this link, if we do not complete this market, make the markets work, the cost to Europe's overall competitiveness will be very high. It is, by the way, an area where perhaps Europe could overtake other economies if it gets its act together.

Now, why is Jorge's chapter important? First of all, we would all say that the general climate around the energy sector is full of challenge, linked to electricity and gas price rises, perceived lack of consumer choice, declining oil and gas production in the EU, and the parallel challenge of raising environmental standards. At the same time, within the industry, there is ongoing and sustained merger activity. Both Vasconcelos and I were associated with the control of a proposed merger between the Portuguese gas and electricity monopolies, which we prohibited. The European Court of First Instance backed our prohibition, but so did the regulator in Portugal!

In Hungary, Denmark and in Spain, we have similar initiatives to concentrate the structure of the industry with the rationale of being able to create a national champion in a wider European market. Our concern and challenge here is not to deny the benefits and efficiencies which can be gained from consolidation in a wider European market, but to ensure that there is sufficient room for competitors to challenge the position of any new consolidated grouping.

At the level of the different policy processes we are engaged in in Europe, our energy ministers, under the UK presidency, are meeting to review progress on liberalisation and see whether any more regulation needs to be put in place and adapted. You can imagine that from a competition agency, I am not in principle particularly attached to the idea of further regulation of the sector. From a competition policy angle, we start with the question: how can we make markets work better? Sometimes regulation can make markets work, but sometimes it can frustrate competition.

Nevertheless, Vasconcelos highlighted a number of regulatory issues which need to be addressed. I think we emphasised too the necessity of increasing transmission and interconnected capacity on long-term investments. We take the view that we have to provide a degree of the certainty and predictability to financial interests who finance new investments in energy by some degree of reservation of capacity and therefore exemption from third-party access rules.

More generally, we also argue, not with a great deal of success, *vis-à-vis* our finance ministers in Europe, that construction of further interconnection capacity can only serve the objectives of a more competitive market and security of supply. In fact, the 2002 Barcelona European Council endorsed this view, although European councils tend to make resolutions which are not kept! The Barcelona Council set the objective that every member state should achieve an interconnection capacity of 10 per cent of its energy consumption. Well, we certainly have got nowhere near 10 per cent today in any of our member states. Clearly, this is an issue which is very important to address. At the national level, for example in the Nordic pool, the level of interconnection is regarded as totally insufficient to make the pool work effectively.

Beyond the infrastructure issues, clearly price trends and the growing level of complaints, not just from potential new entrants, but from consumers, have created a general concern that we need to look more widely than simply at the issue of better regulation. We need to see how these energy markets in Europe are working, and if not why not. This is why we launched an energy sector inquiry in June 2005. Let me add that it is not realised too much outside legal circles that the Commission as a competition agency does not have any particular exclusivity in applying European competition law. Every single competition agency in Europe now applies the same European law. There is one small exception as far as unilateral conduct is concerned. The UK Office of Fair Trading applies European law. The German Cartel Office applies European law. We have a difference in the merger area, where we are applying national merger laws as opposed to European law, but the substantive tests concerned are the same. There has been huge convergence between us. So when I am talking about general concern about the competition concerns in the energy sector, I am speaking, after many debates with the heads of the competition agencies and the national regulators, about the problems.

I was with the Head of the German Cartel Office recently, when he argued very strongly with Dr Bergmann of EON/Ruhrgas about the potential for freeing up the gas market in Germany from the heavy weight of long-term contracts, which prevent any significant liquidity downstream markets for gas. He has not been able to do that through consensus, and now he is doing it through legal means.

The combined efforts of the regulators, the competition authorities throughout the European Union, and ourselves have resulted in the launch of this inquiry, which started in June 2005. We overloaded the industry with a lot of questions in August 2005 when they were all on holiday, and they were not very pleased with us. Nevertheless, we devised the questionnaires concerned in close consultation with the regulators, and seven of the national regulatory authorities have actually seconded their own staff to Brussels to carry out this inquiry. It is an inquiry which produced a first issues paper for the energy ministers in December 2005 and shall have a final report early 2007. It is not a fishing expedition. We are rather interested in identifying concrete conclusions and remedies, which will be subject to a consultation process. Contrary to the UK system of sector inquiries, European sector competition inquiries cannot impose remedies directly on companies. We have to first of all identify the problems, and then decide what are the implications in our various areas of policy – mergers, anti-trust, state aid – but also clearly giving a message to our colleagues on the regulatory side as to what might need to be changed in regulations and what might need to be changed in terms of the work of the regulators.

Going further into the results of our inquiry so far, market concentration is a key issue: the level of concentration in the gas markets is very high. Market entry at the wholesale level is, generally speaking, limited by the incumbents' control of gas import contracts and long-term capacity reservations in pipelines transporting imported gas to national markets. There are only four major sources of gas coming into Europe, but at the moment, they are not competing in any serious sense, except in so far as they are competing to firm up very long contracts, supply contracts, to final consumers. So the scope for competition to take place, bearing in mind the heavy weight of this long-term capacity reservation contractual framework, is very small.

On the electricity side, the generators, due to the characteristics of the market, are able to influence prices by the use of the generation capacity available to them. The level of concentration on the exchanges and on trading platforms is less striking, so we cannot draw the conclusion at the moment as to whether these aspects of the markets are functioning satisfactorily.

As far as vertical foreclosure is concerned, vertical integration, and the limited sales by incumbents on gas hubs, results in very low liquidity on wholesale markets. That contributes to obstacles for new entrants into retail markets. Despite the unbundling requirements of the gas directives, new entrants tend to believe that network operators continue practices which actually favour the related supply company, and long-term contracts between importers and customers clearly lead to foreclosure in certain markets.

There are of course a range of other allegations made about abusive behaviour that inhibits switching between suppliers, but we need to carry out further analysis before drawing any conclusions in the area.

On the electricity side, as far as vertical integration is concerned, there is clearly illiquidity in the wholesale markets, a similar effect of long-term contracts, and similar inhibitions to new entrants.

As far as market integration is concerned, the restrictive clauses in the gas import contracts tend to have encouraged market segmentation, and we have tried to tackle that already by anti-trust action against a number of importers who impose territorial and destination restrictions. But there is still scope for better enforcement in this area. Swaps can substitute for physical transport of gas, and can offer some solutions to congestion, and that has got to be looked at closely.

We referred to interconnectors before as a key element in market integration, but grandfathering of capacity reservation remains a problem, and the incentives to increase capacity are not that clear, as far as we can see. As Jorge himself emphasised, transparency is a huge problem. Transparency about access to networks is vital. Information is notably lacking for cross-border pipelines and entry points into national markets. If we do not have adequate transparency, there is really no level playing field for new entrants at all, and they are often subject to significant risk exposure. Eighty per cent – this is a preliminary figure – of suppliers believe that useful, important or indispensable information is lacking for them on available energy sources.

On price formation, I do not need to mention the notorious links between gas and oil prices, which fail to create the right signals for investment. In electricity, wholesale markets are fairly marginal, so confidence in pricing in those markets is lacking.

We are now going into a great deal of detail, and we hope that by drawing conclusions backed by statistics and replies from energy users, network operations and the incumbents themselves, the inquiry will provide us with a political impetus for change and a political impetus perhaps which will mean that as competition authorities, we shall be able to make a contribution to realising the ambition that Jorge Vasconcelos started with, with his colleagues and Callum McCarthy and others, some 10 years ago.

4. Supply security in competitive electricity and natural gas markets
Paul L. Joskow

INTRODUCTION

Perhaps the most frequently expressed concern about electricity sector liberalisation reforms that I hear from government policy makers is that competitive electricity markets are not consistent with achieving acceptable levels of reliability or supply security. They point to rolling blackouts, voltage reductions and public appeals for emergency conservation in California, Ontario, Chile, New Zealand and Brazil, the network collapses in the eastern and western US, Italy and elsewhere, and what appears to be inadequate investment in new generation and transmission capacity to meet forecasts of 'need'. This question is asked much less frequently with regard to liberalised natural gas markets. However, the decline in UK North Sea production and the expected increase in UK reliance on imports through interconnectors and liquefied natural gas (LNG) shipments to meet future demand has led to similar questions being raised in the UK. Growing demand for natural gas, rapidly rising natural gas prices, disappointing supply responses in North America, and recent cold winter natural gas 'shortage' alerts in the northeastern US, are starting to raise similar questions in the US as well. The increasing use of natural gas to generate electricity has also led to increased interest in the implications for supply security of the resulting linkages between liberalised electricity and natural gas markets.

Are there 'supply security' problems that result from the structure, behaviour and performance of liberalised electricity and natural gas markets, or the way that the transmission and distribution infrastructures they rely upon are regulated, or a combination of both? If so, what can be done to improve performance? Or is it just the concerns of nervous politicians or special pleadings of interest groups that might benefit from regulatory interventions into these markets?

There is no inherent conflict between the liberalisation of electricity and gas sectors and reasonable supply security goals as long as the appropriate market, industry structure, market design and regulatory institutions are developed and implemented. Moreover, there is little evidence that liberalisation has, at least yet, reduced supply security in most developed countries and considerable evidence that supply security has improved in some developing countries that have adopted comprehensive liberalisation programmes. However, the effective liberalisation of the electricity and gas sectors does create a number of challenges for institution building and governance that must be recognised and addressed for liberalised systems to perform reasonably well from a supply security perspective.

In the next section I provide what I consider to be a reasonable definition of what 'supply security' means in liberalised gas and electricity sectors in both the short and the long runs. This leads to a brief discussion of why supply security issues are of more concern in electricity and gas sectors than they are with goods and services bought and sold in other competitive markets. I then turn to a discussion of supply security issues that may arise in the regulated network segments of the electricity and natural gas sectors. Supply security issues associated with the supply of commodity natural gas and investment in new electric generating capacity are discussed next. This leads to a brief discussion of the role of voluntary demand response for supporting good performance of these markets. The chapter concludes with a discussion of growing linkages between liberalised natural gas and electricity markets and their potential implications for supply security. The chapter draws primarily on examples from the UK and the US and compares and contrasts their approaches to liberalisation of electricity and natural gas markets.

WHAT IS 'SUPPLY SECURITY?'

Policy makers are not always very clear about what they mean by 'supply security' and why they are particularly concerned about it in the case of electricity and natural gas. Accordingly, my first task is to define more precisely what it is that I think policy makers mean when they express concerns about 'supply security' in liberalised electricity and gas markets. First, they are concerned about 'involuntary rationing' of demand in the form of controlled rolling blackouts, uncontrolled transmission network failures, distribution network failures, and the process of public appeals and government exertions to reduce demand that accompany 'supply emergencies'. Involuntary rationing of demand can be very costly to individuals and businesses. These costs grow as outages are more sudden, more frequent, of longer duration and the geographic expanse of involuntary rationing expands. Public appeals to reduce demand in response to supply emergencies reflect badly on policy makers and the liberalisation policies they support. Public reactions to such appeals are also sensitive to how frequently policy makers must resort to them.

Second, policy makers are also concerned about high prices, or at least sudden increases in prices, for electricity and natural gas that naturally emerge to balance supply and demand when supplies are 'tight'.[1] Of course, high market prices resulting from a tight supply situation provide the economic signals that provide potential suppliers with the incentives to expand supplies. And periods of relatively high and relatively low prices are to be expected in all competitive markets. Rationing by price is also generally far superior from a social efficiency perspective to involuntary administrative rationing. Nevertheless, it should not be surprising that consumers are unhappy when prices for electricity or natural gas increase significantly. There is something about electricity and natural gas (as well as gasoline, diesel fuel and heating oil) that makes consumers especially unhappy about large sudden increases in prices and about even relatively brief involuntary outages. Energy costs are a significant fraction of consumer budgets and the short-run demand elasticities for these energy sources are very low. As prices rise, consumers cannot easily avoid paying the piper by switching to substitutes. In most developed countries, electricity and natural gas systems have been highly reliable as well for the last few decades and regulation has partially shielded consumers from price volatility.

To further burden elected government officials, involuntary rationing of demand (blackouts) and unusually high prices are highly correlated with one another in both the short and the long runs. In electricity and natural gas markets tight supply contingencies are first revealed in higher prices and associated price-driven demand responses. However, in electricity and natural gas markets, supply and demand cannot always be balanced with prices and related market mechanisms such as interruptible contracts. At some point, conventional price-driven demand response may not be available to reduce demand to match available supply fast enough to satisfy the need to maintain the physical integrity of the network. This leads system operators to turn to involuntary rationing of demand to maintain the integrity of the network. When system operators resort to involuntary rationing they also reduce market efficiency and (typically) create a large gap between market prices and the value of unserved energy or lost load.

Developments in California's electricity markets in 2000–01 became an 'electricity crisis' (Joskow, 2001) both because of involuntary rationing of demand (California ISO, 2001) and because of a sudden and dramatic increase in wholesale electricity prices (California ISO, 2002). Recent electricity crises in Ontario, Brazil and Chile were characterised by a similar combination of high prices, voltage reductions and rolling blackouts. The California electricity crisis also sensitised policy makers to potential market power problems in electricity markets (Borenstein et al., 2002; Joskow and Kahn, 2002) and in the US led to the expanded use of wholesale market price caps and other market power mitigation mechanisms.

Involuntary rationing of demand on electricity and gas networks is not always associated with high prices. Failures of the transmission and distribution network can lead to involuntary outages with no visible effect on market prices and no role for price-driven demand response. The cost to consumers of such outages can be quite high, especially if they are unanticipated and are sustained for a long period of time. In a large-scale network collapse such as those that occurred in the northeastern US and Italy in 2003, tens of millions of people lost their power in a few seconds. When these transmission networks collapsed there was excess demand, a surplus supply of generating capacity, and a zero price. This is not the typical configuration that we see in a textbook model of supply and demand in competitive markets!

Although perhaps an oversimplification, it is useful to group 'supply security' concerns into two categories: short-run system operating reliability and long-run resource adequacy.

1. *Operating reliability*   This dimension of supply security refers to the short-run performance attributes of the system as it works physically to balance supply and demand in real time, given the existing physical capacity of the system. In electricity, the physical capacity of the system encompasses the generation, transmission and distribution network (including metering and control) facilities. In the case of natural gas, it is the physical capability to produce commodity gas, the physical capacity of natural gas storage, transmission (including interconnector), LNG import and distribution facilities. The relevant indicia of performance here include (a) success in maintaining the network's physical operating constraints (for example, frequency, voltage, pressure), the number, duration and resulting costs of non-price rationing (involuntary blackouts), the speed of service restoration when non-price rationing occurs, *and* the overall costs of operating the system given the physical capacity that is in place.

2. *Resource adequacy*   This dimension of supply security in the case of electricity refers to the long-run performance attributes of the system in attracting investment in generation, transmission (including interconnectors), distribution, metering, and control capacity at the right times and the right locations to minimise the long-run costs of power supplies, including the costs of involuntary rationing of various kinds.

In the case of natural gas, the relevant supply segments where long-term investment needs emerge include natural gas production, storage, LNG import terminal capacity, as well as natural gas pipeline transmission, distribution and metering.

Obviously, operating reliability and resource adequacy considerations are interdependent. Operating an electric power or natural gas system reliably is a lot more challenging and costly when efficient investments in supply resources have not been forthcoming. Similarly, protocols to meet short-run reliability criteria may affect incentives for investment in new facilities in the long run. I shall focus here primarily on resource adequacy issues, but we should not forget this interdependence.

WHY WORRY ABOUT SUPPLY SECURITY?

Why should policy makers be worried about supply security in electricity and natural gas markets any more than they worry about supply security in any other competitive market? There are a few reasons: (a) important segments of these industries continue to be regulated; (b) physical and economic attributes of these products make the design of well-functioning competitive markets a significant technical and political challenge; (c) competitive market institutions are still evolving through 'reforms of the reforms' and sometimes subject to residual regulation; (d) liberalisation is incomplete in some areas where electricity and gas are supplied and sold competitively; (e) these markets cannot always be cleared by prices, rely on involuntary rationing under extreme conditions, and the costs of involuntary rationing can be very high.

The title of this chapter commits a common sin in referring only to 'competitive' electricity and natural gas markets. In fact, the phrase 'liberalised markets' used extensively in Europe provides a more productive context for evaluating supply security issues. The liberalisation of the electricity and natural gas sectors involves a complex institutional transformation from industries composed of vertically integrated regulated monopolies (typically state owned) to industries with unregulated competitive segments (for example, generation of electricity, retail supply) and regulated (primarily) monopoly transmission and distribution network segments. For liberalised systems to work well it is necessary to implement sound market institutions and market designs for the competitive segments, vertical and horizontal restructuring, unbundling of competitive and regulated network services, *and* a compatible regulatory framework to govern the regulated network segments. Poorly performing network segments can undermine the performance of the competitive segments and adversely affect supply security directly and indirectly through their effects on the performance of competitive power markets. Liberalisation initiatives have tended to focus a lot on the competitive segments (unbundling, market design, vertical separation, ring-fencing) and much less on the remaining regulated network segments. Outside of the UK, the importance of developing and implementing a good incentive or performance-based regulation framework for the transmission and distribution networks has not been given adequate recognition (Joskow, 2005c). The failure to build liberalised electricity and gas sectors with both good market designs for the competitive segments and good performance-based regulatory mechanisms for the regulated segments can be a major source of supply security problems.

It is also important to recognise that electricity in particular has a set of unusual physical and economic characteristics that create significant challenges for the development of good market institutions, for developing compatible regulatory institutions, and for integrating supply security considerations of various kinds into market and regulatory institutions. Natural gas networks share some of these attributes, though they are quantitatively less important. The differences between some of the attributes of gas and electricity are reflected in both institutional design challenges and in market performance.

Most discussions of electricity sector liberalisation recognise that electricity has some unusual characteristics that create challenges for creating well-functioning competitive power markets. These attributes include: (a) electricity cannot be stored economically; (b) electricity demand varies widely within days, between days, and between months of the year – a factor of three from peak to trough and peak demands are sustained for only a few hours each year; (c) the short-run elasticity of demand for electricity is very low; (d) electric power networks are physically delicate in the sense that they must meet stringent physical criteria for network frequency, voltage and stability to be able to supply electricity from dispersed generators to dispersed consumers at all; (e) supply and demand must be balanced continuously in real time to meet these physical criteria and the associated balancing mechanisms must react very quickly to changes in system conditions, including equipment outages, to meet these physical constraints; (f) most consumers cannot see or respond to short-run price movements that signal supply scarcity at different times and at different locations and which can come and go very quickly; (g) there can be very significant intra-day and day-to-day price volatility to balance demand variations in the presence of capacity constraints and in the absence of storage; (h) a very small fraction of peak electricity demand can typically respond voluntarily to large sudden price increases resulting from sudden imbalances in demand and supply; (i) except for the largest customers, demand typically cannot be physically controlled on an individual basis in the short run so that any administrative rationing must be accomplished on a 'zonal' basis, making individual price-contingent 'priority rationing' contracts[2] infeasible for these customers; (j) as a result, an effective controlled 'last resort' involuntary rationing system must be in place to keep the entire network, or a large portion of it, from collapsing so as to avoid both involuntary rationing on the demand side and idle generating capacity on the supply side.

From a longer-run perspective, changes in the physical infrastructure of an electric power system can take a significant amount of time to be realised. New generating stations and new transmission lines can take several years to plan and build. Procedures for environmental reviews to obtain certifications to build new facilities can add significantly to the time it takes to change the physical capacity of the network. Major transmission facilities are often especially challenging in this regard since they typically traverse multiple local and regional government jurisdictions.

Many of these attributes are not unique to electricity. Rather what makes electric power systems special is the intensity of the individual attributes and the combination of so many of them in a single product. So, empty hotel rooms or airline seats cannot be stored. But the short-run demand for hotel rooms and airline seats is much more elastic than the demand for electricity. And if a big tour bus filled with passengers demanding hotel rooms suddenly shows up in a city where all of the hotel rooms are full, there is no need for a 'hotel system operator' to act quickly to avoid all of the hotels suddenly closing down, thrusting their occupants out on the streets. Indeed, the passengers on the bus are turned away by individual hotel operators and just sleep on the bus while the hotel occupants continue to sleep soundly. If the flights are full when a passenger calls for a reservation he/she can take the train, drive, travel the next day, or take his/her chances by flying standby; a 'stockout' does not disrupt the operation of the airline network. Of course, in the case of airlines an air traffic controller is required for safety reasons and in this sense there is a similarity to the system operator of an electric power network. Furthermore, air traffic control systems have been criticised for not using any economic mechanisms to allocate scarce takeoff and landing slots and congested airspace. The air traffic control system is quite reliable but not economically efficient.

Unlike electricity, natural gas can be and is stored economically, though storage is costly and its ability to replace current production streams limited. Moreover, once gas in storage is released for sale, it may take a significant amount of time to replenish it, while electricity-generating plants that run to meet peak demand one week during a cold snap or heat wave can run again two weeks later if the peak demand reappears, assuming that they do not break down in between. Natural gas networks must also meet physical operating criteria, in particular maintaining minimum physical pressure in the pipes, but the real-time physical operating constraints are less stringent than with electricity since variations in the pressure or packing of the pipeline can accommodate short-run changes in supply and demand relatively easily.[3] The aggregate demand for natural gas has a larger short-run price elasticity than is the case for electricity, largely due to fuel-switching capabilities. Historically, there has been relatively more interruptible demand on the gas side than on the electricity side. Since natural gas can be stored in situ or in storage facilities and demand is more responsive to price spikes, commodity prices for natural gas exhibit much less short-run volatility than do electricity prices.[4] Designing and building new facilities can also take several years as with electric power infrastructure, though existing facilities can often be expanded quickly at modest cost by increasing compressor capacity or adding short loops around bottlenecks on the network. I would argue that creating well-functioning liberalised natural gas markets is less of a technical challenge than is creating well-functioning liberalised electricity markets.

Importantly, liberalised electricity and natural gas sectors also have organisational attributes that are different from those that govern most competitive markets. As already noted, these sectors are composed of competitive segments (electricity generation, natural gas production, wholesale marketing and retail supply) and regulated monopoly segments (transmission and distribution). The performance of the competitive segments depends critically on the performance of the regulated monopoly platforms on which they operate. Actions taken by the monopoly network operator as it balances the system to meet physical operating reliability criteria can affect market prices in the short run and incentives to invest in new facilities in the long run.

In addition, in the case of electricity, market mechanisms that are relied upon for the physical or near physical operation of the system (day-ahead, intra-day, real-time energy markets and operating reserves) are 'designed' by regulators in consultation with stakeholders, rather than evolving naturally via the invisible hand. These market mechanisms may have design features ('flaws') that adversely affect the behaviour and performance of the market. So, for example in England and Wales, the New Electricity Trading Arrangements (NETA) replaced the Pool because it was thought that the Pool had design flaws. In the New England region of the USA, what was viewed as a flawed single-price auction mechanism in the wholesale electricity market was replaced with a locational marginal price (LMP) mechanism that reflects the marginal cost of congestion and marginal losses in prices at each major node on the network (ISO New England, 2005a).

Electricity sector liberalisation must deal with another set of network issues in continental Europe and North America. The synchronised alternating current (AC) networks in continental Europe and the US span large geographic areas that include several countries or states and multiple system operators with 'control area' responsibilities for specified portions of the larger synchronised network. From a physical perspective it is one network. From ownership, control and regulatory perspectives it is several networks. Moreover, although power is traded both within and between individual network control areas, the market designs may differ between them. Coordinating the physical operation of the multiple-system operators and harmonising the market designs in each of them is important for achieving supply security and economic efficiency goals for the entire integrated network.

The studies of the 2003 US and Italian blackouts either state or imply that electricity sector liberalisation *per se* played no role in the blackouts. I think that this conclusion is too cavalier. Liberalisation in North America and Europe *has* placed increased stress on the reliable operation of electric transmission networks in a number of dimensions. Essentially the same transmission network that existed before liberalisation in continental Europe and the US now supports a much greater volume of trading between countries (in Europe) and regions (in the US) than in the past and, as a result, the electricity network runs close to physical operating constraints more frequently. Vertical and horizontal restructuring that has accompanied liberalisation has brought more market participants into the system and complicated coordination issues between suppliers and network operators and between network operators in different countries (in Europe) and different regions (in the US). The harmonisation of market mechanisms in different countries (Europe) and regions (the US) efficiently to dispatch generation and to allocate scarce transmission capacity on the synchronised network they all share is still a work in progress and leads to a sacrifice of some efficiency benefits from competition. Finally, horizontal and vertical restructuring to support well-functioning competitive electricity markets had been (and still is) only partially implemented in much of Europe and the US.

Consider First Energy, the company at the centre of the US blackout. It is a vertically integrated utility (generation, transmission and distribution) which, at that time, was still the system operator in its area.[5] It is fairly clear that it did not view transmission and network operations as a core business for the company and it appears to have devoted limited resources (labour, training, computer and communications equipment) to its transmission business. Inadequate tree trimming and maintenance were identified as the prime initial causes of the blackout. Neither Ohio nor the US Federal Energy Regulatory Commission (FERC) has adopted incentive regulation programmes that would have given First Energy incentives to maintain and operate its system reliably and, indeed, regulatory responsibility for transmission in the US is split between the states and the federal government in such a way as to make good regulation almost impossible. It does not require too much imagination to conclude that *incomplete and ineffective* liberalisation made at least some indirect contribution to this cascading blackout.

Natural gas networks in the United States and Europe have some similar coordination characteristics. There are multiple pipeline owners that must coordinate their pricing, scheduling and balancing protocols to make efficient use of the system for delivering natural gas reliably from dispersed production sources to dispersed consumers. The US gas transmission network relies more on parallel (competing) pipelines than does the European gas network. It is also far more advanced with most aspects of liberalisation. However, the coordination challenges are not as great as in electricity if for no other reason than there is more time to respond to changes in supply and demand conditions on the network than with electricity.

So far, the UK has been spared most of the challenges of operating within a larger physical network with many hands on the wheel. In electricity, there is only a direct current (DC) interconnection with continental Europe and the British Electricity Trading and Transmission Arrangements (BETTA) has internalised network operations between England and Wales and Scotland. In gas, the UK has relied primarily on gas delivered to the beach from the UK North Sea fields, on a limited volume of storage, and relatively little on interconnectors with other European countries or on LNG imports. This situation is now changing and the UK gas network will become increasingly integrated with the only partially liberalised continental European gas system and with a growing world market in LNG.

The unusual combinations of physical, economic and organisational attributes do not mean that liberalised electricity and natural gas sectors cannot yield good performance from cost, price and supply security perspectives, especially compared to the alternative of vertically integrated regulated monopolies. It does mean that creating the necessary institutional infrastructure is very challenging. If we can get it right then we should expect to see good performance in all dimensions, including supply security dimensions. If we get it wrong, there will eventually be serious performance problems.

NETWORK REGULATORY FRAMEWORK

The development and application of a sound regulatory framework for transmission and distribution networks is an important component of an electricity and natural gas liberalisation programme that has good performance attributes from both a cost and security of supply perspective. For the unregulated market segments of liberalised electricity and natural gas sectors to work well, a robust transmission network that can respond quickly to changing supply and demand conditions is essential. The attributes of the regulatory framework affect both the short-run operating reliability and long-run resource adequacy. The regulatory framework that has evolved in the UK over the last 15 years is the international gold standard for electricity and natural gas network regulation within a liberalised sector context.

From a short-run operating reliability perspective the challenge is to apply a regulatory framework that exhibits a proper balance between incentives to reduce operating costs, capital expenditures and incentives to maintain or improve reliability in both the short and the long runs.[6] Regulators in liberalised electricity and natural gas sectors were fairly quick to adopt price-cap mechanisms (RPI-X) as an (apparently) simple way to provide high-powered incentives for cost reduction while, through the periodic reset of the base price level (P_0), conveying the benefits of lower operating costs to consumers (Beesley and Littlechild, 1989). In the UK, the improvement in productivity, measured over the decade following privatisation and restructuring, is impressive (Domah and Pollitt, 2001).

One of the well-known problems with a pure price-cap mechanism is that it may provide incentives to reduce network reliability, in terms of the frequency and duration of network outages and the speed with which new suppliers and consumers are connected to the network, as they stimulate network owners and operators to reduce operating costs (Joskow, 2005c). In order to deal with this potential problem, network regulatory frameworks have been extended to incorporate targets for various dimensions of reliability and financial penalties and rewards for falling short of or exceeding them. The UK has been a pioneer in this regard, though US regulators have begun to implement similar 'quality of service' regulatory mechanisms. However, achieving the right relative marginal incentives for cost reduction and service quality changes remains a challenge, especially building consumer valuations for network reliability and other dimensions of service quality directly into the regulatory mechanism. And there continues to be the potential for new technologies to make it possible to 'unbundle' some aspects of reliability or service quality so that individual consumers can express their individual preferences for service reliability.

Of course, price-cap regulation is not as easy to implement in practice as it may appear to be in theory. Mechanisms must be put in place to set and reset P_0 and X. P_0 in turn must reflect both forecasts of efficient operating costs *and* a budget for capital expenditures to replace ageing equipment and for new equipment to support changes in supply and demand for electricity and natural gas, consistent with achieving both operating reliability and resource adequacy goals. Moreover, once a capital budget is approved, 'mundane' issues like the depreciation rate, the debt/equity ratio, and the cost of capital must be resolved. Although rarely discussed in the academic literature on price-cap mechanisms (Joskow, 2005c), the capital budgeting process and the determination of the cost of capital and associated allowed rate of return have very important implications for the long-run supply security attributes of transmission and distribution networks from a resource adequacy perspective. Imperfections in the regulatory framework here can have serious adverse network security consequences going forward and also undermine the performance of the competitive electricity and gas segments that rely on the network.

Developing a good forward budget for capital expenditures for the transmission network owner is a very challenging problem. It requires that the regulator implement an investment planning process in which the network owners offer their proposed investment plans and the regulator, with the help of its own consultants and other stakeholders, must ultimately evaluate them. The regulator can know the firm's efficient capital needs over the next five years only imperfectly and the network owner will always know more about its best estimate for future capital needs than does the regulator – a standard asymmetric information problem. Moreover, even the network owner can know its efficient capital needs only with considerable uncertainty, since future investment needs will necessarily depend on contingencies as they evolve (demand growth, interconnections, environmental and safety regulation changes) over the 'fixed price' period. Ofgem (Office of Gas and Electricity Markets) adopted a particularly clever 'menu of incentive contracts' approach in its recent Distribution Network Operator (DNO) price review (Ofgem, 2004) to resolve differences in views about future capital needs between the regulator's consultant and the DNOs. The DNOs could accept a capital budget close to that recommended by the consultant and get a higher expected return and a higher-powered cost-sharing formula or a capital investment budget further from the consultant's recommendation with a lower expected return and a less powerful cost-sharing formula (ibid.).

However, given the inherent uncertainties about future efficient levels of capital expenditures and the possibility that the networks will underspend in the face of a hard capital budget and a price-cap mechanism, I do not think that there is any way to avoid some kind of *ex post* review of deviations from the capital budget to determine whether they were efficient and to provide for recovery of efficient overspend and recapture of underspend compared to approved capital expenditure budgets that did not reflect efficiencies. This places a significant but necessary burden on the regulator.

One of the things that always puzzled me about US regulation of electric utilities during the 1970s and 1980s was the amount of time devoted to arguing about whether the net-of-tax cost of equity capital was say 11 or 12 per cent (nominal). The effect on retail electricity prices of any decision within this range is tiny and imperceptible to consumers once it is included with all of the other elements that go into the retail prices that they see. The effects of regulatory decision about the cost of capital on consumer prices are even smaller today as the scope of regulation has been reduced to network charges only. However, the effects on the network owner's incentives to invest can be very large. The US FERC has historically chosen to allow gas pipeline owners allowed rates of return on equity that are at the high end of a zone of reasonableness because FERC has been very focused on stimulating investment, reducing congestion and increasing reliability. This is one reason why investment in natural gas pipeline capacity has proceeded reasonably well in the liberalised US market and there is little congestion on the natural gas pipeline network.

FERC has recently proposed new policies that would promote increased investment in electric transmission investment by reducing regulatory uncertainty and increasing the profitability of transmission investments in response to growing concerns about the consequences of inadequate electric transmission investment and obligations imposed on FERC by the Energy Policy Act of 2005 (US FERC, 2005b). The Act requires FERC to adopt incentive or performance-based electric transmission-pricing mechanisms that benefit consumers by reducing the cost of delivered power and ensuring reliability by reducing transmission congestion. The US provides an unfortunate case study of how a poorly developed regulatory framework for electric transmission can undermine investment incentives and how insufficient investment can in turn undermine the performance of wholesale power markets and reduce reliability. The existing framework for supporting transmission investment in the US is seriously flawed. Regulatory responsibilities are split between the states and the federal government in sometimes mysterious ways (Joskow, 2005a, b). FERC initially supported what I consider to be a flawed 'merchant investment' model for electricity transmission investment (Joskow and Tirole, 2005) and confused issues of who pays for transmission upgrades with questions about whether such upgrades are mediated through market mechanisms or regulatory mechanisms or a combination of both. Transmission investments driven by reliability considerations and transmission investments driven by congestion cost reductions are inherently interdependent but have been treated by FERC and some system operators in the US as if they were completely separable (Joskow, 2006b). The US does not even collect statistics on transmission investment and transmission network performance that are adequate to evaluate the performance of the network (US EIA, 2004).

Accordingly, it should not be surprising that there has been little progress in developing and applying a coherent incentive regulation framework for transmission. Moreover, there has been little if any investment in transmission facilities to increase interregional transfer capability. As a result, as new generating capacity has been added in the US and as wholesale market activity has expanded, there is growing congestion on the network, increased use of administrative transmission load relief procedures, and the system runs much more closely to the margins of operating reliability constraints, making it more susceptible to network failures and involuntary rationing of demand (Joskow, 2005b).

Inadequate investment in electric transmission infrastructure has unfortunate implications for both electricity prices for consumers in constrained import areas and for reliability. For example, the eastern US has abundant generating capacity at the present time. However, due largely to transmission constraints, the prices for power vary widely across the region. Table 4.1 reports data on forward prices for monthly contracts for January/February 2006 at various locations in the eastern US as quoted in October 2005. The prices vary from a low of $94/MWh (Ohio) to a high of $204/MWh (New York City). Natural gas, which has a more robust pipeline transmission network, exhibits much smaller locational basis differences under normal winter operating conditions, though the infastructure in the Northeast is only barely adequate to meet demand under extreme weather conditions.[7]

Table 4.1   Forward wholesale power prices, monthly contracts for January/February 2006 (on October 7, 2005)

Location	Price ($/MWh)
Boston	$194
New York City	$204
Buffalo, New York	$130
Pennsylvania (West)	$115
Ohio	$94
Ontario, Canada	$120

Source: Platt's Megawatt Daily, October 7, 2005.

In addition to the effects of transmission congestion on wholesale power prices and the social costs of congestion, a congested transmission network makes it more challenging to achieve efficient wholesale market performance. Congestion increases market power problems and the use of highly imperfect regulatory mitigation mechanisms to respond to them. Congestion makes it more challenging for system operators to maintain reliability using standard market mechanisms, leading them to pay specific generators significant sums to stay in the market rather than retire and to rely more on out-of-market (OOM) calls that depress market prices received by other suppliers. In New England, the amount of generating capacity operating subject to 'reliability contracts' with the independent system operator (ISO) has increased from about 500 MW in 2002 to over 7000 MW projected (including pending contracts) for 2005 (ISO New England, 2005a, p. 80) and will add hundreds of millions of dollars of 'uplift' costs to electricity consumers' bills in 2006.

Another relevant issue that must be addressed is where to draw the line between investments in *regulated* monopoly network elements and investments in network elements that will be determined by market forces and whose prices will be *unregulated*. As previously noted, in the US, FERC at one time envisaged that electric transmission network investments, aside from interconnection facilities linking generators with the grid, would be guided by market forces. FERC expected to rely extensively on market signals (locational price differences) and unregulated merchant (or voluntary market participant-driven) investment to expand the capacity of the grid (Joskow and Tirole, 2005), turning to regulated investments identified through an open planning process only as a last resort. Unfortunately, this led to almost no investment in the electric transmission network for several years.[8] In the US, the role for merchant investment in electricity infrastructure now seems to be focused on electric transmission interconnectors between regions, though only one has been built and one is under construction. Both have been secured by long-term contracts with a municipal utility which can pass along the associated costs in regulated prices charged to retail consumers.

I have serious doubts about the viability of a merchant investment framework for electric transmission investment in the near term, even for interconnectors, especially in Europe and the US where wholesale and retail electricity markets in different countries (Europe) and different regions (US) are still in a state of flux. In the case of electricity interconnectors between countries and regions, merchant investors should be given an opportunity to develop projects, but a meaningful regulatory backstop should be available as well to expand interconnector capacity to reflect opportunities to access cheaper power supplies and to increase the reliability of the system, especially its ability to respond quickly to significant changes in supply and demand conditions which may have low probabilities of being realised. In this regard I approve of the analysis applied by the Dutch regulator in its review of the NordNed interconnector project in December 2004[9] and by the policies on interconnector financing being developed by the European Commission.

On the natural gas side there has been much more success with the development of individual long-distance pipelines and expansion projects with the financial backing, through contracts or ownership positions, of groups of shippers and large customers. In the US, the development of new pipeline capacity depends primarily on voluntary contractual agreements between pipelines, shippers, local distribution companies (LDCs) and large consumers, operating under the shadow of FERC regulation of maximum transport prices. However, in the US, as in the UK, the liberalisation process of the natural gas sector is now reasonably mature and the market and regulatory mechanisms are fairly stable. Commercial arrangements are honoured, and one rarely hears concerns in the US about the Canadians cutting off their exports of gas during tight supply situations. There have been some questions raised about whether pipeline investment has expanded adequately to meet growing demand for natural gas in the electricity sector, especially in the Northeast which historically has a weak gas transmission network. The traditional reliance on long-term contractual commitments with shippers and large consumers is also being tested as liberalisation in the US has moved market participants to shorter-term contractual arrangements.

An important question for the UK, as it looks forward to relying more on imports of natural gas to meet demand as production from the UK North Sea areas declines, is how it will mesh its liberalised natural gas market with what are only partially liberalised markets in Europe. In particular, will commercial arrangements between market participants in different countries be honoured or will governments in Europe try to 'capture' gas that might otherwise be exported for their own citizens during supply emergencies using out-of-market mechanisms and government-induced behaviour that restricts the transportation of gas when it is most valuable? Partially liberalised gas markets in continental Europe can lead to higher prices and more frequent demand rationing in the UK as it relies more on imports than would be the case in a well-functioning competitive European gas market.

Finally, we come to natural gas storage facilities. Pipeline transportation and underground storage are complementary components of a natural gas system. While mainline gas transmission lines provide the crucial link between producing area and marketplace, gas storage facilities help to maintain the system's reliability and its capability to transport gas supplies efficiently and without interruption. The capability to store gas as backup ensures supply availability in downstream markets during periods of heavy demand by supplementing pipeline capacity. Storage also enables greater system efficiency by allowing more level production and transmission flows. In some instances, development or expansion of the pipeline network is tied inexorably with storage and vice versa.

Are storage facilities properly part of the regulated gas pipeline network or part of the unregulated gas production and supply sector? It depends on what kind of storage we are talking about and what its purpose is. Dispersed 'fast response' gas storage facilities are needed to respond to short-lived pipeline network outages or constraints that would otherwise lead to reliability problems, including unacceptable reductions in pressure or service curtailments. These facilities should be under the control of the gas pipeline network operator (the facilities can be owned or contracted) and a component of the regulatory contract.[10] It would also be reasonable for a regulated gas transmission or distribution network owner to have the flexibility to evaluate trade-offs between expanding delivery capabilities by expanding the capacity of the pipeline or expanding local storage capacity instead to meet peak demand. However, as long as the gas market itself is functioning well, and in particular that price-contingent demand response or other types of voluntarily negotiated interruptible contracts rather than involuntary curtailments are relied upon to balance supply and demand, there is no reason why gas storage facilities designed for other than short-term reliability reasons should not be left to the market. Ten years of US experience with deregulation of entry into gas storage and open access to gas storage facilities controlled by interstate pipelines has been quite good. The current policy focus is on the provision of information to the market about the status of gas storage inventories to improve market performance.[11]

NATURAL GAS RESOURCE ADEQUACY

Competitive natural gas production markets work very well when they are allowed to work without government interference. Suppliers respond quickly to price movements by increasing or decreasing exploration and development activity, injecting gas into storage or taking it out, and adjusting physical production where this is feasible. There are liquid financial markets to allow buyers and sellers to hedge risks and express their views on future changes in supply and demand conditions. Rising natural gas prices have led to a huge expansion in the development of LNG export and import facilities in the last few years. Suppliers do have to confront environmental and certification processes for major new production facilities, especially LNG facilities, and at least in the US this is a significant constraint on expanding LNG import capabilities, as well as on extending exploration and development activity to protected off-shore areas and Alaska. Policy makers need to ensure that environmental and related project certification reviews are conducted in a fair and efficient way so that new facilities are not unduly delayed and their costs increased unreasonably.

Dry gas production in the lower 48 states of the US has or soon will peak and supply and demand are forecast to be balanced by growing imports of LNG (and possibly with gas from Alaska and proximate areas in northern Canada if the necessary pipelines are built to move the gas down into the lower 48 states).[12] The UK is in a similar situation, looking for increased imports from Europe through expanded interconnectors and expanded LNG imports to meet future demand as production from the UK fields in the North Sea continue to decline. The growing reliance on imports by the US and the UK does raise some issues. First, the UK will be relying much more on the natural gas supply markets in continental Europe which are only partially liberalised. The big question here is whether pipeline suppliers controlled by other EU countries will honour commercial commitments during supply emergencies or divert supplies to their own citizens using OOM mechanisms and the 'socialisation' of recovery of the associated costs. Such policies can lead to higher prices and more rationing of demand in the UK during tight supply conditions than would be the case if there were a well-functioning competitive European gas market. The UK clearly has an interest in promoting full liberalisation and getting government out of the business of allocating gas supplies or controlling prices when supplies are tight.

Second, the primary sources of LNG exports are also the primary sources of petroleum exports (International Energy Agency, 2005). They are concentrated in politically unstable areas of the world. To the extent that one is concerned about 'oil supply security', relying on the same suppliers for LNG is not a move in the right direction. Since LNG trades in world markets, these concerns are global and not limited to individual countries. Increasing global diversification of LNG import supply sources can help to mitigate politically motivated supply disruption. I shall leave it to others to discuss potential diplomatic and military responses to these concerns.

Finally, the increasing reliance of many countries on LNG imports, combined with expanded storage capacity, is already leading to international linkages between natural gas markets in different regions that historically have been thought of as being isolated regional markets. These changes will eventually lead to a world market price for natural gas determined by movements of LNG serving to arbitrage locational price differences. This is not a 'problem', but requires recognition in traditional 'supply security' evaluations. Gas will move around until the arbitrage opportunities are exhausted. This should help rather than hurt on the supply security front as long as governments do not interfere with market pricing and the associated allocation of scarce supplies across locations and consumers.

ELECTRICITY GENERATION RESOURCE ADEQUACY: MARKET AND REGULATORY IMPERFECTIONS

I turn now to the investment incentives provided by liberalised electricity sectors to stimulate efficient investments in generating capacity at the 'right' times and in the 'right' places to balance supply and demand at minimum cost in the long run. Unlike, the situation for natural gas supplies, at the moment, there is considerable concern in the US, Canada and other countries that competitive wholesale electricity markets do not provide adequate incentives to stimulate adequate investment in generating capacity to meet reliability standards. Various proposals for regulator determined capacity obligations, capacity prices and long-term contracting obligations placed on retailers and/or on the system operator are now being considered (California Public Utilities Commission, 2005; Cramton and Stoft, 2005; Joskow and Tirole, 2006).

At first blush, it is puzzling that policy makers should be worrying about investment in new electric generating capacity. Between 1990 and 2002 there was 26,000 MW of new generating capacity added in the UK, or about 40 per cent of the initial stock, while nearly 20,000 MW was retired (DTI (UK), 2002). In the US, roughly 200,000 MW of new generating capacity entered service between 1999 and 2004, an increase in total US generating capacity of about 30 per cent (Joskow, 2006a) from the level in 1998. There has been little new investment in generating capacity in the Nordic countries or Northern Europe in the last few years, but these countries entered the liberalisation era with excess capacity. The drying up of investment has sensibly been viewed as a sound market response to a system that persistently had excessive investment in generating capacity (Von der Fehr et al., 2005).

Despite the enormous quantity of new generating capacity that entered service between 2000 and 2004, and the existence of excess capacity in most regions of the country, US policy makers are now very concerned about future shortages of generating capacity resulting from retirements and inadequate investment. Many of the merchant generating companies that made these investments subsequently experienced serious financial problems and several went bankrupt. The liberal financing arrangements available to support these projects during the financial bubble years are no longer available and project financing for new generating plants is difficult to arrange unless there is a long-term sales contract with a creditworthy buyer to support it. Rising natural gas prices have changed the economic attractiveness of the combined-cycle gas turbine (CCGT) technology that has dominated the fleet of new plants. The quantity of new generating capacity coming out of the construction pipeline is falling significantly, and most of the new capacity under construction now in the US is either being built under traditional regulatory arrangements or benefits from various subsidies and contractual benefits available to renewable energy, primarily wind.

Very little investment in new merchant generating capacity is being committed at the present time in the US. System operators in the Northeast and California are projecting shortages and increases in power supply emergencies three to five years into the future, recognising that developing, permitting and completing new generating plants takes several years.

On the one hand, a market response that leads prices (adjusted for fuel costs) and profits to fall and investment to decline dramatically when there is excess capacity, is just the response that we would be looking for from a competitive market. For 25 years prior to the most recent market reforms, the regulated US electric power industry had excess generating capacity which consumers were forced to pay for through cost-based regulated prices. The promise of competition was that investors would bear the risk of excess capacity and reap the rewards of tight capacity contingencies, a risk that they could try partially to reallocate by offering forward contracts to consumers and their intermediaries. At least some of the noise about investment incentives is coming from owners of merchant generating plants who would just like to see higher prices and profits.

On the other hand, numerous analyses of the performance of the organised wholesale electricity markets in the US indicate that they do not appear to produce enough net revenues from sales of energy and operating reserves (ancillary services) into the market to support investment in new generating capacity in the right places and consistent with the administrative reliability criteria that are still applicable in each region. Moreover, while capacity obligations and associated capacity prices that are components of the market designs in the northeastern US wholesale electricity markets produce additional net revenue for generators over and above what they get from selling energy and ancillary services, the existing capacity pricing mechanisms do not appear to yield revenues that fill this

Table 4.2   Theoretical net energy and ancillary services revenue for a new combustion turbine peaking plant (PJM, $/MW-year)

Year	Net energy and ancillary service revenue
1999	64,445
2000	18,866
2001	41,659
2002	25,622
2003	14,544
2004	10,453
Average	29,265
Annualised 20-year fixed cost ~ $70,000/MW/year	

Source: PJM State of the Market Report, 2005.

'net revenue' gap. That is, wholesale prices have been too low even when supplies are tight.

The experience in the PJM Regional Transmission Organisation[13] in the US is fairly typical. Table 4.2 displays the net revenue that a hypothetical new combustion turbine (CT) would have earned by selling energy and ancillary services in PJM's spot markets if it were dispatched optimally to reflect its marginal running costs and market spot prices in each hour for the years 1999–2004. In no year would a new peaking turbine have earned enough net revenues from sales of energy and ancillary services alone to cover the fixed costs of a new generating unit and, on average, the scarcity rents contributed only about 40 per cent of the capital costs of a new peaking unit. Based on energy market revenues alone, it would not be rational for an investor to invest in new CT or CCGT capacity in the PJM region. PJM has capacity obligations that are imposed on load serving entities (LSEs)[14] and there is a market where qualifying capacity entitlements are traded. Capacity obligations in PJM were carried over from its origins as a centrally dispatched power pool into its competitive market design. Sales of capacity entitlements provide another source of revenues for generating units. However, even adding in revenues from sales of capacity at market prices, the total net revenues that would have been earned by a new plant over this six-year period would have been significantly less than the capital costs of an investment in new peaking capacity.

This phenomenon is not unique to PJM. Every organised market in the US exhibits a similar gap between net revenues produced by energy markets and the fixed costs of investing in new capacity measured over several years time (New York ISO, 2005, pp. 22–5; US FERC, 2005a, p. 60). There is still a significant gap when capacity payments are included. The only exception appears to be New York City where prices for energy and capacity collectively appear to be sufficient to support new investment, though new investment in New York may be much more costly than assumed in these analyses (US FERC, 2005a, p. 60). Moreover, a large fraction of the net revenue there comes from capacity payments rather than from energy market revenues (New York ISO, 2005, p. 23).

How can we explain the empirical observation that if investors in new generating capacity are expected to rely only on revenues from sales of energy and ancillary services it would not be profitable to invest in new generating capacity? Obviously, there is something about these markets that keeps prices too low. There are three attributes of electricity and electricity networks that I discussed earlier that interact with imperfections in existing wholesale market institutions to cause this 'net revenue gap problem'. First, individual generating plants are needed to run, and are economical to run in a well-functioning wholesale market, for widely varying fractions of the year to meet demand; from 8760 hours during the year (base load) to perhaps 100 or fewer hours per year (peaking). Second, there is relatively little price-contingent demand response and related quick-response interruptible contracts available in most regional US electricity markets. In the US, demand response under contract to system operators accounts for only 2 to 3 per cent of peak demand in most regions (US FERC, 2005a, p. 212). Due to transmission constraints, the fraction of peak demand that can be managed with demand response in some subregions is much smaller. Moreover, some of the interruptible contracts were negotiated under the assumption that there would be no interruptions. Customers who thought that they could get a price discount with no interruptible pain either do not respond to curtailment notices or quickly cancel their contracts. Third, in order to operate the network reliably, system operators purchase frequency regulation services and operating reserves to allow the system to continue operating reliably if there is a sudden failure of a large generating plant or major transmission line and to respond to short-term variations in demand. Operating and related replacement reserves typically amount to about 10 per cent of peak demand. When operating reserves fall below a certain level (for example, 7 per cent of peak demand), the system operator will take action to reduce demand to keep operating reserves from falling further in order to avoid a network collapse (Joskow and Tirole, 2006). Thus, one can think of the capacity constraint as being binding when generating capacity falls below about 110 per cent of peak demand.

The first attribute means that the marginal investment in generating capacity that just balances supply and demand efficiently in the long run will run only a few hours on average in any year. Moreover, the number of hours this 'peaking' capacity runs will vary widely from year to year depending on variations in the supply/demand balance from year to year. As a result, for investments in peaking capacity to be financially attractive, the associated capital costs must be recovered from market revenues during a relatively small number of hours. Prices during these hours must rise above the marginal operating cost of this peaking capacity if investment is to be economical on a total cost basis. For example, if the annualised fixed costs of a peaking turbine are $80,000 per MW/year and it runs only 50 hours on average in a year then it must be expected to sell its output at prices that yield, on average, a margin (net of operating costs) of at least $1600/MWh over the generating unit's life. However, prices will rise above marginal operating costs in a competitive market only when a supply constraint is reached and 'scarcity prices' are set by demand bidding for the opportunity to have access to generation from this scarce generating capacity.

Figure 4.1 illustrates a wholesale electricity market equilibrium where supply and demand are cleared at a quantity that is below the maximum generating capacity on the system. The price reflects the marginal cost of operating the last generator that profitably supplies to clear the market. Generators with lower operating costs earn some competitive market rents at this price and these rents help to pay for their capital costs. Figure 4.2 depicts a situation in which generating capacity is fully exhausted and price is determined by demand response actions. At this equilibrium price, competitive market 'scarcity rents' are produced to help to pay for the capital costs of the inframarginal capacity as well as for the capital costs of the peaking capacity. In reality things are a little more complicated because demand and supply are stochastic and system operators must hold operating reserves to ensure that they can respond very quickly to, for example, unplanned outages of generation or transmission equipment. This creates an additional set of demand contingencies where increases in demand are accommodated by reducing operating reserves below target levels. When the network operates with lower levels of operating reserves, the probability of a network collapse increases and the marginal social cost of further reducing operating reserves increases as well. At some point the system operator will no longer allow operating reserves to fall further and instead will implement rolling blackouts to avoid a more costly system collapse (Joskow and Tirole, 2006).

An electric power system with traditional levels of reliability would find itself in 'scarcity conditions' due to either operating reserve deficiencies or rolling blackouts only a few hours each year (for example, 50). When these contingencies arise, the efficient market-clearing price can be quite high, reflecting the value of lost load or unserved energy; as much as 10–15 thousand $/MWh. In a well-functioning wholesale electricity market a

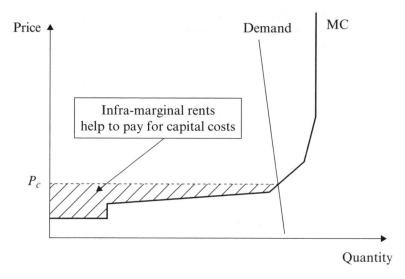

Figure 4.1   Wholesale market equilibrium below capacity constraint

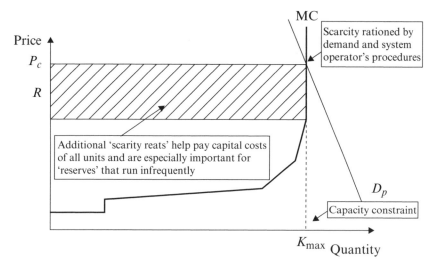

Figure 4.2   Wholesale market equilibrium at capacity constraint

large fraction of the net revenues earned by generating units that run for only a small fraction of the year are realised during these high-priced 'scarcity' hours. If prices are not right during these hours it will distort investment incentives, lead to underinvestment in peaking capacity and increase the probability of rolling blackouts or a network collapse. Accordingly, investment (and retirement) incentives on the margin are extremely sensitive to price formation during a relatively small number of high demand hours. Unfortunately, without adequate demand response, the short-run aggregate demand curve eventually becomes vertical and cannot be relied upon to balance (vertical) supply and demand when generating capacity is fully utilised or to determine a clearing price. Under these 'scarcity' conditions, administrative allocation and pricing rules, as well as small changes in behaviour by the system operator can have a very large effect on prices.

If we look at the distribution of spot prices for New York and New England this is clear (New York ISO, 2005; ISO New England, 2005a). A peaking plant that runs 50 hours a year needs net revenue of about $1600/MWh to cover its capital and other fixed costs. The highest hourly price in New York between 2002 and 2004 was $1000 and the average price for the highest-priced 50 hours about $300/MWh. Wholesale prices for electric energy are too low to attract adequate investment to balance supply and demand at conventional levels of reliability in the long run. Why are prices so low? The primary contributing factors are:

1. All of the organised markets in the US have wholesale market price caps and other market power mitigation mechanisms in place. The price cap is typically $1000/MWh (except in California where it is $250/MWh). (It is A$10,000 in Australia!) These caps are too low to allow prices to rise high enough during operating reserve deficiency conditions or when involuntary demand rationing is being imposed. However, it cannot just be the price caps because the price caps are rarely hit even during operating reserve deficiency conditions.
2. The absence of adequate demand response to be called upon (or relied upon) to reduce demand so that operating reserve and capacity constraints are not violated also ends up depressing prices. Appropriate price formation requires the existence of adequate demand response so that there is relatively little short-term demand response in most US electricity markets. There is not enough active demand to bid up the price to market-clearing levels.
3. Because system operators do not expect that rising prices will balance the system, they take various 'reliability' actions when they anticipate that the system will be running close to its limits. These actions all have the effect (though not the goal) of suppressing prices. The system operator may start calling on replacement reserves before market prices rise to reflect the scarcity conditions. They may issue emergency appeals before prices rise to signal that there is a supply emergency. They may

reduce voltage by 5 per cent, effectively reducing demand *and* reducing prices. However, voltage reductions are not really free. Equipment runs less efficiently and savings now will partially be compensated for by increased consumption later. By reducing demand in this way under operating reserve deficiency conditions, market prices are depressed and provide incorrect price signals. They may use OOM calls on selected generators that have the effect of paying some generators premium prices but depress the market prices paid to other suppliers. They make up-front payments to small emergency generators to allow them to be called upon during supply emergencies, but these payments are restricted to a small subset of generators and are not available to all generators providing supplies at the same time. They will begin to curtail demand involuntarily before prices rise to levels consistent with the value of unserved energy.

4. Reliability standards have been carried over from the old regulated regime. They have not been re-evaluated as part of the liberalisation process. Even if demand were fully represented in the market, there were no price caps, and system operators allowed prices to rise to clear the market before taking administrative reliability actions, it is not clear that the market would yield the levels of reliability that are reflected in current reliability rules. For example, the reliability council that covers New England and New York has a requirement for installed reserve capacity margins that is consistent with an implicit value of unserved energy of about $150,000/MWh. This is at least 10 times higher than the highest estimates of the value of unserved energy that I have ever seen. A well-functioning market would be satisfied with a lower reserve margin. On the other hand, without adequate demand response, involuntary rationing is likely to impose a much higher average cost of unserved energy than would voluntary price response.

There are at least three kinds of approach that can be taken to resolve these perceived electric generation resource adequacy problems. One approach is to fix the imperfections in the spot market. That is, get rid of the price caps, work hard to develop more market-based demand response, require system operators to integrate their reliability actions to movements in market prices and to rely on generally available market mechanisms to balance the system, and to re-evaluate reliability criteria to ensure that they reflect reasonable measures of the value of reliability to consumers. US policy makers are not enthusiastic about lifting the price caps. It has proved difficult to convince system operators in the US to rely more on market mechanisms during extremely tight supply contingencies. Efforts are under way to expand demand response, but progress has been slow.

A second approach is to impose (better designed) forward capacity obligations on LSEs (or retail suppliers in UK parlance) that require them to contract forward for generating capacity to meet their peak demand plus an administratively determined reserve margin. LSEs would then have to contract in advance for installed generating capacity that is expected to be available to meet their peak demand (plus a reserve margin) as well as to buy energy (forward or in the balancing market) to meet realised demand. The installed capacity reserve margin obligation is set to reflect the system operator's reliability criteria (for example, 14 to 18 per cent reserve margin at a 'competitive' peak demand level). The price for this capacity acts as a sort of 'safety valve' to produce the net revenues required to attract investment in generation consistent with engineering reliability criteria (Joskow and Tirole, 2006). All generators get the benefit of the associated capacity prices and, in principle, the demand side should see this price as well. Variations on capacity and forward contracting obligations have been tried in the US and are now being refined (California Public Utilities Commission, 2005).

A third approach is to require the system operator to solicit bids for long-term contracts with new generators only in order to acquire additional reserve capacity that is not being provided by the market. This approach effectively involves price discrimination between existing generators and new generators that have access to the long-term contract option. In light of the pricing issues identified in the organised US wholesale markets, this approach is likely to lead to ISO procurement crowding out market-based entry of new generating plants. This in turn is likely to distort the mix of generating technologies that end up being built. There is presently a lot of enthusiasm in the US for this approach, largely because it makes it unnecessary for customers to pay the full market value of capacity to existing generators.

There is another set of deterrents to investment in new generating capacity in the US and some other countries. The future regulatory and market environments are very uncertain. Some states have embraced liberalisation reforms and others have not. There is a continuous set of reforms of the previous reforms of wholesale market institutions. Infirmities in retail competition programmes have delayed the development of a strong competitive retail supply segment that could do more long-term contracting (or acquisitions) with generators. Given all of this policy uncertainty and the continuing 'reform of the reforms' it is not hard to figure out why potential investors in new generating capacity are unwilling to commit capital unless they can get long-term contracts with creditworthy buyers.

The UK's electricity sector is in much better shape from a generation resource adequacy perspective than is the electricity sector in the US. It has a reasonably stable and well-developed set of market institutions. Retail competition has evolved nicely. There are no price caps. The system operator must go to the markets first to balance the system. It is incentivised to balance the system efficiently. The market and regulatory frameworks for electricity in the UK are by far the best on earth. This suggests that the UK should be cautious about making significant additional changes to its wholesale electricity market institutions. There is significant value in market and regulatory stability. If it is not badly broken, my advice is not to try to fix it.

THE DEMAND SIDE

In both electricity and natural gas markets, operating reliability and resource adequacy issues are significantly reduced when there is a large active and credible demand side that is available to allow supply and demand to be balanced with market mechanisms, associated price movements, and with a minimum of administrative intervention by the system operator to meet reliability standards. Reliable network operations can be maintained with traditional market mechanisms, the consumers who place the lowest values on service will be curtailed (voluntarily) first, market prices will rise to reflect the value of unserved energy, and investors can be more confident that they will be paid the true competitive market price once they enter the market.

Increasing demand response in competitive electricity markets has proved to be difficult. Obviously, customers who cannot see the real time price because they do not have a real-time meter and are billed based on load profiles are not going to show any demand response during power supply emergencies, apart from feeling as though they are doing their civic duty by responding to emergency appeals. And real-time meters and associated data processing are still relatively expensive compared to the savings that smaller customers are likely to realise from installing them, taking account of the reality that they are not going to sit and watch the meter all day and night. New technologies are likely to be required to make it easier for customers to pre-programme their appliances and equipment to respond to changes in prices or system conditions. Efficient levels of demand response will only be stimulated if prices are allowed to rise to levels far above the wholesale market price caps that regulators have imposed in the US during 'scarcity conditions' in order to give consumers appropriate incentives to participate in demand-side programmes. Moreover, the ability of the distribution or transmission network operator to physically control consumption of individual customers on behalf of their retail supplier may be more important than relying on real-time meters (Chao and Wilson, 1987). The customer would then simply contract to have his/her load reduced or curtailed or certain appliances turned off or cycled when pre-specified wholesale market price levels or system contingencies are reached. Day-ahead price signals and curtailment notices make these types of priority rationing contracts more appealing to consumers. The key here is to have the communications and control capability linking the network operator with individual consumer locations. In the US, air-conditioner cycling programmes, relying on signals sent over the electric distribution lines (but it could just as well be the internet or a radio signal), have been especially popular with consumers. A lot more can be done here.

The natural gas industry has always had a lot more demand response capability than has the electricity industry. Dual-fuel capabilities in power generation and industry made it feasible and potentially economical for consumers to switch to petroleum when supplies of natural gas were tight. This capability allowed them to contract for less costly interruptible pipeline capacity and to switch to cheaper petroleum products when natural gas prices rose during cold snaps due either to limitations on the volume of commodity gas available or to regional or local network deliverability constraints. Increased reliance on daily metering and pricing of gas also increases price-responsive demand.

It is my impression that traditional demand response capability in the natural gas industry has declined in the US and probably in the UK (National Grid, 2005). This decline is due to changes in industry composition, the retirement of conventional steam-generating plants that could burn either oil or natural gas, the construction of some CCGT units without dual-fuel capabilities or only limited oil storage, and environmental constraints on burning oil rather than gas (ISO New England, 2005b). This suggests that increased demand for natural gas during extreme weather conditions will be more difficult to manage with demand response, require higher prices to balance supply and demand, lengthen the duration of curtailments of interruptible customers, and increase the possibility of involuntary curtailments. If this impression is correct it also suggests that this will change the economics of investment in gas storage capabilities and increase incentives to expand storage capacity.

INTERACTIONS BETWEEN GAS AND ELECTRICITY MARKETS

This leads directly to a brief discussion of supply security issues that may arise as a consequence of the interaction between liberalised gas and electricity sectors, in the context of increased reliance on CCGT capacity. In a region like New England where the spot electricity market clears with gas-fired capacity about 85 per cent of the hours, the economic relationships are straightforward. CCGT generators transform gas into electricity. If the wholesale price of electricity is high enough to make it profitable they will buy the gas and produce the electricity. If the price of electricity is not high enough to make manufacturing electricity with natural gas profitable, generators with gas and pipeline contracts will sell them to others who value them more highly. For gas-fired generating capacity to be in the bid-based dispatch in the electricity sector, electricity prices must be greater than or equal to the marginal cost of manufacturing electricity with gas. Basically, a set of simple arbitrage conditions will simultaneously determine the allocation of gas between the end-use sector and the electricity-generating sector, and the prices of electricity and natural gas.

What could happen that might restrict the efficient arbitrage of natural gas between these two markets? The New England cold snap of mid-January 2004 provides an excellent example and also further illuminates the issues surrounding generation adequacy discussed earlier (ISO New England, 2004 and US FERC, 2005a). The third week in January 2004 was the coldest week in New England in about 50 years. Demand for natural gas was at an all-time high due to high heating demand and both the import capacity of the pipelines and the delivery capacity of the distribution networks were stressed. Pipelines implemented strict balancing rules and imbalance penalties. Natural gas in New England traded as high as $75/mmbtu ($7.50/therm) on the peak day (ISO New England, 2004 and US FERC, 2005a). Local gas distribution companies relied on gas drawn from local 'peak shaving' storage facilities and gas released from the electricity sector to meet the unusually high gas demand from residential and commercial consumers with gas space heating. In the end there were no involuntary curtailments on the gas side, though a longer cold snap would have been problematic as local storage could have been exhausted.

While electricity demand in New England peaks in the summer, the winter peak demand is not too much lower. In January 2004 the peak electricity demand was about 10 per cent below the peak summer demand. Although there was a significant surplus of installed generating capacity to meet the peak electricity demand, a large fraction of the gas-fired capacity was unavailable due to either declared mechanical problems or decisions to sell the gas to the end-use market rather than use it to produce electricity. ISO New England struggled to schedule enough generation to meet demand to avoid rolling blackouts or a network collapse and had to implement emergency protocols as generation supply deficiencies loomed. While the system ran for a time with insufficient operating reserves, there were no involuntary outages of customers (and very little demand response) in the end. There are several observations from this experience (US FERC, 2005a):

1. The spot gas market worked well to allocate scarce supplies of gas and pipeline capacity, though gas prices did rise to extraordinarily high levels for a brief period of time.
2. There were incompatibilities in the 'time-lines' with which the spot gas and spot electricity markets operated and this hindered efficient arbitrage of gas between electricity and end-use sectors. For example, gas supply arrangements had to be made several hours before the day-ahead market and the specification of day-ahead schedules for the electricity market operated. The gas market also had much less intra-day flexibility than the electricity market.
3. The gas delivery infrastructure was barely adequate to meet peak day demand. The gas pipeline and distribution network infrastructure was the most constrained and the source of the gas supply constraints. Gas demand had expanded much more quickly than pipeline delivery capabilities into the region as nearly 10,000 MW of new gas-fuelled generating capacity was installed between 1999 and 2004. The generators' reliance on non-firm transportation arrangements and their poor credit ratings reduced pipelines' incentives to expand capacity. Distribution networks operated at more than 100 per cent of design capability. Limited electricity import capabilities also reduced the ability of the region to access electricity from neighbouring regions.
4. The electricity spot market worked poorly and prices were too low. The ISO's protocols for managing supply emergencies, especially its reliance on out-of-market mechanisms and non-market orders to generators, depressed spot prices below competitive levels. Despite the fact that the ISO declared that there was an operating reserve deficiency and struggled to balance supply and demand, spark spreads for CCGT capacity were zero or negative (US FERC, 2005a). This distorted incentives for allocating gas between the electricity and end-use markets and provided inadequate 'scarcity rents' to signal new investments.
5. During extremely cold weather, generator availability declines due to everything from frozen coal piles to frozen valves and hoses. This suggests that assumptions about equipment availability during extreme weather conditions need to be carefully tested.

The growing linkages between gas and electricity markets means that the performance of both markets can be affected adversely by market and regulatory imperfections in the other market as well as its own market. Market design, regulatory and reliability policies therefore need to be compatible across both liberalised gas and liberalised electricity markets.

CONCLUSION

Where electricity and natural gas sector liberalisation has followed the right path and has had the opportunity to mature and stabilise, as in the UK, there does not appear to be a significant supply security problem. On the gas side in the UK, the growing need to deal with what are only partially liberalised European gas markets, to facilitate expansion of LNG import facilities, and to expand the interconnector and internal pipelines infrastructure to accommodate these new gas supply sources, appear to be the greatest challenges. The institutions and understanding to confront these changes successfully appear to be in place, though the regulatory process will have to adapt to significantly increased capital budgets and the need to provide adequate investment incentives. Ofgem appears to have met this challenge in the 2004 electricity distribution price review. The UK will have to be a strong advocate for continued liberalisation of European gas markets for reasons of self-interest rather than simply ideology.

While I am reasonably optimistic about electric generation resource adequacy in the UK, I am also of the view that the jury is still out on the issue. To be sure, the structural features that plague the organised electricity markets in the US are not present in the UK. However, I believe that there is a tendency to take too much comfort from the experience with entry of new generating capacity in the UK during the 1990s. The conditions that led to the big influx of new generating capacity in the UK during that time were particularly attractive. The legacy fleet of generating plants included a lot of old inefficient coal-fired generating capacity. With low gas prices it was economical to build CCGTs to replace them. High electricity price–cost margins resulting from generator market power made entry even more attractive (Wolfram, 1999). There was also significant exit and a meaningful amount of mothballed plant remained that can be returned to service relatively quickly if forward prices are high enough. These attractive conditions for entry no longer prevail. Carbon prices and other environmental constraints are likely to lead to more retirements of old coal plant in the next several years. The renewable energy programme creates additional supply-side uncertainty. The ability to finance merchant generating plants has changed. So, we should not draw too much comfort from the investment patterns of the 1990s. At this point the best strategy is to keep the government's hands off the generation market and closely to monitor developments to determine whether there are market failures that adversely affect generating capacity investment incentives.

In the US, the primary challenge on the gas side is to facilitate a speedier and less costly process for expanding LNG import authority. On the electricity side there is a lot of work to do to improve wholesale and retail market design, unbundling, horizontal and retail restructuring, and incentive regulation of transmission and distribution networks. If there are going to be serious supply security problems, the areas of the US that have tried to liberalise the electricity sectors but have done so incompletely or incorrectly are the places where supply security problems are most likely to emerge in the next five years.

NOTES

1. By 'tight' I mean (loosely) that supply capacity constraints are being approached and relatively small shifts in demand lead to large swings in prices.
2. Chao and Wilson (1987) develop the theory of priority rationing for the case where individual consumers can be rationed by the system operator.
3. Generating plants that provide frequency regulation, reactive power support and spinning reserves on an electric power network play a similar role.
4. The intra-year spot prices for natural gas vary by one order of magnitude while the unconstrained intra-year spot prices for electricity vary by as much as three orders of magnitude.
5. The Midwest ISO (MISO), the independent system operator for a large portion of the transmission networks in the midwestern US had only taken over limited control area responsibilities by August 2003.
6. See Joskow (2005c) for an extensive discussion of the theory and practice of incentive regulation for electricity transmission and distribution networks.
7. US FERC (2005a, p. 145). Note that the large locational basis difference between Henry Hub (Louisiana) and New York in January 2004 corresponded to an extremely cold weather event during which imports of natural gas into portions of the Northeast were constrained by limitations on pipeline capacity. This event is discussed in more detail in the section on interactions between gas and electricity markets, below.
8. Most of the observed transmission investment is for regulated investments required to build interconnections between the network and new generating units.
9. 'Decision on the Application of TenneT for Permission to Finance the NordNed Cable . . .', December 23, 2004.
10. Just as electricity network operators contract for frequency regulation, operating reserves, and replacement reserves with generators.
11. US FERC (2005a).
12. US EIA (2005). Exports to the US from the conventional production areas in Alberta also appear to have peaked.
13. PJM is the system operator for the transmission networks in the Mid-Atlantic states and portions of several midwestern states.
14. An LSE is equivalent to a retail supplier in the UK. However, in PJM the bulk of the retail supply is still provided by regulated distribution companies which procure power to serve retail customers.

REFERENCES

Beesley, M. and S. Littlechild (1989), 'The regulation of privatized monopolies in the United Kingdom', *Rand Journal of Economics*, **20**(3): 454–72.
Borenstein, S., J. Bushnell and F. Wolak (2002), 'Measuring market inefficiencies in California's restructured wholesale electricity markets', *American Economic Review* **92**(5): 1376–405.
California Independent System Operator (ISO) (2001), *Operations Economic Report 2001*, December, Folsom, CA, USA.
California Independent System Operator (ISO) (2002), *Third Annual Report on Market Issues and Performance*, January, Folsom, CA, USA.
California Public Utilities Commission (2005), 'Capacity markets White Paper', August 25, San Francisco, CA, USA.
Chao, H. and R. Wilson (1987), 'Priority service: pricing, investment and market organization', *American Economic Review* (77): 899–916.
Cramton, P. and S. Stoft (2005), 'A capacity market that makes sense', *Electricity Journal*, **18**, August/September: 43–54.
Department of Trade and Industry (DTI) (UK) (2002), *United Kingdom Digest of Energy Statistics 2002*, London: DTI.
Domah, P.D. and M.G. Pollitt (2001), 'The restructuring and privatisation of the regional electricity companies in England and Wales: a social cost benefit analysis', *Fiscal Studies*, **22**(1): 107–46.
International Energy Agency (2005), *World Energy Outlook*, Paris: IEA.
ISO New England (2004), 'Final Report on Electricity Supply Conditions in New England During the January 14–16, 2004 Cold Snap', October, www.iso-ne.com, accessed December 15, 2005.
ISO New England (2005a), *2004 Annual Market Report*, New England: ISO New England.
ISO New England (2005b), *Power Generation and Fuel Diversity in New England: Ensuring Power System Reliability*, August, New England: ISO New England.
Joskow, P.L. (2001), 'California's Electricity Crisis', *Oxford Review of Economic Policy*, **17**(3): 365–88.
Joskow, P.L. (2005a), 'The difficult transition to competitive electricity markets in the United States', in J. Griffin and S. Puller (eds), *Electricity Deregulation: Where To From Here?*, Chicago: University of Chicago Press, pp. 31–97.
Joskow, P.L. (2005b), 'Transmission policy in the United States', *Utilities Policy* (13): 95–115.
Joskow, P.L. (2005c), 'Incentive regulation in theory and practice', NBER Regulation Project, http://econ-www.mit.edu/faculty/download_pdf.php?id= 1220, accessed December 19, 2005.
Joskow, P.L. (2006a), 'Markets for power in the United States: an interim assessment', *The Energy Journal*, **27**(1): 1–36.
Joskow, P.L. (2006b), 'Patterns of transmission investment', in F. Leveque (ed.), *Competitive Electricity markets*, Cheltenham, UK and Northampton MA, USA: Edward Elgar Publishing, http://econ-www.mit.edu/faculty/download_pdf. php?id=1133, accessed September 21, 2006.
Joskow, P.L. and E. Kahn (2002), 'A quantitative analysis of pricing behavior in California's wholesale electricity market during summer 2000', *The Energy Journal*, **23**(4): 1–35.

Joskow, P.L. and J. Tirole (2005), 'Merchant transmission investment', *Journal of Industrial Economics*, **53**(2): 233–64.

Joskow, P.L. and J. Tirole (2006), 'Reliability and competitive electricity markets', *Rand Journal of Economics*, forthcoming, http://econ-www.mit.edu/faculty/download_pdf.php?id=917, accessed September 21, 2006.

National Grid (2005), 'Winter Outlook Report 2005/06', www.ofgem.gov.uk/temp/ofgem/cache/cmsattach/12493_214_05.pdf, accessed December 19, 2005.

New York Independent System Operator (ISO) (2005), '2004 State of the Markets Report', prepared by David Patton, July, www.nyiso.com/public/webdocs/documents/market_advisor_reports/2004_patton_final_report.pdf, accessed December 19, 2005.

Office of Gas and Electricity Markets (Ofgem) (2004), 'Electricity Distribution Price Control Review: Final Proposals', 265/04, November, London, www.ofgem.gov.uk/temp/ofgem/cache/cmsattach/9416_26504.pdf?wtfrom=/ofgem/whats-new/archive.jsp, accessed January 20, 2005.

US Energy Information Administration (EIA) (2004), 'Electricity Transmission in a Restructured Industry: Data Needs for Public Policy Analysis', December, DOE/EIA–00639. www.eia.doe.gov/oss/TransmissionDataNeeds-DH.pdf, accessed December 19, 2005.

US Energy Information Administration (EIA) (2005), *Annual Energy Outlook 2005*, www.eia.doe.gov/oiaf/aeo/index.html, accessed December 19, 2005.

US Federal Energy Regulatory Commission (FERC) (2005a), *State of the Markets Report*, www.ferc.gov/EventCalendar/Files/20050615093455-06-15-05-som2004.pdf, accessed July 6, 2005.

US Federal Energy Regulatory Commission (FERC) (2005b), 'Promoting Transmission Investment Through Pricing Reform', Notice of Proposed Rulemaking, Docket RM06-4-000, November.

Von der Fehr, N.-H., E. Amundsen and L. Bergman (2005), 'The Nordic market: signs of stress', *The Energy Journal*, Special Issue, 71–98.

Wolfram, Catherine (1999), 'Measuring duopoly power in the deregulated UK electricity market', *American Economic Review*, **89**: 805–26.

CHAIRMAN'S COMMENTS

Sir John Mogg

Notwithstanding that Paul is a non-executive director of National Grid Transco (NGT), there's no such thing as regulatory capture. I admit to blushing on behalf of my predecessors for the accolades that Paul has rained upon the UK regulatory framework. His opening remarks that it sets an international gold standard for gas and electricity, within a liberalised context, are very flattering.

It would not be surprising that I welcome and support the general thesis, notably that there is no inherent conflict between having a liberalised markets regime and security of supply. We are at a crucial moment notably, winter 2006, the severity of the weather is unknown but the position is perhaps better than in 2005.

But Paul made the important caveat, about the devil being in the detail; that you need to have crucially an appropriate set of market rules; an appropriate industry structure, and regulatory institutions to manage the process. Non-intervention requires the right sort of structure. Among the case studies, that of New Jersey made me freeze with anxiety. My view is of a practical regulator, with the experience of our tiny blackouts just a few weeks before I took over, and how we have benefited from those, fortunately very rare events – to deliver the National Grid's transmission record, which is 99.99999 per cent of security confidence. We must learn from what happened and how that could be avoided. But we must first identify what to deal with in the event of it happening and how to respond and how to minimise the damage. In these days of terrorism, we now have to confront issues that cannot rest on the standard preparatory engineering structures.

I ask myself, why it is that the academics, many notable academics, tend to concentrate on electricity. Yes, it is zippy, with gas lumbering along at 30 miles an hour, but, for Europe for example, there are many issues that relate to gas that should also come up during the discussion.

I share Paul's healthy distrust of political intervention. Any independent regulator would endorse that. In the European context, it is difficult to see how government will not be involved in generation. Most of us would be surprised if government simply stood aside. The long-term diversity of supply issue also is an area where one would look for government's external involvement. The focus on security of supplies is undeniably pertinent to our present situation.

I was interested in Paul's views on the influence of the supply side to alleviate the transmission difficulties. A further issue is the way the non-liberalised EU system, given the rollout of a more liberal approach into continental Europe and the tensions it creates, will be dogged by questions about future LNG global arrangements too. There are the odd indicators of changing attitudes towards liberalised markets. I was in Berlin in September 2005, invited by the new German regulator to explain the virtues of incentive regulation. We get many overseas visitors to Ofgem to listen to what we have to say, and the developments in the EU especially with an emerging presence of the Council of European Regulators are further signs.

Is there any causality between market liberalisation as Paul tends to think, and the blackouts? Most immediately, in the UK, if you look at the meteorological forecasts, we face the one in 50 winter. We have had recent experience of a continental freeze; will they make the flow of natural gas through the inter-connector less than it might be? Are people actually abusing the situation in Europe, filling up their storage and declining to push where the market is demanding it? This will be a major concern for the UK regulator.

The problems with planning are real, and they are not only for LNG terminals, for the development of infrastructure, and for the development of the pipelines. They cause great problems for operators. Generators particularly would like to have clarity from government Indeed clarity, and predictability of policy are centrally important for industry, be it for the environment, regulation or energy policy itself. Paul has marvellously conveyed the complexity and the opportunities of learning from both sides of the Atlantic.

5. The end to the postal exception?

Dermot Glynn and David Stubbs

INTRODUCTION AND OVERVIEW

With the recent proposal of the European Commission to move towards full postal liberalisation by 2009, this is a good time to reflect on the development of postal regulation in Europe and the UK.

This chapter's main conclusion will be that, on balance, the postal sector in the European Union (EU) has in the past suffered from delay in the pace of reform, and regulators and policy makers should support moves to end the 'postal exception', by which is meant the delay in postal reform compared to other network-based industries.

To set the scene we begin with a brief history of European and UK postal regulatory development to understand the nature and evolution of the postal exception. We shall then briefly review European postal market development and emerging market trends in the sector. We shall conclude by offering some recommendations about how deregulation may best be effected in the sector, suggesting that the universal service obligation could be reduced in scope, opening the way to a regulatory regime focused on ensuring reasonable access by entrants to essential services and eventually to removing retail price controls.

One caveat to note at the outset: good comparative data on the sector are difficult to find and while we have endeavoured to use the best available research there remain deficiencies in establishing a precise comparable view of market and regulatory development. In part these deficiencies stem from a reluctance of market players to release information, and in part they stem from a lack of detailed regulatory oversight in some member states in areas such as accounting separation.

The 'Postal Exception': A Brief History of Postal Regulation

The regulatory history of the European postal sector has been one of a generally slower progress towards deregulation and the opening of markets to competition than has happened in other network industries. Fears of potential political repercussions from the employment and industrial relations effects of postal restructuring and the rationalisation of the post office network, combined with the lobbying power of the national post organisations (referred to as national posts, or universal service providers: USPs), have made policy makers cautious about deregulation in this sector.

These concerns led to a 'postal exception' in the sense that the model of deregulation applied to other comparable sectors has not yet been applied as fast or as rigorously to the postal market. This postal exception has been manifest in reluctance to deregulate the sector so as to allow competition for mail services; and reluctance to move towards the privatisation of the USPs.

The postal sector at national level remained largely unreformed at the time of the formal achievement of the EU internal market in 1992. National posts (the USPs) were statutory monopolies, still largely run as public corporations. Rather than ratifying a reform already achieved in some member states (while promoting it in others), the European Commission (EC) found itself promoting reform across most of the EU and facing a blocking minority (which initially included the UK) in the European Council able to delay reform.

Against this background, the Postal Green Paper of 1992 set out the objectives of Community regulation of postal services as being:

1.   to ensure the maintenance of a universal postal service;
2.   to improve the quality of services; and
3.   to move towards the internal market for postal services.

These proposals were not universally welcomed, and several years elapsed before the next important step was taken.

The Postal Directive of 1997 (97/67) (the Framework Postal Directive) was the means through which member states agreed a harmonisation of the interpretation of the Treaty (of the European Union) in the postal sector. This involved a general definition of regulatory principles in areas including pricing (affordable prices geared to costs) and accounting separation (between reserved and non-reserved and universal reserved and non-reserved services). The postal directive limited the services which member states could continue to reserve to their USPs to mail services below 350 grams and five times the price of the fastest standard category tariff. The directive required that member states set up independent national regulators.

The Amended Postal Directive of 2002 (2002/39) harmonised further the interpretation of regulatory principles in relation to access pricing (this was to take account of avoided costs) and cross-subsidisation (which was only to be permissible for universal services) and the member states agreed to next steps in the reduction of possible exclusive rights for mail services to 50 grams in 2006. Most importantly, the Amended Postal Directive also set a timetable for the full accomplishment of the internal market for end 2009, subject to a study by the Commission and the agreement of the member states. Application of these principles in the UK has recently been accelerated.

The Postal Services Act of 2000 set up Postcomm (the Postal Services Commission) with duties to safeguard the universal postal service (a primary duty), to promote competition and to regulate Royal Mail's prices. Condition 9 of Royal Mail's licence (agreed in 2001) requires it to negotiate access for potential competitors to its postal facilities. In 2003 the market for bulk mail services was opened. In this way the services reserved to Royal Mail were reduced at a faster pace than the EC required, and from 1 January 2006 any business has been able to offer any postal service anywhere in the UK, subject only to getting a licence from Postcomm with Royal Mail, publicly at least, welcoming this.

Throughout the process so far, in the UK and in the rest of the EU, the primary aim of regulatory intervention has been to ensure the universal postal service. This is defined in the Amended Postal Directive as the delivery and collection of postal items at least five times a week; a high quality of service; and non-discriminatory access for other providers and customers to the incumbent's service infrastructure.

In nearly all the 25 EU member states, this definition of universal service has been interpreted essentially as continuing the services currently provided by the national USP. In the UK, and in the Netherlands, however, moves have been made to exclude bulk mail from the definition (which appeared to require some strenuous interpretation of the requirement as set out in the Amended Postal Directive). This was a significant move.

The EU USPs are predominantly state owned. The exceptions are Deutsche Post and the Dutch company TNT. Denmark Post has (at end 2005) a minority private shareholding (22 per cent is owned by CVC Capital Partners) and negotiations are continuing to sell 49 per cent of Belgian La Poste. There is also some expectation that private shareholdings might be introduced in Italy, and Greece, although the position is not clear. The state-owned USPs are organised either as government corporations or as public limited companies with 100 per cent state ownership.

The Four Main Operators

It is worth saying a little more about the four main operators. These include the USPs from the three largest member states together with the Dutch USP, TNT, which is prominent in the parcels and express market due to its acquisitions in this sector.

- *DHL (Deutsche Post)* is the most profitable of the EU USPs enjoying significant margins on mail products and consequently, it has recorded annual EBIT (earnings before interest and tax) of more than €2 billion on mail services. DHL had largely completed its first round of European acquisitions by the end of 2002 and is now engaged in trying to cut costs, obtain operational synergies and unify its brand for its varied portfolio of businesses. This process is known as the STAR programme, and it is claimed to have realised savings of €800 million. DHL had a turnover of about €43 billion in 2004 and it now operates in 220 countries with an assured presence in all European markets and a workforce of 380,000 of whom over 170,000 are employees outside Germany. Fewer than half the German employees are now civil servants. A new labour flexibility has apparently been a major ingredient in its increasing efficiency; DHL now handles about 140,000 items per employee per annum.[1] Key areas of planned expansion appear to be postal markets in Japan and China as well as the US parcels markets. For example, DHL is projecting that 20 per cent of its revenues will come from China by 2010. The recent bid for Exel suggests that DHL may still be seeking to cement its leading status in the logistics sector. DHL shares rose from €10 at year end 2002 to €16.38 in January 2004 with a dividend of over €500 million and dividend per share of €0.50.

- *Dutch TNT (TPG)* also enjoys high margins for its mail products and consequently significant profits. Turnover in 2004 was nearly €13 billion and the workforce in 2005 was around 160,000. Global presence is secured through the 'Spring' venture begun in 2000 with Royal Mail and Singapore Post. TNT also provides upstream and downstream services through its Cendris subsidiary. Its key targets for growth appear to be in the postal markets in Japan and China, and in the freight forwarding and postal consolidation markets more generally. A main concern for TNT has been its mail volume decline, which is forecast at 3 per cent annually, possibly as a result of increased competition in the Dutch market. In response to this, TNT has launched its own cost-efficiency programme, which it estimates has generated extra productivity of about 5 per cent between 2001 and 2003.[2] The financial performance of the company has been sound with TPG shares rising from €15.82 in December 2002 to €19.68 in January 2005.

- *French La Poste* group has Europe's third largest postal network, covering 80 per cent of the European market, giving it presence in 20 countries. It has a workforce of about 300,000 and a turnover of around €19 billion (2004). Key acquisitions have included the DPD

German parcels network and UK Mayne Nickless parcels company, which has been absorbed into the GeoPost group. La Poste has partnership links with Sweden Post and Fedex and working agreements on express parcels services with Poste Italiane and with Correos (Spain). La Poste's strategy now includes a cost-efficiency programme which involves closing down the internal operator Ditipack and the loss-making parcels DPD France network. La Poste is also heavily involved in the French financial services market and appears to be poised to become a major player in the French mortgages market.

- *Royal Mail* retreated from its acquisitions policy but retains a presence in the Dutch and German postal markets. Its turnover was around €12.5 billion in 2004 and by the end of 2005 its workforce stood at about 195,000, reduced by 34,000 from March 2002.

Economic Trends in the Sector

Within this regulatory framework, the economic performance of the sector has been changing. Data are limited, and much of what we have comes from individual, unrelated, studies. There is inevitably some risk of inconsistency, as a result.

Overall, USP postal revenues in the EU are estimated at about €88 billion in 2002, rising to about €90 billion in 2004 (when telecom, for comparison, was €236 billion). Direct employment was 1.8 million (1.7 million in 2004), more than in telecoms or energy sectors; confirming that post remains a very large-scale employer. Aggregate output in the USPs was estimated by the EC to be growing at about 1–2 per cent a year.

The USPs are all major employers of unskilled and semi-skilled workers. The political importance of the sector is also reinforced by the value that customers evidently attach to the service (in opinion polls, where quality of service is generally found to be more important than price and in reactions when rural post offices are threatened with closure).

USP revenues have grown at substantially different rates in different countries, reflecting differences in price levels, and also differences in letter post volumes. During the period from 1998 to 2002, the large EU countries showed relatively little growth, whereas in Poland, Hungary, Slovenia, Latvia, together with Spain, much greater increases were recorded. By 2002 over half of the €88 billion revenues came from mail, but €36 billion came from parcels and express services.

Another major feature of demand is that it is now significantly concentrated in a limited number of key customers. For example: in each of French La Poste, Deutsche Post and Royal Mail between 50 and 60 per cent of revenues come from the largest 3000 accounts; and the household sector – with between 25 million and 40 million households – contributing less than 15 per cent of revenues. Therefore the business economics of these USPs depend on what they earn from these largest customers, including many that are able to negotiate discounts from the uniform tariff for pre-sorted mail, and many that are potential customers for ancillary services.

The USPs' shares of the EU mail market broadly correspond to the size of the different economies; letter mail is still predominantly in the hands of the national USP (over 95 per cent in many cases). However in parcels the overall EU market is more concentrated, with DHL (Deutsche Post) having achieved a leading position.

More generally, as the market moves towards deregulation, evidence is emerging that postal operators compete in a changing and in some respects dynamic market. In particular it is clear that there are opportunities for postal operators:

1. to compete in unaddressed mail services;
2. to expand horizontally and vertically into upstream and downstream services and ancillary markets; and
3. to expand through mergers and acquisitions (M&As) and into international postal markets.

Horizontal and vertical expansion
There is now a wide range of related services provided by USPs and other postal operators. In part these stem from the legacy of USPs as providers of non-postal services such as financial services (post banks) and retail services (post offices). However, they also increasingly reflect the opportunities for expansion into ancillary services such as unaddressed mail and upstream and downstream services such as printing services and mail-room management.

There are a number of sectors into which USPs have moved by acquisition. By end 2004 Deutsche Post appears to be the only USP that had acquired a letter post company; 10 USPs had bought one or more parcel companies; 10 had bought an express delivery company; and seven had bought businesses dealing with unaddressed items. There had also been vertical expansion into printing services, mail preparation; and mailroom management. M&A activity continues.[3]

Within an overall mature postal sector, significant changes are taking place. Revenues are growing, especially for parcels and express. DHL alone now probably has over 40 per cent of the EU parcel market. Demand is concentrated on important business customers; indeed, the proportion of mail volumes now originating with a business customer is often over 80 per cent. Within the overall picture, the variations between individual USPs remain great.

Policy Implications

What do these trends and the experience of regulatory policy thus far imply for the next stages of EU postal development? Are we indeed coming to the end of the 'postal exception' with new policies designed to open markets and actively encourage the development of competition?

The primary case for delayed postal reform (as distinct from the regulation of dominant suppliers) in the sector is based upon concerns that there should be a universal service, and that the universal postal service obligation imposes burdens upon the USP such that it may not be possible to finance universal service provision in a fully competitive market, without 'reserved areas'. Indeed a universal service obligation (USO) with a uniform geographic tariff and without a reserved area could be a recipe for profitable entry by entrants less efficient than the incumbent.

The primary strength of the rationale for reserving parts of the market from competition depends then on:

1. the importance of the USO as a service of general economic interest; and
2. the scale of the burdens imposed by USOs.

As we have seen, the European Community universal service requirement is extensive including five deliveries and collections a week, at 'affordable' prices. In addition most member states (including the UK) have added a requirement for universal geographically averaged tariffs.

Is there a continuing justification for this intervention; that is, for a USO in postal services? Clearly, the means of communication open to individuals and households through telephone, and electronic methods, are more widespread than in say 1992. Although access to alternative means of communication is less in poorer parts of the EU, it is hard to imagine that a need for a means of personal communication any longer justifies the USO in (for example) the UK.

The USO requires that the services be 'affordable'. We estimate that the average number of letters posted each year in the UK in 2003 was about 40; and for the EU as a whole the average would have been less than 25. The EU average stamp price is about €0.30. This means that the average EU adult spends about €10 per annum on letters; and in the UK, about £10–15. Obviously there must be substantial variations around the average, and there may be a small number of people for whom the 'affordability' of the postal service is a genuine issue. However, it appears unlikely that there are not enough, surely, to justify a major regulatory intervention of this kind.

The business customers, who now originate most of the mail by volume, obviously value the service; and some of the correspondence is of great inherent importance. However, such customers have bargaining power, and are not generally providing an essential service, so their interests do not justify the continuation of the USO still less at geographically standard tariffs.

Similar considerations lead to doubt about whether there is a long-term need for retail price controls. These are clearly unnecessary for the bulk mail business; and cannot be justified in order to protect the pockets of individuals spending so little on the service.

The 2002 Postal Directive requires that competitors should be able to access parts of the overall network service, at charges taking account of avoided costs; and if this is made effective (through bottom-up assessments of the efficient levels for such charges) there should be enough actual and potential entrants to protect the consumer wanting a competitive offering. There is also the possibility of recourse to action against a dominant USP which was thought to be behaving in an anti-competitive way, through a case based on Article 82 (there have been a number of cases of this kind against Deutsche Post, for example).

The argument for removing, at the right time, retail price controls is underlined by the desirability of avoiding a situation in which entry might be profitable purely because of the regulations, not because the entrants had a competitive offering. Such inefficient entry must be a risk with widely varying regional costs, a uniform geographic tariff, and no or limited 'reservations'.

Conclusions

The conclusions that follow from the assessment are:

1. That there has hitherto been a 'postal exception' to the general policy of opening access to markets once wholly supplied by network industries. This exception is evidently derived more from political considerations than from particularly difficult economic or technical issues.
2. That the business strategy policies followed in different countries and by different USPs have varied quite widely, including some aggressive expansions into world markets, both within post and in adjacent sectors. This is now in many respects a varied and dynamic sector.
3. That the nature of the core business has changed substantially, with business customers and bulk deliveries becoming much more important.
4. In the light of these developments and of the development of alternative means of communication, the regulatory intervention requiring USPs to supply a universal service, specified in detail and often including a uniform geographic tariff, is hard to justify. It is doubtful whether, if it were a new proposal, it would it pass a modern regulatory impact assessment.

5. There will continue to be a need for sector and/or competition policy regulation in order to guard against possible abuses of still dominant positions. This will involve an emphasis on defining efficient access arrangements and charges.

Finally, it is hard to see a justification for the long-term regulation of retail prices in this sector.

THE DEVELOPMENT OF EUROPEAN POSTAL REGULATION

We begin with a brief history of European postal regulation up to end 2005.

The 'Postal Exception'

The regulatory history of the European postal sector has been one of a generally slower progress towards deregulation than some other network-based industries. Fears that post may become technologically obsolete and of the political fall-out from the employment effects (or industrial relations effects) of postal restructuring and the rationalisation of the post office network (combined with the lobbying power of national posts, the USPs) have made policy makers generally nervous about deregulation in this area.

These fears appear to have led to a 'postal exception' where the model of deregulation applied to other comparable sectors has not been applied as fast or as rigorously to the postal market. This postal exception has taken two key forms:

1. a reluctance to introduce competition and to deregulate the sector; and
2. a reluctance to move towards the privatisation of the USPs.

A reluctance to deregulate the sector

A slow pace of reform at national level leading to a delayed reform at European level The postal sector at national level remained unreformed at the time of the formal achievement of the internal market in 1992. National posts (the USPs) were statutory monopolies, still largely run as public corporations. Rather than ratifying a largely achieved reform in some member states while promoting it in others, the EC found itself promoting reform across most of the EU with a blocking minority in the European Council able to delay reform.

This legacy of delayed reform at national level contributed (alongside remaining political concerns) to the EC being unable to gather the necessary support from the member states for a rapid sector reform.[4] This has led the Commission to move the postal file to DG Internal Market to speed up the pace of reform.

Typically EU deregulation would include the following steps:

1. full market opening;
2. increasing harmonisation of regulatory principles and practice; and
3. gradual movement towards a European regulation initially through a European group of regulators to spread best practice, with possible later moves towards a European regulator.

However, these steps are not yet achieved with the key milestones of postal regulation at European level including the following.

The Postal Green Paper of 1992 aimed to address the problems of poor quality of service in some EU member states which appeared to be creating regulatory border effects limiting the potential for the development of a European postal market. It set out the objectives of Community regulation of postal services:

1. to ensure the maintenance of a universal postal service;
2. to improve the quality of services; and
3. to move towards the internal market for postal services.

The Postal Directive of 1997 (97/67) (the Framework Postal Directive) through which member states agreed a gradual reduction of the services which could be reserved to the USPs and a harmonisation of the interpretation of the Treaty (of the European Union) in the postal sector through a general definition of regulatory principles in areas including pricing (affordable prices geared to costs) and accounting separation (between reserved and non-reserved and universal reserved and non-reserved services). The postal directive limited the services which member states could continue to reserve to their USPs to mail services below 350 grams and five times the price of the fastest standard category tariff. The directive also required that member states set up independent national regulators.

The Amended Postal Directive of 2002 (2002/39) harmonised further the interpretation of regulatory principles in relation to access pricing (take account of avoided costs) and cross-subsidisation (only permissible for universal services) and the member states agreed to the next steps in the reduction of possible exclusive rights for mail services to 50 grams in 2006. Most importantly, the amended directive also set a timetable for the full accomplishment of the internal market for the end of 2009, subject to a study by the Commission and the agreement of the member states (see Box 5.1).

BOX 5.1   THE AMENDED POSTAL DIRECTIVE
(DIRECTIVE 97/67 AS AMENDED BY
DIRECTIVE 2002/39)

Guaranteed universal postal service for all EU citizens

Articles 1, 3, 4 and 5: daily (five days a week) delivery and collection from a reasonable access point.

Article 12: Non-discriminatory access to postal universal service value chain, prices should be geared to cost; access prices should take account of avoided costs.

Article 7: Possibility of special rights for USPs – reserved areas of up to 100g for letters, reducing to 50g in 2006.

Article 9: Licensing possible in scope of universal service, authorisations outside scope of universal service.

Article 13: Terminal dues fixed in relation to costs.

Improved quality of service for universal services

Article 16: Quality of service standards set.

Article 18: Quality of service targets for cross border mail – D+3 and D+5.

Article 20: Standardisation and the work of the CEN (European Committee for Standardization).

Article 19: Customer complaints procedures.

Accomplishment of the internal market

Article 7: Reducing scope of 'reservable' services – 50g letters.

Article 23: Possible end date for possibility of special rights subject to a study on the impact on universal services in each member state of full accomplishment of the internal market.

Article 22: Set up of independent national regulators to police incumbent USPs.

Article 14: Accounting separation – principle of the full distribution of costs.

Article 16: Independent auditing.

Source: Europe Economics (2005), www.europe-economics.com.

This leaves postal regulation at a fairly early stage of harmonisation and of deregulation, with agreement not yet reached on the final timetable for liberalisation of mail services or on the further harmonisation of key regulatory principles such as access price determination.

While an end date for full competition has been agreed in the telecoms and energy markets it remains a topic for debate in post. Further, the electronic communications directives of 2002 have included a more detailed harmonisation of key principles including the universal service obligation and have been followed by a definition of the concept of significant market power. While the Committee for European Postal Regulators, the CERP, has begun to make progress towards regulatory cooperation and best practice, it can be argued that it remains at an early stage in this process compared to similar regulatory groups in electronic communications and the energy sectors, in part at least because it still includes ministries as well as regulators.

The delayed calendar has also been important in that the substantial reform of the sector is occurring after the date of the accession of the new member states, bringing with it new problems of their adaptation to new market conditions.

A cautious national application of the Community framework While the calendar of reform at Community level has been relatively tardy, the Community framework does allow for a deregulation of postal services, subject to the requirement to safeguard a minimum universal service for EU citizens and to ensure quality of service for cross-border mail. However, in practice, member states have transposed and applied the Community framework in a cautious manner.

In particular, there remain the following significant regulatory barriers to effective competition in the EU postal market:

1. *Undefined universal service obligations* Regulators in the member states have largely started from the assumption that universal services constitute the mail and standard parcel services currently provided by their USPs, while allowing their USPs some exemptions to universal service requirements for the most expensive areas served. Further, few of the member states have conformed in any obvious way to the directive's requirement for a universal service which evolves in line with market developments and customer needs apart from in the UK and the Netherlands which have begun to re-appraise the need for a universal service which includes bulk mail, as shown in Figure 5.1.

2. *Exclusive rights in the sector* As shown in Box 5.1, the next step in the reduction of 'reservable' mail services (that is, those services which a

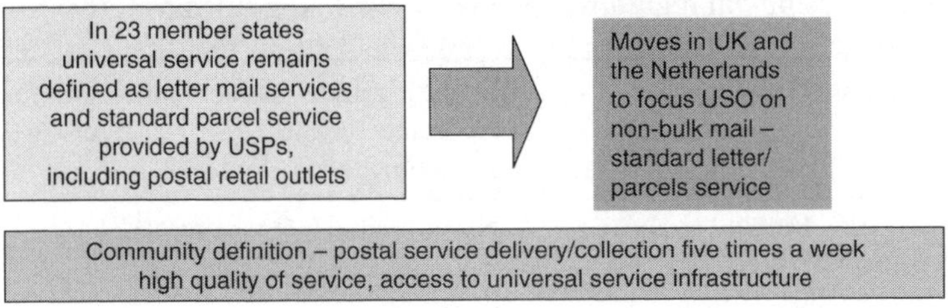

In 23 member states universal service remains defined as letter mail services and standard parcel service provided by USPs, including postal retail outlets

Moves in UK and the Netherlands to focus USO on non-bulk mail – standard letter/parcels service

Community definition – postal service delivery/collection five times a week high quality of service, access to universal service infrastructure

Note: Some member states such as Sweden have set obligations for a universal services infrastructure and all comply with directive requirements.

Source: Europe Economics (2004), based on European Commission studies, and press reports.

Figure 5.1   Universal service obligations in the EU25 member states, 2005

member state may reserve to their USP) is to 50 grams. This still allows member states to reserve about an estimated three-quarters of postal mail volumes to their USP.[5] Table 5.1 shows that while many member states have chosen to continue to reserve domestic and incoming cross-border mail, direct mail and outgoing cross-border services, a number of member states have moved to open their postal markets more quickly.[6] Notable examples include the UK, the Netherlands, Sweden, Estonia, the Czech Republic and Slovenia.[7] Further, Spain has a liber-alised local mail market and of the EFTA (European Free Trade Association) states Norway has moved to open its postal market in 2009.[8] This has resulted in a different speed of liberalisation across the EU with early starters, Sweden, the Netherlands, Spain and now the UK enjoying (limited) competition for mail services.

3.   *Other regulatory barriers*   As well as the potential for the exclusive rights detailed above, there are a number of other regulatory barriers to effective competition in the market in the member states. These include:

●   the use of apparently excessive licensing or authorisations condi-tions (in the EC's view, presently done in 12 member states);[9]
●   the use of a universal service compensation fund (presently imple-mented in Italy);[10] and
●   the exemption for USPs from value-added tax (VAT) on their stan-dard services.

Figure 5.2 shows that the USPs in most member states are exempt from VAT for their postal services. VAT exemption is seen by many

Table 5.1   Remaining exclusive rights for the USPs (EU25), 2005

Member states	Domestic and incoming cross-border	Direct mail	Outgoing cross-border
Estonia (EE), Finland (FIN), Sweden (SE), UK	No or relatively minor reserved area		
Czech Republic (CZ), Netherlands (NL), Slovenia (SI)	X		
Spain (ES)*, Italy (IT)	X		X
Austria (AT), Belgium (BE), Germany (DE), Denmark (DK), France (FR), Ireland (IE)	X	X	
Cyprus (CY), Greece (GR), Hungary (HU), Latvia (LT), Lithuania (LU), Luxembourg (LV), Malta (MT), Portugal (PT), Slovakia (SK)	X	X	X
Poland (PL)*	Reserved area still exceeds limits of directive		

Note: * Polish reserved area still exceeds limits of directive while Spain has liberalised local mail.

Source: European Commission, 2004, staff working paper annex to the report on the application of the amended Postal Directive (Directive 2002/39/EC).

potential entrants as a vital barrier to end-to-end entry into the market, providing USPs with a direct commercial advantage on prices to those customers unable to reclaim VAT. However, some USPs have argued that the exemption also disadvantages them, as they cannot claim back VAT on their own contracting costs and the EC (DG Taxud) has argued that the revenue effects for USPs of ending the exemption would not be significant.

The delayed privatisation of the USPs
Another element in the postal exception has been limited privatisation in the sector. From Figure 5.3 we can see that only in Germany and the Netherlands do we now have fully (Germany – DHL) or almost fully (Netherlands – TNT) privately owned USPs. Denmark has sold 22 per cent of its shares in Denmark Post to CVC Capital Partners and negotiations are currently proceeding about the sale of 49 per cent of the stock of Belgian La Poste. Other member states which have indicated they are likely to pursue privatisation include Italy, Belgium and Greece.

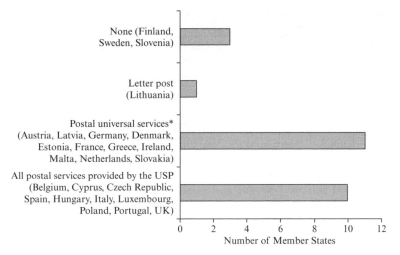

Note: * Services included those in the USO and provided by the USP.

Source: European Commission staff working paper annex to the report on the application of the Postal Directive (Directive 97/67/EC as amended by Directive 2002/39/EC), Brussels, 23 March 2005.

Figure 5.2   VAT exemptions in the EU25 member states, 2005

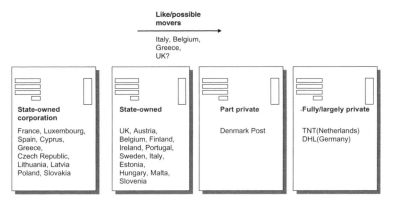

Source: Europe Economics (2004), based on European Commission studies, and press reports.

Figure 5.3   Private ownership of the USPs, 2005

Thus the postal sector has entered a sequence of reform in which in some cases full market opening will occur without privatisation, and in other cases privatisation occurred before a tradition of effective regulation in the member states.

Summary

In this section we have argued that postal sector reform has been delayed
compared to other sectors and that this delay constitutes a postal exception. This has been due to reluctance in the member states to progress
postal reform due to concerns over the maintenance of universal postal services and political concerns over employment and postal office networks.

The 'postal exception' can be seen through the relative delay in the calendar of postal reform, cautious transposition and application of the
Community framework in the member states and limited privatisation of
postal services. This has resulted in a sequence of postal reform which is
unusual in that it has been primarily driven at European level, and progress
towards market opening has generally occurred before that towards privatisation and sector reform at national level (apart from in Germany and
the Netherlands).

In many respects postal sector reform remains incomplete in the member states. While the Community framework allows for complete market
opening, significant regulatory barriers remain at national level to the
development of competition in the mail market, not least the continued
granting of exclusive rights (or reserved services) to the USPs (with the
exception of the UK, from January 2006).

THE DEVELOPMENT OF THE POSTAL MARKET

The Relative Importance of the Sector

The European postal sector (operators who provide postal services and
who operate on the postal value chain) remains important in revenues and
also in employment creation. This is shown in Table 5.2, which provides an
indicative summary of the revenues, employment and growth in comparable sectors.

The political importance of the sector is underlined by the relative concentration of unskilled and semi-skilled employment in the national posts
(USPs), which are major employers in every EU member state. Further, EU
citizens value their daily contact with postal services and appear to resent
any move to withdraw postal services.[11]

Recent Revenue and Volume Growth

Figure 5.4 shows that despite the relatively slow overall growth in real
output predicted above, parts of the European postal services market have

Table 5.2 *The postal sector compared to telecoms, electricity and gas,*
2002

Sector	Revenues	Employment	Predicted annual growth of output
Post[1] (USP and non-USP postal revenues and employment)	€88 billion	1.8 million	1–2%
Telecoms[2]	€236 billion	1.5 million	3–4%[3]
Electricity and gas	€224 billion[4]	0.9 million[5]	1–2%

1. 2002 figure from WIK Consult (2004): 'Main Developments in the European Postal Sector', study for the European Commission, final report, Bad Honnef, July.
2. 2002 figure from the European Commission based on Eurostat.
3. This growth figure from 1998 overstates current growth in the electronic communications market which was estimated at 3–4% by the European Commission in 2003.
4. 2001 figure from Eurostat based on GVA (gross value added).
5. 1998 figure from Eurostat.

Sources: Europe Economics based on information from Eurostat statistics (2005) and European Commission studies; www.europe-economics.com.

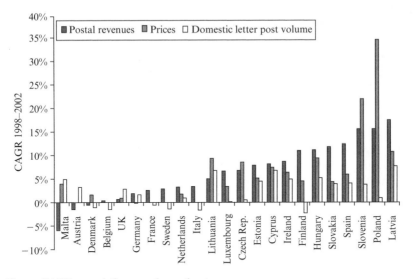

Note: CAGR: cumulative annual growth rate.

Source: WIK Consult (2004): 'Main Developments in the European Postal Sector', study for the European Commission, final report, Bad Honnef, July.

Figure 5.4 *USP revenues, prices and volume growth: (EU25 CAGR),*
1998–2002

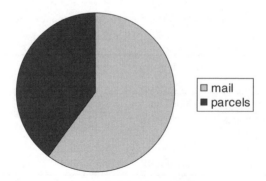

Source: Composed from 2002 figures in WIK Consult (2004), 'Main Developments in the European Postal Sector', study for the European Commission, final report, Bad Honnef, July.

Figure 5.5   EU25 mail and parcel revenues, 2002

been experiencing rapid revenue growth, even taking account of the M&As of the major players. Only in Denmark, Malta and Austria have postal revenues actually declined and even then only significantly in Malta where possibly there are special local market conditions.

In general, revenue growth reflects increased prices and only to a lesser extent volume growth, although from the figure it appears that mail volume growth has been variable across the member states, and possibly also that revenue growth may be led more from parcels and express products (given that generally postal revenue growth outstrips that of mail volumes growth).[12]

Of the €88 billion 'postal' revenues generated by the EU postal sector in 2002, €52 billion came from mail and €36 billion from parcels and express products (see Figure 5.5).[13] However it should be noted that USPs may have regulatory incentives to underplay mail volumes and also that it is felt by some regulators that internal sampling techniques and revenue-allocation techniques used by USPs lean towards overestimating parcel and packet volumes and underestimating letter mail volumes. Some recent research into mail forecasting has concluded that such forecasts have generally underestimated future volume growth and overestimated the potential impact of factors such as e-substitution.[14]

The Concentrated Demand for Postal Services

The demand for mail services is concentrated among major customers, some of whom can use alternative media to promote or communicate to customers. This is shown by Figure 5.6. This suggests that USP business economics largely depend upon the revenues they can make from these customers both from postal services and ancillary or upstream and

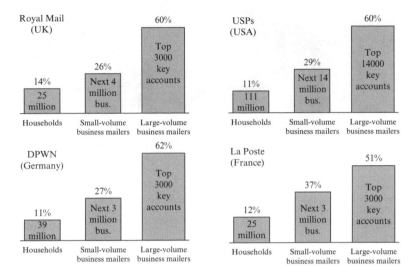

Source: F.H. Nader (Adrenale Corporation) (2005), 'Mail Trends', research for Pitney Bowes on effects of e-substitution.

Figure 5.6   Concentration of postal mail volumes with key customers

downstream services. (This is a point to which we shall return.) Larger customers in the market achieve significant discounts from the uniform tariff, for example for pre-sorted mail.

Market Shares

In Figure 5.7, we can see that the EU mail market is dominated by DHL, La Poste (France) and Royal Mail, each with about 20 per cent of the market. This roughly corresponds to the size of their national GDP as a proportion of total EU GDP, reflecting the traditional correlation between mail volumes and GDP. Other major players include Poste Italiane, TPG (TNT) and Correos (Spain).

The EU parcel market is more concentrated and in Figure 5.8 it can be seen that DHL has the largest market share with up to 40 per cent of the volume. This partly reflects the scale of its acquisitions (particularly of DHL) and the relative size of the German parcel market.

The Profitability of the USPs

From Figure 5.9, we can see that in general USPs have been profitable and since 2003 both La Poste and Royal Mail have returned to profitability.

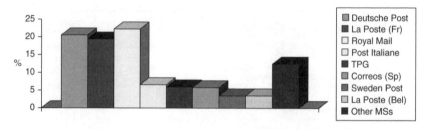

Source: WIK Consult (2004), 'Main Developments in the European Postal Sector', study
for the European Commission, final report, Bad Honnef, July.

Figure 5.7   EU25 USP market shares in domestic letter volumes, 2002

Source: WIK Consult (2004), 'Main Developments in the European Postal Sector', study
for the European Commission, final report, Bad Honnef, July.

Figure 5.8   EU25 USP market shares in parcel volumes, 1999

However, it should be noted that profitability as reflected in these data
does not equate to 'postal' profitability in that financial performance
includes performance in non-postal activities and postal retail outlets. The
profitability of the USPs has tended to vary according to national strategy
for the USPs with regulation as well as business success being a key factor.

The EU postal sector is extremely diverse with modern conglomerate
international businesses such as DHL and TNT sitting alongside very small
domestically focused USPs.

The Four Main Operators

The four main operators include the USPs from the three largest member
states in terms of GDP together with the Dutch USP, TNT, which is prominent in the parcel and express market due to its acquisitions in this sector.

● *DHL (Deutsche Post)* is the most profitable of the EU USPs enjoying significant margins on mail products and consequently, annual

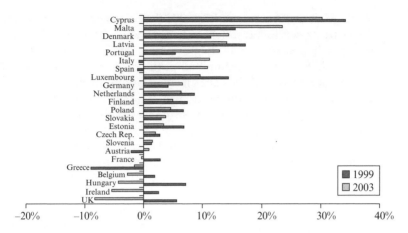

Source: WIK Consult (2004), 'Main Developments in the European Postal Sector', study for the European Commission, final report, Bad Honnef, July.

Figure 5.9   Profitability of the EU25 USPs, 1999–2003 (EBIT/revenues)

EBIT of more than €2 billion on mail services. DHL had largely completed its first round of European acquisitions by the end of 2002 and is now engaged in trying to cut costs, obtain operational synergies and unify its brand for its varied portfolio of businesses. This process is known as the STAR programme, and it is claimed to have realised savings of €800 million. DHL had a turnover of about €43 billion in 2004 and it now operates in 220 countries with an assured presence in all European markets and a workforce of 380,000 of whom over 170,000 are employees outside Germany; less than half the German employees are now civil servants. This new flexibility has apparently been a major ingredient in its increasing efficiency; DHL now handles about 140,000 items per employee per annum.[15] Key areas of planned expansion appear to be postal markets in Japan and China as well as the US parcel markets. For example, DHL is projecting that 20 per cent of its revenues will come from China by 2010. The recent bid for Exel suggests that DHL may still be looking to cement its leading status in the logistics sector. DHL shares rose from €10 at year end 2002 to €16.38 in January 2004 with a dividend of over €500 million and dividend per share of €0.50.

• *TNT (TPG)* again enjoys high margins for its mail products and consequently significant profits. Turnover in 2004 was nearly €13 billion and the workforce in 2005 was around 160,000. Global presence is secured through the 'Spring' venture begun in 2000 with

Royal Mail and Singapore Post. TNT also provides upstream and downstream services through its Cendris subsidiary. Its key targets for growth appear to be in the postal markets in Japan and China, and in the freight forwarding and postal consolidation markets. A main concern for TNT has been its mail volume decline, possibly as a result of increased competition in the Dutch market, which is forecast at 3 per cent annually. In response to this it has launched its own cost-efficiency programme, which it estimates has generated extra productivity of about 5 per cent between 2001 and 2003.[16] The financial performance of the company has been sound with TPG shares rising from €15.82 in December 2002 to €19.68 in January 2005.

- *La Poste* has Europe's third largest postal network, covering 80 per cent of the European market, giving it presence in 20 countries. It has a workforce of about 300,000 and a turnover of around €14 billion (2003). Key acquisitions have included the DPD German parcel network and UK Mayne Nickless parcel company, which has been absorbed into the GeoPost group. It has partnership links with Sweden Post and Fedex and working agreements on express parcel services with Poste Italiane and with Correos (Spain). La Poste's strategy now includes a cost-efficiency programme which involves closing down the internal operator Ditipack and the loss-making parcel DPD France network. La Poste is also heavily involved in the French financial services market and appears to be poised to become a major player in the French mortgages market.
- *Royal Mail* retreated from its acquisitions policy but retains presence in Dutch and German postal markets. Its turnover was around €12.5 billion in 2004 and by the end of 2005 its workforce stood at about 195,000, reduced by 34,000 since March 2002.

Key Market Trends

As the market moves towards deregulation, evidence is emerging that postal operators compete in a changing and in some respects dynamic market. In particular it is clear that there are opportunities for postal operators:

1. to compete in unaddressed mail services;
2. to expand horizontally and vertically into upstream and downstream services and ancillary markets; and
3. to expand through mergers and acquisitions and into international postal markets.

Horizontal and vertical expansion

Figure 5.10 identifies some of the related services provided by USPs and other postal operators. In part these stem from the legacy of USPs as providers of non-postal services such as financial services (post banks) and retail services (post offices). However, also, increasingly they reflect the opportunities for USPs and other operators to expand into ancillary services such as unaddressed mail and upstream and downstream services such as printing services and mail-room management.

Table 5.3 further illustrates this horizontal and vertical expansion by listing the acquisitions of the USPs in unaddressed mail companies, freight and logistics, printing services, mail preparation companies, hybrid mail companies and mail-room management companies. Compared to these acquisitions it is noticeable that only DHL had so far acquired a letter mail company.

The development of European postal networks

DHL and TNT (and to a lesser extent La Poste) have also moved to create European postal (parcel and express) networks. DHL and TNT have achieved this through an active policy of acquisitions as shown in Tables 5.4 and 5.5.

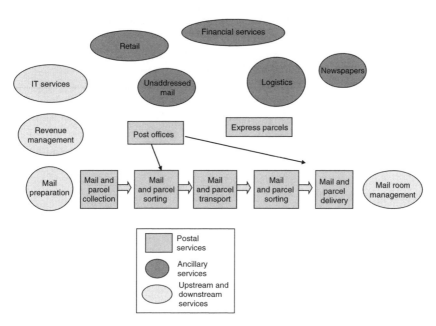

Source: Europe Economics (2004), based on European Commission studies, and press reports.

Figure 5.10   Blurring sector boundaries and new opportunities for postal operators

Table 5.3   The main operations of companies acquired by EU USPs, 2005

Operations	No. of USPs acquiring companies	List of USPs active in the acquisition of companies
Horizontal expansion		
Letter post	1	DE
Parcels	10	AT, BE, DK, ES, FIN, FR, IE, IT, PT, SE
Express	10	BE, DE, FR, IE, IT, LT, NL, PT, SE, SI
Unaddressed items	7	AT, BE, DE, FIN, FR, NL, PT
Freight logistics	4	DE, IE, SE, SI
Vertical expansion		
Printing services	5	DE, FIN, IE, NL, SI
Mail preparation	4	DE, FIN, IE, PT
Hybrid mail	3	NL, PT, SI
Mail-room management	3	BE, NL, PT

Note: For country abbreviations, see Table 5.1.

Source: European Commission staff working paper annex to the report on the application of the Postal Directive (Directive 97/67/EC as amended by Directive 2002/39/EC), Brussels, 23 March 2005.

Table 5.4   DHL acquisitions, 1997–2002

Company	Year	Country	Division
Air Express International	1999	USA	Air freight
Yellowstone	1999	USA	Publications/catalogues distribution
ASG	1999	Sweden	Logistics
Royal Nedloyd	1999	Netherlands	Parcels
MIT	1999	Italy	Parcels and Express
Danzas	1999	Switzerland/Europe	Logistics
Global Mail	1998	USA	International mail
Ducros Services Rapid	1998	France	Parcels/express
Securicor	1998	UK	Parcels/express
DHL	1998–2002	Europe wide	Express/courier
Belgian Parcel Distribution	1997	Belgium	Parcels
Sevisco	1997	Poland	Parcels

Source: Europe Economics (2004), based on European Commission studies, and press reports.

Table 5.5   TPG acquisitions, 1999–2004

Company	Year	Country	Division
Wilson Logistics Group	2004	Sweden	Logistics
Full Service	2003	Italy	Mail
Docvision	2003	Netherlands	Mail
Werbeagentur Fischer	2003	Germany	Mail
Dimar Group	2002	Czech Republic and Slovakia	Mail
Transports Nicolas	2002	France	Logistics
Cerilly (Steic/PMS – ELS)	2002	Italy	Mail
MDS	2001	Netherlands	Mail
Bleckmann Group	2001	Netherlands	Express
T.E.I.	2001	Thailand	Express
Lason UK Group/CENDRIS	2001	UK	Mail
Advanced Logistics Services (ALS)	2001	Italy	Logistics
CD Marketing Services Group Ltd	2001	UK	Mail
Logistics Taylor Barnard	2000	UK	Logistics
CTI Logistx	2000	USA	Logistics
Schrader Group	2000	Germany	Logistics
Barlatier	2000	France	Logistics
Mendy	2000	France	Logistics
Omnidata	1999	Netherlands	Mail
Jet Services SA	1999	France	Express
Tecnologistica	1999	Italy	Logistics

Source: TPG website, http://group.tnt.com.

Table 5.4 shows that DHL's policy of acquisitions has been focused in the express and logistics markets both in the EU and more recently the USA. These acquisitions have made it the major player in the European logistics market (through Danzas) and a major player in express (through its acquisition of DHL). From a regulatory perspective it is noticeable that in pursuing expansion in international markets DHL has been prepared to withstand significant losses, in particular for its US operations. Its position in the EU logistics market will be cemented further if the Exel acquisition is allowed to proceed.

Table 5.5 shows that TPG has moved more gradually to acquire network penetration including recently mail companies in Europe. We can see also a more European focus, although it also appears to be moving to expand also in the Japanese postal market. Its programme of acquisitions in the

Table 5.6   Recent acquisitions in the European postal and logistics sectors

Operator	Company acquired	Type of business	Country
Deutsche Post	Exel (not yet completed)	Logistics	UK
Deutsche Post	Unipost (38 per cent stake)	Mail	Spain
Deutsche Post	Speedmail	Bulk mail	UK
Deutsche Post	KarstadtQuelle*	Logistics	Germany
UPS	Messenger Service Stolica	Parcels and express	Poland
Deutsche Post	Koba	Mail	France
Swiss Post	Porta a Porta	Logistics	Italy
UPS	Menlo	Air freight forwarding	Europe wide
Italian TNT	Servizi Distribuzione	Express	Italy

Note: * This acquisition appears to have run into difficulties and is not yet complete.

Source: Press reports and company press releases.

sector appears far from complete, and it may well be that mail deregulation sparks off a fresh wave of activity.

Table 5.6 underlines that this process has not yet finished in the sector, with a new wave of acquisitions (December 2004 onwards), including the acquisition of mail providers.

The development of competition for unaddressed mail
USPs also compete in the unaddressed mail market, and although they have fairly small market shares in their domestic unaddressed mail markets they can use unaddressed mail volumes to supplement addressed mail volumes where they have spare capacity.

The development of new services
USPs such as Finland Post are also gaining significant new revenues by diversifying into new services such as e-messaging (see Table 5.7).

Summary

● From the above we can see that postal revenues are growing and that most USPs are profitable. Letter volume growth is more mixed with volumes growing strongly in some member states and declining in others. Parcel and express products are enjoying stronger growth.
● The three largest USPs represent about 60 per cent of mail revenues in the EU and DHL by itself represents around 40 per cent of the parcel market.

Table 5.7 Finland Post's business sectors, 2002

Finland post group's net turnover by business sector	Share of net turnover %	Net turnover 1 Jan.–30 June 2003 MEUR	Net turnover 1 Jan.–30 June 2002 MEUR	Change %[1]
Messaging	63	363.7	418.0	−13 (+2)
Electronic messaging	12	67.0	61.7	+9 (+2)
Logistics	20	133.7	52.1	+157 (+2)
Other business activities	3	38.9	44.3	−12 (+3)
Group activities	2	11.5	76.4	
Internal net turnover		−52.4	99.6	
Consolidated net turnover	100	562.4	552.9	+2 (+1)

Note: 1.   Comparable change in brackets.

Source: Finland Post website.

- The demand for postal services is largely concentrated among key customers.
- Key market trends include significant horizontal and vertical expansion by the USPs, the development of European postal networks and the movement by the USPs into new services.
- It appears that EU USPs have significant opportunities to expand their revenues upstream and downstream from the postal value chain and into ancillary markets. These opportunities derive in large part from their existing customer base which is served by the national distribution network which provides the universal service, that is, they derive significant competitive advantages through national distribution.
- This is also notably the case in the opportunities which the growing e-commerce related traffic may offer to postal distributors.
- The larger posts are moving to expand into international markets, for example with Deutsche Post most famously becoming the largest European logistics operator and establishing operations in the US, Japan and China.
- In these respects it can be argued that the EU postal market is a dynamic market and that EU USPs have significant opportunities to expand their revenues.

- However, while the German, French and Dutch USPs have moved to establish European parcel networks, reflecting their greater financial muscle, Royal Mail has retreated from its initial M&A policy. (We shall consider the UK market in more detail in the next section.)

THE CASE FOR THE POSTAL EXCEPTION REVIEWED

We have seen then that postal regulation is exceptional in its delayed progress towards sector reform and deregulation, and that the postal market has dynamic features, with significant revenue growth opportunities for successful market players. In this section we shall review the case for prolonging the postal exception, considering its rationale in more detail, and comment upon the costs and benefits of current approaches.

The Rationale for the Postal Exception

The primary case for delayed postal reform (as opposed to the regulation of dominant suppliers) in the sector is based upon concerns that there should be a universal service, and that the universal postal service obligation imposes burdens upon the USP such that it may not be possible for the USP to finance universal service provision in a fully competitive market, without 'reserved areas'. Indeed a universal service obligation (USO) with a uniform geographic tariff could be seen as a recipe for profitable entry (also referred to as 'cherry picking'), including that by entrants who may be less efficient than the incumbent.

To some extent the concerns which led policy makers to move slowly in post have also been based upon a view of postal services as a market likely to face declining volumes and revenues and of USPs as likely to face financial problems unless supported by state funds. The primary strength of the rationale for reserving parts of the market from competition depends then on:

1. the importance of the USO as a service of general economic interest; and
2. the scale of the burdens imposed by USOs.

Some Different Approaches to Measuring Universal Service Costs

It is clear that any regulatory obligation which requires a national daily delivery and collection at a uniform tariff will impose some additional burdens on the USP.

The first major study undertaken to measure universal service costs in the EU member states was for the EC in 1998.[17] This considered the net costs of the universal service to be 'when a postal administration is obliged by the government to supply customers or services in circumstances where the overall revenues generated from doing so are less than the costs of supply, taking into account any revenue benefits from providing the universal service' (NERA, 1998, p.iii, executive summary).

This was termed the 'net avoided cost' (NAC) approach, which sought to assess the revenue gain or loss that the USP may have if it was not obliged to provide the universal service. This was to be estimated by adding together losses made by the USP on services where revenues did not meet incremental (or avoidable) costs and netting off these losses against the financial benefits of universal service provision. The study estimated the costs of the universal service as ranging from 8 per cent of delivery costs in Austria to zero in France, Greece, Denmark and Finland.

In the discussions surrounding the next steps of Community regulation, such findings proved controversial. In particular USPs were concerned that, under this static analysis, the losses they might incur as a result of the USO under different steps of postal market opening would not be clear.

Royal Mail's economists then developed their own technique for identifying universal service costs in a competitive market, known as the 'entry pricing' model. This approach used a spreadsheet model to measure the impact of the USO (in particular the geographically averaged uniform tariff) on the USP's finances by seeking to assess where they would lose revenues to competitors in a competitive environment. Here the cost of the universal service was defined as the reduction in profit levels caused by USOs (in particular the uniform tariff) under different scenarios of weight and direct mail liberalisation.

This approach has subsequently been refined further, notably at the Institut d'Économie Industrielle (IDEI) at Toulouse University, to include additional analyses of the effects of the pressure of competitive entry on the uniform tariff pricing of the USP in a competitive environment and the potential welfare implications of competition in the market.

American economists have also applied entry pricing models to simulate the potential effects of competition on the United States Postal Service, deriving what has become known as the 'graveyard scenario'. This occurs where a USP increases its prices to offset revenue losses (and as a result increased average unit costs due to loss of economies of scale), thereby generating increased future switching. Further refinements of this type of modelling have been made by economists working with Poste Italiane to consider the potential for a graveyard spiral in EU posts, particularly where a smaller volume per capita post may be vulnerable to increasing average costs (due to the initial steepness of the average cost curve) as it loses volumes.

The findings of these approaches

In theory the NAC method and the entry pricing methodology might produce similar results. However, in practice, given that the NAC method uses estimates of incremental costs and that there are difficulties in fully establishing the advantages to the USP of providing the universal service and the likely scale and impact of competitive entry, it is unsurprising that their results have often proved widely different.

For example, the UK regulator, Postcomm, used consultants who undertook a NAC analysis of Royal Mail's service provision. Their conclusion, based on similar incremental costings data to that which had populated Royal Mail's entry pricing model, was that the NAC was, in context, not a substantial burden (about £80 million). Royal Mail's entry pricing model had, however, predicted that if the weight defining the protected mail market was reduced to 50 grams and direct mail was liberalised, the USP could lose all their 'normalised' profit.

This Rationale Reviewed in the Context of Today's Market

As the market has changed and mail market competition has become a reality in the sector, the primary rationale for protecting parts of the USP markets from competition (as opposed to the regulation of the dominant supplier) has begun to look increasingly unfounded.

The need to update the rationale for the USO

While the universal postal service was doubtless important for all citizens at the time when post performed an essential unique function as a means of communication, this is no longer the case. There are many available alternative modes of communication, most of which are not regulated as postal services are. Moreover, the nature of the service is changing towards distribution of business-originated and direct mail rather than personal correspondence.

We can see from Table 5.8 that it is businesses rather than consumers that increasingly originate (and pay for) mail and that this is a general trend across the postal sector. In most of the countries shown, between 80 and 90 per cent of post volumes are now originated by business distributors.

These factors may suggest to policy makers that in future significant intervention in the postal market which protects only a declining number of consumers who post mail may become disproportionate. This may be

Table 5.8   The increasingly business nature of mail volumes, 1970–2003

Country	Business-originated post					
	1970	1970	1985	1985	2003	2003
France	69%	7 B	82%	11 B	88%	15 B
Germany	75%	8 B	86%	10 B	90%	14 B
Netherlands	78%	2 B	87%	2 B	89%	5 B
UK	74%	7 B	85%	9 B	86%	17 B
USPS	80%	66 B	86%	119 B	89%	169 B
Italy	NA	NA	NA	NA	80%	3 B
Spain	NA	NA	NA	NA	74%	3 B
Switzerland	NA	NA	NA	NA	86%	3 B
Sweden	77%	3 B	86%	3 B	88%	3 B

Source: F.H. Nader (Adrenale Corporation) (2004), 'Mail Trends', research for Pitney Bowes in reference to the substitution debate.

Table 5.9   Development of competition in the EU mail market, 1998–2003 (%)

Country	USPs' letter post market share in liberalised markets					
	1998	1999	2000	2001	2002	2003
Germany	99.2	98.7	98.4	97.6	97.0	96.0
Denmark	100.0	100.0	100.0	100.0	100.0	98.0
Spain	–	–	–	–	–	90.0
UK	–	–	–	–	–	99.7
Netherlands	98.0	98.0	98.0	98.0	95.0	95.0
Sweden	95.6	95.1	95.7	94.8	94.2	93.4
Slovenia	98.0	98.0	98.0	98.0	98.0	98.0

Source: European Commission staff working paper annex to the report on the application of the amended Postal Directive, (Directive 97/67/EC as amended by Directive 2002/39/EC), Brussels, 23 March 2005.

particularly the case where that regulatory obligation to provide a universal service also requires a geographically averaged uniform tariff (which was not, one should note, a feature of the EU directives).

The limited effects of mail market opening on universal services
In practice as shown in Table 5.9, where the mail market has been partially opened to competition, in Germany, Spain, Sweden, the Netherlands and the UK end-to-end competition has been slow to develop (even many years after market opening in the case of Sweden and Spain).

While explanations for this vary, it appears that the concentrated demand for postal services (if this carries a reduced likelihood of customer switching), natural monopoly characteristics in relation to postal delivery and also the incumbent early-mover advantage as a national postal distributor have all acted to restrict competition.

The concentration of demand   The concentrated nature of the demand for postal services (see the previous section) may imply that customer switching is less likely to occur as a response to geographic price differentials where contracts range across products and across geography.[18]

Detailed route-by-route analysis of the type involved in entry pricing models seems incongruous compared to the reality of large contracts with customers, which contracts may range across postal and non-postal products. This incongruity is further evidenced by the emergence of competitive end-to-end entry (where it has occurred) which appears to have been built upwards from key customers.

Natural monopoly characteristics   Postcomm has suggested that meaningful competition for end-to-end services is unlikely to occur at least in the short run in the UK mail market due to barriers to entry including significant economies of scale advantages for the USP in delivery.[19] In the light of this, it has moved to ensure that third-party access to parts of the Royal Mail service is available to entrants.

Figure 5.11 shows the cost curve of the United States Postal Service which has been found to be similar in shape to that of EU USPs.[20] This suggests that there are significant economies of scale, particularly in postal delivery.

In practice, where end-to-end competition has occurred it has been largely for city to city international business mail (as in Sweden) or based around a gradual network build-up serving a few major customers (as in the Netherlands) with a delivery specification of once every few days to ensure sufficient volumes.

Incumbent early-mover advantage   The USPs enjoy early-mover advantage in their home markets as national postal distributors. While it has been argued that there are no significant capital expenditure entry costs[21] any national distribution network involves significant labour costs and can only be economic to the extent that there are sufficient volumes. In general only the USPs have these volumes (and customers) and it can be argued that end-to-end entrants would need to build up these volumes over considerable time organically via one or two large customers or unaddressed mail networks before they could offer national distribution on a regular basis. During this time entrants would be vulnerable to competitive response

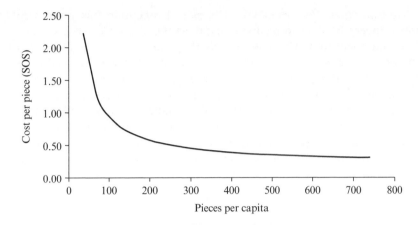

Source: Bob Cohen, M. Robinson, G. Scarfiglieri, R. Sheehy, V.V. Comandini, J. Waller
and S. Xenakis, 'The role of scale economies in the cost behaviour of posts', December
2004, draft paper.

Figure 5.11   Economies of scale in postal services

from the USPs, highlighting the importance of appropriate regulation of a
dominant supplier.

Summary
There are significant doubts about the remaining strength of the rationale for
a postal regulation built around the protection of universal services as opposed
to a need to control a dominant supplier. The case for a USO looks weaker
when there are alternative modes of communication for EU citizens, for many
of which alternatives there are no regulatory obligations. If competition is to
occur largely through third-party access then the access price is crucial.

The Costs and Benefits of the Postal Exception

In the light of this weakening rationale for the USO, extending the postal
exception could only be justified if it could be demonstrated that it was
having a beneficial impact on the market in some other respects. What then
have been its costs and benefits?

The costs of the postal exception
Identifying the costs of the postal exception involves a consideration of the
effects which a protracted reservation of mail services and an asymmetry in
the regulatory treatment of, and national strategy for, postal services across
member states have had on the market.

Mixed incentives for operators   The postal exception has given USPs mixed incentives depending upon their market conditions, national regulation and ownership. This is summarised in Figure 5.12. The interplay of these factors has influenced the balance of the strategies adopted by the USPs between defensive and expansive options (though all USPs are understandably reluctant to cede ground in home postal markets).

Larger players, sometimes with a favourable national regulation and with private ownership profit-maximisation incentives, have moved to build up European parcel markets largely through programmes of acquisitions and have also entered unaddressed mail markets creating the possibility of regional or even European mail market networks in the future.

Regulatory asymmetry, national strategy and market distortions   Regulatory asymmetry as a reflection of national strategy for the USP has also possibly created market distortions. Where national implementation of the Community Framework has been concerned primarily with the development of a 'national champion' or global postal operator, as perhaps in Germany and the Netherlands, then the USPs have been most able to pursue expansive strategies. Here, differences in the application of regulation rather than a healthy rivalry between firms seems to be playing a significant role in determining the apparent competitive success or otherwise of the USPs. It has sometimes been suggested that the sequence of reform in these member

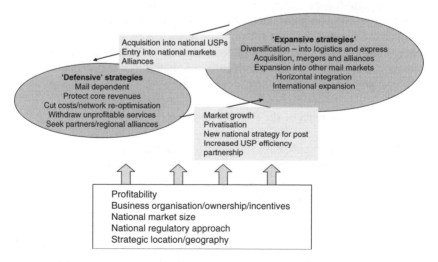

Source: Europe Economics (2004), based on European Commission studies, and press reports.

Figure 5.12   Some influences on USP business strategies

states, where expansion has occurred before full privatisation, could have led to financial indiscipline.[22]

Competition law concerns and the reliance on competition law enforcement In this context, where businesses have enjoyed special rights for some services while competing in others and have had profit-maximisation incentives and favourable national regulation, it is unsurprising that there have been many complaints of abuse in the sector. There have been a significant number of competition cases brought, the main ones of which are summarised in Figure 5.13. These complaints have focused on allegations of predatory pricing of competitive products (cross-subsidised through excessive prices on universal or reserved services), and of insufficient independent regulation of access conditions and illegal state aids. While these cases suggest that the application of competition law may redress some of the deficiencies in the national application of the Community framework, over-reliance on competition law enforcement at national level could increase regulatory uncertainty.

Weaker incentives for cost efficiency, innovation and customer responsiveness Lack of competition for the main mail services with fairly constant volumes and revenues has provided some USPs with apparently safe returns and perhaps therefore incentives for satisficing rather than for cost-efficient and innovative service delivery. Where this has been combined with national ownership of the USP, then incentives towards increasing efficiency may be weaker, resulting in a failure to progress the postal sector.

Different national strategies are again important here and we have noted how the Scandinavian postal services, DHL, TNT and La Poste have diversified into information technology services, express and logistics while other USPs have retained more traditional product specifications.

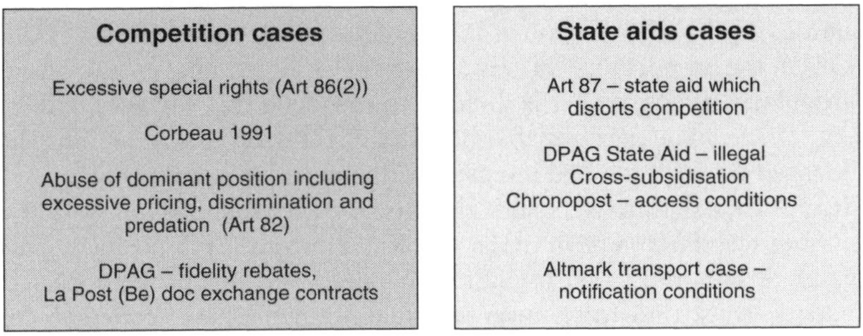

Competition cases	State aids cases
Excessive special rights (Art 86(2)) Corbeau 1991 Abuse of dominant position including excessive pricing, discrimination and predation (Art 82) DPAG – fidelity rebates, La Post (Be) doc exchange contracts	Art 87 – state aid which distorts competition DPAG State Aid – illegal Cross-subsidisation Chronopost – access conditions Altmark transport case – notification conditions

Note: DPAG is Deutsche Post, now known as DHL.

Source: Europe Economics (2004), based on European Commission studies, and press reports.

Figure 5.13   Main competition cases in the European postal sector

Table 5.10   Impact of liberalisation on the efficiency of USPs

Country	Reduction in workforce (%)	Over time period
New Zealand	40	1988–2001
Sweden	30	1990–2000
Germany	37	1990–1999
Great Britain	15–20	2002–2005

Source: Bob Cohen, 'Testimony before the President's Commission on the
Postal Service', February 2003; www.prc.gov/pres_comm/cohen.pdf.

The variable effects of the postal exception can also be seen in the
response of the USPs to possible competition. This is shown in Table 5.10.
Where postal reform has been most developed we can see that there have
been the greatest efforts towards cost efficiency. (New Zealand Post is privatised and New Zealand is fully open to competition.) Early movers in this
respect include the Netherlands, where postal efficiency improvements are
ongoing, and DHL[23] which through its STAR programme aims to take
advantage of organisational synergies while also addressing labour rigidities as its workforce continues to move away from civil service patterns of
employment.

We can see further evidence in Figure 5.14 of the scale of possible
efficiency gains in the productivity improvements made by Sweden Post
since Swedish postal reform and market opening in the early 1990s.

However, in non-liberalised markets such as France and Belgium, the
USPs have generally acted much later to instigate significant programmes
of rationalisation and cost cutting. Anecdotal evidence suggests that
overall there remains wide scope for increased efficiency in the sector.
This view is supported by Figure 5.15, which shows a wide variance
in unit costs, the organisation of infrastructure and inputs in (EU15) USPs.

Given the importance of economies of scale to the postal business
(particularly in delivery) it is difficult to reconcile this variance with economic efficiency, suggesting that political imperatives may sometimes have
influenced the location and intensity of the postal infrastructure.

It appears also that the postal exception has acted against innovation and
customer responsiveness in the sector. Key innovations in postal engineering (use of hub-and-spoke organisation, parcel-sorting automation) and in
products (track and trace, inventory management) have tended to come
disproportionately from the competitive express operators. Further, anecdotal evidence suggests that responsiveness to customers changes markedly
with the development of competition.

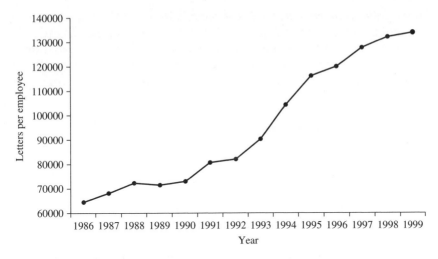

Source: Frontier Economics (2002), 'The impact of liberalisation on efficiency', a report prepared for Postcomm, January.

Figure 5.14   Sweden Post: letters per employee, 1986–1999

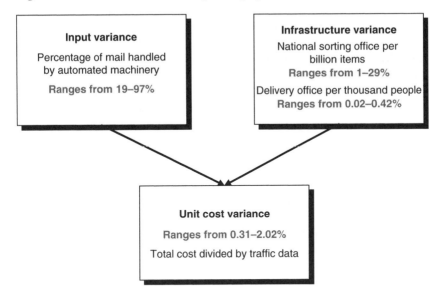

Source: Europe Economics (2004), based on European Commission studies, and press reports.

Figure 5.15   Cost/infrastructure variance across (EU15) member states, 2002

Gains from sector reform seen in comparable sectors A cost of the postal exception can also be seen in that the postal sector has not enjoyed the gains in productivity and lower prices seen in other comparable industries where an earlier reform has taken place. Compared to other sectors, Royal Mail has achieved relatively low efficiency gain – historically of around 2.9 per cent.[24]

The benefits of the postal exception

The postal exception has been fuelled by political nervousness about the effects of deregulation of mail services and, with this in mind it could be argued that a cautious liberalisation of the sector has acted at least to prevent some of the negative scenarios predicted by those reluctant to reform from unfolding. For example, we can see that during the period of the postal exception the following positive trends have occurred:

1. *Improved quality of service* The quality of postal services has improved particularly in those member states where previously it was very low.
2. *Postal market employment has grown* Over the period of the postal exception, employment in the sector has grown despite a slight contraction in employment in the USPs.

The effects of the postal exception on the UK

The UK postal market has suffered an unusual pattern of postal reform. At the beginning of the reform process in Europe, Royal Mail had a number of significant commercial advantages over its rivals: relatively efficient operations, early corporatisation and the ending of civil service employment rigidities.

However, while, as we have seen, some member states had a clear strategic response to the reform of the sector (creating national champions) and others either opened the market to competition (Sweden) or continued largely as before, it can be argued that in the UK political and regulatory uncertainties in the 1980s and 1990s resulted in confused incentives to Royal Mail which may have delayed its commercial evolution. Initial plans for privatisation were abandoned in the early 1990s and other politically led interventions such as the separation of Parcel Force from the rest of the business created recurring regulatory uncertainty for the company.

Over time the result of this uncertainty appears to have been to prevent the company from taking the decisions necessary to take full advantage of emerging business opportunities. This conclusion appears consistent with Royal Mail's current concerns about a potential lack of investment in the sector and also perhaps its recent moves to update its product mix towards better meeting the needs of its customers.

Further indications of this can also be seen in the relative lack of diversification of Royal Mail upstream and downstream of the postal value chain compared to other major European USPs and in the later nature of its introduction of cost-efficiency programmes. This is also reflected in the corporate structure of Royal Mail compared to the other three larger USPs (or 'superposts') (Figure 5.16). This has left Royal Mail more dependent on mail revenues (though not profitability) than its main competitors, and possibly more vulnerable to greater competition for these services. Table 5.11 illustrates this.

This then leaves the UK in a rather unique position. On the one hand, Royal Mail remains anecdotally one of the more efficient EU USPs[25] with the advantage that it does not employ a largely civil service workforce and has therefore potentially greater scope for making quick efficiency gains than other USPs. Further it retains incumbent advantage in a market which it can be argued is dynamic and growing. On the other hand, Royal Mail is facing a pace of structural change which is faster than that which has been

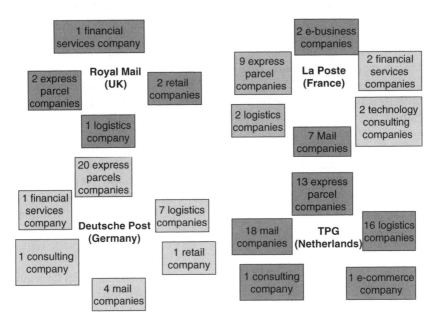

Source: Presentation slides by H Makitalo, Finland Post: 'How well the international postal system is able to meet and reflect the needs of international business', 2004 Rutgers Conference.

Figure 5.16   Conglomerate superposts

Table 5.11   USP revenue percentages, 2003

Operator	Mail %	Parcels and express %	Logistics %	Other %	Total %
DHL[1]	30	41	15	14	100
TNT	31	36	33	0	100
La Poste[2]	59	12	06	23	100
Royal Mail	76	13	0	11	100

Notes:
1. DHL includes subsidiaries from a wide range of sectors.
2. La Poste is a major player in the French financial services market.

Source: Europe Economics (2004), based on European Commission studies, and press reports.

imposed on other USPs, which have been more sheltered from competition during their adaptation. Further, Royal Mail may be the only major USP which does not have the potential to compete for parcel and express services on a European basis.

Nevertheless it may only have been through the pressures imposed by the regulator and by potential competition (and the new leadership of Royal Mail) that it has begun to shake off the legacies of statutory monopoly and regulatory uncertainty. Further, the process of deregulation itself, while challenging to the company, may well be to its long-term benefit, imposing a still relatively early efficiency and optimum business model on the company. It remains to be seen whether the M&A policies of its rivals constitute sound investment and diversification or the financial indiscipline sometimes associated with monopolies.

In any case as we approach January 2006 and a UK postal market fully open to competition it is a significant moment for Royal Mail. Either it can continue to respond positively to the new regulatory certainties or competitors (at least those taking advantage of third-party access) will now capture parts of its market.

Summary

The rationale for the postal exception has been based on the need for a universal postal service and concerns that regulatory intervention in the market is necessary to ensure that such a service is maintained in a competitive environment. This rationale looks less convincing in the light of the development of alternative communications networks and the shift of mail business away from personal correspondence to direct mail and other business originated products.

Reflection on the costs and benefits of the postal exception suggest that this exception has significant costs in terms of lower incentives for efficiency, innovation and customer responsiveness and that regulatory asymmetry in the market may generate market distortions.

Finally, with the positive signal set for the end date for full mail market opening in the UK the regulatory debate should move on to discussions about how to further deregulate the market while protecting efficient competitors (and customers) from a still dominant supplier.

CONCLUSIONS AND RECOMMENDATIONS

In conclusion, we shall outline a model for ending the postal exception.

The Principles of Better Regulation and Regulatory Impact Assessment

The principles of good regulation suggest that regulatory intervention should be proportionate, accountable and consistent. Regulatory impact assessments require setting clear policy objectives, identifying the rationale for regulatory intervention and carefully assessing the impact of different policy options.[26]

We can see in the pattern of consultations and analyses which Postcomm has undertaken since 2001 an approach which appears largely consistent with these principles; initial scoping of the meaning and interpretation of its statutory duties and consultation on different policy options, followed by detailed empirical research on the key questions or analysis. Postcomm stands out among European postal regulators in seeking an explicitly evidence-based approach to policy making, and in the transparency of its process.

Moving to End the Postal Exception

In our previous analysis of the postal exception we have noted that postal deregulation remains delayed compared to other sectors, while underlying sector development remains strong and dynamic. We have also seen that reservation in the sector applied differently in different countries may have distorted market development. The rationale for regulatory intervention, concern over the viability of universal service provision, appears weaker than in the past, given that the justification for universal postal services as an essential means of communication is fading.

In light of the above we conclude that the current level of regulatory intervention in the sector (the postal exception) is disproportionate to its objectives. How, then, is it best to proceed towards deregulation?

Third-party Access and Light Touch Regulation

At this time we should aim to reduce the scope of regulatory intervention, while protecting potential efficient competitors and customers from the dominant supplier. After the complete opening of the UK market as planned, the following steps would seem appropriate:

1. update the universal service obligation, in line with customer needs;
2. regulate access prices to Royal Mail's essential facilities ensuring efficient charges for the use of these facilities, through a bottom-up modelling of Royal Mail's technical and operational efficiency and ensuring appropriate accounting and managerial separation; and
3. pave the way for retail price deregulation.

This model of deregulation is reflected in Figure 5.17, which illustrates the different elements of the regulation across the postal value chain. In this model:

1. Regulation of third-party access prices (through an access code and through managerial and accounting separation) would become the main element of price control in the sector.
2. Bottom-up modelling of a notional efficient operator would be used to create the basis for the access charges, in order to protect customers and other operators from access prices based on inefficient costs.
3. USOs and other regulatory interventions which may act to increase the efficient price of the delivery network would be regularly reviewed to asses their proportionality and impact.

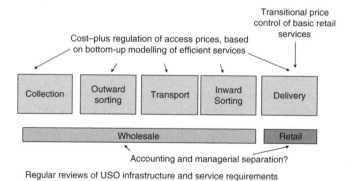

Source: Europe Economics (2004), based on European Commission studies, and press reports.

Figure 5.17   A prospective model for future postal regulation

4. Retail prices would be gradually deregulated (including the easing of uniform tariff restrictions).

The Advantages of This Model

This model would have the following advantages:

1. it would generate greater transparency in the market;
2. the scope of regulatory intervention in the market would be considerably reduced;
3. postal customers would have effective choice upstream with third-party access arrangements based on transparent access prices;
4. Royal Mail would receive positive incentives to be efficient and to compete for customers upstream and downstream of its postal delivery business; and
5. the universal postal service will be maintained only so far as appropriate to the choices made by customers and proportionate in terms of its costs.

The Importance of Bottom-up Modelling

The efficiency of the USP and ensuring efficient costs (for example, if delivery is a natural monopoly) is a key issue in ensuring an appropriate deregulation and control of a dominant supplier. Unlike in comparable sectors there has been little bottom-up modelling or 'greenfield' assessment of postal efficiency. Such an approach, consistent with regulatory practice in the telecoms sector, would be useful not only in revealing more fully any inefficiencies in the delivery network, but also could provide information about the extra organisational burdens imposed by specific USOs allowing us to cost these requirements.

A Process of Regular Review

There could then be an explicit process of periodic review and analysis for key elements forming the rationale for the regulatory interventions for example:

1. as stated previously, reviewing regularly the extent of USOs in terms of their costs and benefits in relation to actual customer needs as senders and receivers of mail;
2. reviewing the appropriateness of quality of service regulation in relation to its costs and benefits and actual customer needs. (For example, it has been argued that current speed of transit regulatory targets are

out of line with customer needs and also that they impose significant cost constraints on USPs); and

3. licensing obligations: where licensing is felt necessary (to monitor the market for example) it could be reviewed regularly with a view to reducing licensing obligations and moving towards general authorisations of market players.

Closing Remarks

As noted at the outset, this is a critical time in the development of postal regulation with the postal exception under scrutiny both in the UK and in the EU generally. We have seen how postal deregulation has been delayed at both European and national levels constituting a postal exception. We have also observed signs of dynamism in the EU postal market, particularly in the new opportunities for postal operators to expand into new services.

Looking again at the rationale for regulatory intervention in the postal sector, we have noted that the justification for a USO, particularly one that includes a uniform tariff, appears to be fading as other modes of communication become available. Further, we have seen that it appears unlikely that end-to-end entry in the market will threaten USP dominance in postal delivery.

We argue then that we should move now to further deregulate the postal sector. In doing so we should review whether there is a continuing justification for the USO, particularly questioning the need for a uniform tariff. Third-party access to Royal Mail's essential facilities, with access prices based upon bottom-up efficiency modelling appears the most likely way to facilitate the entry of efficient competition into the market and to protect customers. There are substantial doubts about the effectiveness or justification for a continued regulation of retail prices, since the amount spent on postal services by individuals is so little, and since business users have alternatives and negotiating strength.

Finally, in this debate it is important to remember that regulatory intervention should always be a last resort and to expect regulators to outline how they plan to deregulate as well as regulate.

NOTES

1. HSBC, 'First Past the Post'.
2. Ibid.
3. This section has been completed through our review of postal news websites and operator websites.

4. The requirement for a co-decision procedure in EU postal regulation means that Postal Directives have to be agreed by the European Commission, European Council and the European Parliament.

5. According to the WIK Consult (2004): 'Main Developments in European Postal Sector', study for the European Commission, final report, Bad Honnef, July.

6. Under the directive the reservation of outgoing cross-border services is only permitted under exceptional circumstances.

7. Estonia has reserved services previously liberalised in setting universal service obligations to Estonia Post.

8. Finland has not been included in this list as its entry tax has effectively foreclosed the market.

9. European Commission staff working paper annex to the report on the application of the Postal Directive (Directive 97/67/EC as amended by Directive 2002/39/EC), Brussels, 23 March 2005. Information from 2004.

10. Ibid.

11. For example the Euro Barometer surveys undertaken by DG Sanco show a consistent level of public support for universal postal services. However these surveys tend not to link this estimation with any cost analysis. The move to conjoint analysis in the surveys for Postcomm and Postwatch has revealed a more sophisticated picture of customer and consumer needs which appears to place higher value on quality of service than on price.

12. While letter mail volume figures are more flat and variable, it can be argued that the effects of regulatory gaming in the preparation and presentation of these figures make them less reliable.

13. For example, EU parcels and express volumes grew from €32 billion in 2000 to €36 billion in 2002.

14. F.H. Nader (Adrenale Corporation), 'Forecasts', 24 February, 2005, commissioned research by Pitney Bowes.

15. HSBC, 'First Past the Post'.

16. Ibid.

17. NERA: 'Cost and financing of universal service obligations in the postal sector in the European Union', study for the European Commission, 1 November 1998.

18. For example, see the recent work by Bob Cohen on this issue, Cohen et al. (2005), 'Will entrants into a liberalized delivery market attract investors', in M.A. Crew and P.R. Kleindorfer (eds), *Regulatory and Economic Challenges in the Postal and Delivery Sector*, Boston, MA: Kluwer Academic.

19. From the Postcomm, 'Competitive market review: proposals for tackling barriers to entry in postal services', November 2005.

20. See the source article by Bob Cohen and others.

21. See the 'Light is Right' papers issued for DHL and TNT: Paul de Bijl, Eric Van Damme and Pierre Larouche, '"Light is Right". Competition and access regulation in an open postal market', Tilberg Law and Economics cenetre (TILEC), 4 June 2005; Matthias Finger, Ismail Alyanak and Pierre Rossel, 'The universal postal service in the communications era. Adapting to changing markets and customer behavior', College of Management and Technology, École Polytechnique Fédérale de Lausanne (EPFL), June 2005.

22. Here it is notable that press reports have recently suggested that DHL is finding it difficult to achieve its anticipated network integration and consequent synergy.

23. The figures for Germany are thought to be exaggerated somewhat by the effects of reunification.

24. LECG (2006), 'Future efficient costs of Royal Mail regulated mail activities. Bottom-up review of Royal Mail's strategic plan: final conclusions', January, www.lecg.com.

25. Though this of course is not the same as saying it is efficient *per se* when the sector remains generally variable in efficiency.

26. 'Handbook on Impact Analysis', Europe Economics at www.europe-economics.com, annual reports for DHL, TNT, La Poste and Royal Mail, 2004.

CHAIRMAN'S COMMENTS

Nigel Stapleton

I must preface my remarks by indicating that I was appointed for a three-year term as Postcomm chairman – it ends in January 2007. So in disagreeing with some of Dermot and David's conclusions, it is not because their proposals might be doing me out of a job; it is for more deep-rooted reasons that I challenge some of the points they have made.

Their chapter starts by talking about the development of the postal market across Europe, and that is a very interesting and helpful bird's-eye view. There are three points that I would add to that overview.

First of all, that the nature of regulation varies substantially across the EU, and all the directive said was that the regulator had to be independent of the USP, the universal service provider. Here in the UK, the government have taken that directive, I believe, further than any other country in Europe has so far done, in the sense that Postcomm is a postal regulator that is independent of government. Although each of the commissioners are appointed by the Secretary of State for Trade and Industry we are accountable not to the DTI, but only to Parliament, in the first instance through the Trade and Industry Committee. No other country in Europe, as far as I am aware, has gone this far in terms of independent regulation of the postal sector.

Given that most of the USPs are clearly state owned we have – in France and in many of the largest jurisdictions – the situation where a government department regulates the USP. This approach I would regard as stretching the definition of independence and the credibility of independent regulation a little bit too far. So one of the things that has got to be looked at in terms of the planned third directive is whether independent regulation, as defined in the second directive, really means what it says.

Second, the chapter talks about the fact that it was only in the Netherlands that there was a mood to narrow the scope of the USO just to non-bulk mail. This is only partly true because here in the UK, Postcomm has proposed that many bulk mail products should be removed from the USO. Royal Mail is still to agree our proposals, because they would like to see all bulk mail products removed from the USO. We are recommending that Mailsort 1400 and Cleanmail should be kept within the USO, because otherwise small and medium-sized business will not have access to a bulk mail product. So in the UK, the change in the definition of the USO is still in the melting pot, and we wait to see the Royal Mail's reaction. Postcomm's stance is that smaller business does not have the degree of buying power that you suggested.

Third, the chapter includes some very interesting observations on the different strategies of the European national operators. I would take those observations a little further. In summary, we need to recognise that there are three distinct strategies being followed by the national operators across Europe.

TNT and DHL are clearly adopting a strategy of, in a sense, trying to build up a European mail business. Essentially they are looking at any place where deregulation is starting to happen and establishing a presence in those areas where there is an opportunity because of deregulation. TNT, for example, has even managed to create a presence – apparently a profitable presence – in Italy, against the background where, 'Italy being Italy', it is the only European country that has been deregulated, and then has taken some of the deregulated area back into the state monopoly again! Yet TNT has still been able to create a successful presence there. So we have those two companies which are trying to build cross-Europe mail businesses.

We have others that have gone down the vertical integration route, by extending their activities into database management and mail preparation for some of their larger customers. Clearly, these are also part of the growth strategies being pursued by the Dutch and German national operators. We have a great example with the state-owned USP in Finland that is using that route and stamping its presence not as a national mail operator but as a vertically integrated company across the Baltic states – a very interesting and thus far successful strategy. Finland Post clearly has got the support of its government to do that.

Then we have – the best examples here being Italy and France – the national operators that are really saying well, it is all about financial services, and mail is an afterthought so to speak.

The fact that we can look across Europe and see one postal industry but three distinctly different strategies has implications for how regulation will go forwards.

Clearly this is an issue for Postcomm in the UK where many people are arguing that the biggest threat to Royal Mail is that the Dutch and German national operators, who currently enjoy a greater degree of protection from competition in their home markets, are starting to come into the UK. I commented upon that argument at the UK mail conference (1 November, 2005), pointing out that actually there is a lot more competition in the Dutch and German markets than most people would observe. More importantly, a tenth of Royal Mail's profits are now generated from successfully competing with the Dutch and the Germans in their own backyard. We find it rather difficult for Postcomm to understand the worries that Royal Mail have about competing with the Dutch and the Germans in the UK when they have been so successful competing with them on their home patch.

These are my three points, therefore, about the chapter's introduction. Let me come to the points where I might challenge its conclusions.

Dermot and David say that the USO in the UK is financed by cross-subsidisation. That I would agree is indeed partly the case. However, I would also argue that it is financed by economies of scale, and in terms of ensuring the viability of the USO, it is much more the scale of the USO, and what the Royal Mail would freely acknowledge to be the unique selling point of their USO that keeps the USO strong and viable. So what we at Postcomm are seeing as most important to the USO going forward is that the scale economies are fully exploited. Actually the degree of cross-subsidisation is substantially exaggerated by Royal Mail with their catchphrase 'We lose 5p on every first class letter and 8p on second', because when you look at their regulatory accounts, they do lose money on stamped mail. However, they only lose an overall £3 million on total retail mail, because they make money on other retail channels like franked mail. So the degree of cross-subsidisation in the USO is, when you look at the detail of their regulatory accounts, not as great as you have suggested.

There is another remark I should like to make, building on the chapter's point that 86 per cent of the revenues in the UK and more than 80 per cent in most other jurisdictions is from business mail. This really demonstrates the importance of direct mail as the crucial revenue stream for a mail operator. We have got to recognise that direct mail is a very price-sensitive product, because all the large direct mailers have sophisticated models which measure response rates versus the cost of radio, television, press and other sources of advertising. Royal Mail's ability to continue to secure large-scale economies relies, therefore, upon direct mail continuing to be a cost-effective way of promotion for major businesses. If it does not, then the economies of scale that underpin the USO will be highly challenged.

The chapter makes the point that a USO in post is not necessary in the UK for people to keep in touch. I would disagree, because the USO, first and foremost, is directed to quite a degree towards vulnerable groups, including the elderly and those people living in rural areas. As we in Postcomm go on our road shows round the country, the feedback we get from those people who are concerned that competition is going to challenge the USO certainly does not tell us that they do not need the post. Yes of course we have telephones, yes of course we have e-mail, but particularly when we are looking at vulnerable groups and others, those are exactly the people who rely a lot more on the mail than the average person in the population. So from our point of view, we would contest that the USO is not necessary for people to keep in touch.

We at Postcomm would also have a different perspective on the affordability point. Dermot and David are absolutely right that people in the UK only pay on average something like a tenth of the amount on post that they do on gas, and electricity, and only about a fifteenth of the overall amount of what they pay on telecoms. The average spend of a person on stamps is something like 50p, but I would not argue that that means affordability is not an issue. Here again, for vulnerable groups, a 50p spend – going up, as Royal Mail would like it to go up in their price control proposals to us – to 78p, is, out of their level of disposable income, quite a significant increase.

That brings me on to say that I am not totally convinced of the argument that there was no justification for continuing with retail price control. There are probably two things that are left out of the otherwise very compelling analysis that you have presented. One is that practically every national postal operator is, and for some time to come is likely to remain, a natural monopoly. Monopolies rarely become, in my experience, efficient unless they are challenged. Certainly that is a statement that can reasonably be proved in terms of what has happened in the UK. It is no accident that quality of service and efficiencies in the Royal Mail have moved forward as the regulatory regime has become tougher. Taking my earlier point about economies of scale and how direct mailers can so easily switch to other media, the biggest challenge to the future of the universal service is if the monopolies are not challenged to become more efficient, and if, as a result of that, the scale of economies are not as significant as they ought to be.

Dermot and David say that business customers have the buying power. Yes, they do, but then you could argue that they are more likely to use that buying power in moving to other media if the monopolies are not challenged, rather than by moving to other mail providers. They also say that third-party access to Royal Mail's last mile would introduce all the competition that is needed. However, on that point there is some quite interesting information in Postcomm's Competitive Market Review, which was published in early November 2005. To inform the review we surveyed 1200 mail customers – which is a pretty large sample – and we asked whether they wanted to see the emergence of end-to-end competition. The majority said that they did, because they do not want to see their mail being handled by an access operator and then handed to Royal Mail for handling over the last mile. They want one carrier to handle their mail end to end. Their major objection to access is if the mail does not arrive, they do not know who to blame – is it the access operator or is it Royal Mail? There are quite a lot of other issues that our survey has revealed which suggests that from the perspective of UK mail customers – and obviously I have no experience other than the UK customer – they really want end-to-end competition.

They do not see access as the alternative in the way that the chapter's otherwise very compelling analysis was suggesting and indicating.

I have deliberately focused on the few points which I would challenge, but let me state that it is an excellent and a very thought-provoking chapter, and I agree with a lot more than I challenged.

6. Developing the framework of rail regulation

Chris Bolt

INTRODUCTION AND OUTLINE

In November 2003, I gave a Beesley lecture on the topic of 'Regulating London Underground' (Bolt, 2005), in my role as statutory Arbiter for the London Underground Public–Private Partnership Agreements. Little did I expect then to be invited to speak again so quickly, or to do so in the joint capacity of PPP Arbiter and also, from 5 July 2004, Chairman of the Office of Rail Regulation (ORR), the body which took over on that date the functions and duties of the Rail Regulator.

Much has happened since then. Eleven days after my appointment as ORR Chairman was announced, the Secretary of State for Transport, Alistair Darling, announced a Rail Review. The resulting White Paper (DfT, 2004) was published in July 2004, 10 days after the creation of the Office of Rail Regulation. There has now been legislation, in the form of the Railways Act 2005, to provide the basis for implementing those changes which required legislation.

Previously, I compared the structure and 'regulation' of London Underground, through the PPP Agreements, with that of the national rail network. I concluded:

> [A]lthough there are clearly many issues with the PPP which cannot be assessed at this early stage in the life of the agreements, I suggest there are two main features which tend to favour the PPP arrangements:
>
> - the smaller number of direct contractual relationships, and in particular the responsibility of Infracos for both track and signalling and rolling stock maintenance and renewal; and
> - the clear 'customer' focus on London Underground, within Transport for London, which is not mirrored in the national rail network. (Bolt, 2005)

In reaching this conclusion, I was not intending to suggest that the structure and regulatory regime for the national rail network could not deliver an effective outcome in the public interest; and I was certainly not arguing for changes in that structure.

Although the primary driver for the Rail Review was perhaps the perception of loss of government control over public rail funding, the White Paper identified five main failings in the structure of the privatised railway, including the two I had identified. The failings identified by the Department for Transport (DfT) were:

- a complex and confusing public sector structure, with too many overlapping responsibilities and no clear command of strategy;
- a regulatory system and contractual structure which do not give the Government direct control of the level of public funding for the railways;
- an over-complex private sector structure, with Government often far removed from the impact of the decisions that it takes;
- a relationship between track and train companies based on false and sometimes perverse market incentives, that in many cases do not reflect customers' needs; and
- a lack of operational leadership in the private sector, with no-one clearly accountable for the delivery of improved performance and reliability. (DfT, 2004)

In this chapter, I want to look forward rather than back. So I shall not discuss in any detail whether these criticisms were valid, but shall instead consider whether the changes now being made are likely to lead to a more customer-responsive and efficient railway or, as some commentators have suggested, are merely the prelude to a further period of instability with further changes in prospect within a few years.

This chapter is therefore in four main sections:

- a brief review of the conclusions of the Rail Review, and the changes that are now being introduced;
- how ORR will be approaching its new expanded responsibilities;
- how the framework of rail regulation might need to develop – through the next Periodic Review and beyond – to deliver the rail review objectives of better value for money in terms of safety, performance and cost, for rail users and taxpayers; and
- some conclusions – in particular on whether the changes made following the Review can indeed be expected to help deliver a more efficient, better performing railway which meets more effectively the needs of its users.

THE RAIL REVIEW AND THE RAILWAYS ACT 2005

In his Foreword to the White Paper, the Secretary of State identified under-investment as one of the problems facing the railway. But he went on to say:

> There are two further problems caused by privatisation in the early 1990s that remain. An inefficient and dysfunctional organisation coupled with a failure to control costs. This White Paper sets out a number of reforms that provide a coherent and effective management structure for the railway. It makes clear what is properly the job of Government, and gives Network Rail clear responsibility for day to day management of the network, whilst enabling train companies to build their businesses by carrying more passengers and improving their customer focus. This new structure is robust enough to stand the test of time and will give the industry badly needed stability, but it also allows sufficient flexibility to respond to changing circumstances. It maintains the public and private partnership that is crucial if we are to encourage even more passengers to travel by rail. (DfT, 2004)

At its simplest, the White Paper conclusions can be summarised in three 'Ss': strategy, Scotland and safety. I consider these in turn.

One major change was to abolish the Strategic Rail Authority (SRA), only created by the Transport Act 2000, to replace the former Office of Passenger Rail Franchising (OPRAF). This change was not intended to question the need for a rail strategy, despite the arguments in the House of Lords that the absence of a specific duty on Ministers to develop a strategy would have this effect, but instead to recognise that the development of strategy was a key role of central government and could not be delegated effectively. This was seen as all the more important in railways for two reasons: the substantial amounts of public financial support for the private companies providing infrastructure and train operating services, with the responsibility this gives Ministers in establishing value for public money (while leaving delivery to the private sector), and the need to link rail strategy firmly to other transport (and indeed wider planning and environmental) policies.

The need for Government to establish strategic policies for the main utility sectors is not a new issue. Without seeking to compromise the independence of regulators in determining the regulatory targets and allowed revenue for the companies they regulate, or the freedom for the companies themselves to determine how to deliver those targets, commentators such as Dieter Helm have long argued for clear statements of government strategy for the key utility sectors (see, for example, Helm, 2005).

In the same vein, the Government had previously recognised the need in particular for guidance to regulators on social and environmental objectives. As the Government response to the 2001 report by the Better Regulation Task Force (BRTF) on economic regulators notes:

> Economic regulation cannot be pursued in a vacuum. Decisions on economic regulation can have social and environmental effects. Regulators need to understand the social and environmental impact of their activities and consider these potential impacts in making choices about which regulatory route to take. Regulatory objectives in relation to social and environmental matters have been a long standing feature of utility regulation. (BRTF, 2002)

More recently, the BRTF has commented favourably on this aspect of the Rail White Paper in updating its assessment of progress on recommendations made in that report.

However, the abolition of the SRA has other consequences. Network Rail has already taken on the SRA's role in developing Route Utilisation Strategies (RUSs) (essentially medium-term assessments of the potential demands for passenger and freight rail services on different parts of the network and the options for meeting those demands, including through more effective use of the existing network). This, combined with a new 'overall responsibility for the performance of the network' (as the White Paper put it), changes in quite important ways the role of Network Rail, and the dynamics of its relationships with train operators. For example, what will prevent Network Rail carrying out its role in a way which minimises its own costs – what is sometimes referred to as a 'producer-led railway' – rather than best meeting the needs of rail users? I shall come back to this issue in more detail below.

A further consequence of the abolition of the SRA is the transfer of its responsibilities for franchise award and franchise monitoring to the DfT, along with responsibility for taking forward major projects such as the replacement for the High Speed Train and for introduction of the planned new European Rail Traffic Management System (ERTMS). While perhaps these changes have administrative convenience, they raise very different issues from the transfer of rail strategy. For example, the need for franchise award, monitoring and enforcement to be free from political influence will be essential if private companies are to continue to participate in providing train services through franchise agreements.[1] And the history of the nationalised industries does not suggest that civil servants are well placed to take major investment decisions.

It is indeed explicitly recognised in the White Paper that 'Central Government is not always best placed to take decisions on the transport needs of different communities'. This is the rationale for the second major change introduced by the White Paper, which is to transfer responsibility for rail strategy and funding in Scotland, together with the management of the ScotRail franchise, to Scottish Ministers.[2] Although the details are different, there will also be increased roles for the Welsh Assembly Government and for Transport for London (TfL) to specify services in their areas of responsibility and to fund additional services above those specified and funded by Central Government. The English Passenger Transport Executives, while losing their status as co-signatories to the franchise agreements, will have similar powers to specify changes in services in their areas.

For these devolved arrangements to work effectively, it is essential that all parties have access to robust and consistent data. So the White Paper proposed that ORR should 'act as a single repository for rail industry data'. ORR has since consulted on the basis for what we prefer to call an 'information network' (ORR, 2005a).

One particular area which requires development of improved information, if devolved decision making is to be effective, is in respect of costs. The principles for this costing are well established (see, for example, Beesley, 1997), but the knowledge of actual costs is still less well developed than needs to be the case. That is the reason why ORR has encouraged Network Rail to develop an infrastructure cost model, which will both help to underpin its own assessment and planning of future expenditure requirements and provide better information for train operators and funders about the implications of changing service patterns.

Better costing is also key to effective implementation of one of the other changes in the Railways Act, which concerns 'network modifications' – the term used in the Railways Act for closures. It is clearly essential that before any closures are considered, steps are taken to reduce expenditure to levels consistent with services being operated, as well as to increase patronage and revenue. That done, decisions should then be based on the incremental costs, over the longer term, of keeping services operating (noting that some costs cannot easily or quickly be avoided even if services cease). Decisions can then be taken either on a commercial basis, or, where social benefits are important, on the basis of a better understanding of subsidy requirements.

The third major change in the Rail Review is to transfer responsibility for rail safety regulation from the Health and Safety Executive to ORR. The aspiration in the White Paper was stated as follows: 'Bringing regulation of all aspects of the rail industry – safety, reliability and efficiency – together under a single public regulator, will streamline the regulatory system, reduce bureaucracy, and ensure that these issues are looked at as a whole and not in isolation from one another'. This is not a simple matter, given that the framework of safety regulation is being changed in parallel to reflect the provisions of the EU Rail Safety Directive.

Although the decision to transfer safety regulation was taken before the ORR Board was appointed, we see considerable opportunities to improve the effectiveness of both economic and safety regulation as a result of the merger. The basis for this is the recognition that good management improves all aspects of performance – including both safety and service while still reducing costs – so that there is no necessary conflict between promoting improved services and improved safety while achieving greater efficiency. Of course, decisions on major investment in new safety measures which go beyond reasonable practicability, to meet societal concerns, will still need to be taken by Ministers. But the merging of economic and safety regulation will allow these proposals to be more effectively appraised, and will ensure that implementation of agreed proposals is done in a cost-effective way.

THE CONTINUING IMPORTANCE OF INDEPENDENT REGULATION

One other important change to the framework of regulation in the Railways Act 2005 is the modification of the periodic review process to require the main funders (the Secretary of State, in respect of England and Wales, and Scottish Ministers) to specify clearly to ORR the rail services that they wish to fund, and the funding available. I shall discuss below the preparation that ORR is making for the next Network Rail review. But it is worth considering here the implications of the change for independent regulation, in particular to challenge the view that the Railways Act has undermined independent regulation.[3]

At the time of the 2003 Access Charges Review, there was much discussion of the alleged inability of Ministers to control the amount of public funding going into the railways. In reality, options existed, even then, for the SRA and Ministers to modify their service requirements, to reflect the significant increase in costs being experienced by Network Rail, before the Regulator reached his decisions on the outputs that Network Rail needed to deliver to support the required level and performance of train services and the funding they required. The fact that Ministers are now required by statute to do this does not therefore prejudice independent regulation. It is entirely proper that the elected Government should determine the extent of public funding of railway services, and the pattern of services that it wishes to buy. What would be unacceptable would be if this were to be translated into decisions by Government about the way those services were to be provided by Network Rail, or the revenue they should be allowed to deliver that efficiently. But those decisions are left very clearly by the Railways Act to ORR.

Nor, as some have suggested, does the new responsibility for ORR to determine what outputs should be provided, if funders' requirements do not match the funding they are prepared to make available, change this position. Parliament has clearly decided that funding should be the constraint; ORR's job is then the essentially 'technical' one of deciding which services would offer best value for money, in terms of the section 4 public interest duties under which it operates. Indeed, the fact that the Railways Act 2005 draws a clear distinction between the 'what' and the 'how' reinforces independence. It also allows explicitly for the possibility that priorities may be different in different parts of Great Britain. So ORR takes account in a formal and transparent way of information provided by public funders on the services they propose to be supported by public funds, and any other guidance they may give, but alone has to determine both how those aspirations are to be balanced against bids for access to the network by other operators and the outputs and funding for Network Rail to support that pattern of access.

Of course, carrying out this role requires extensive dialogue with public sector funders. But that, too, does not undermine independence. As the first Rail Regulator, John Swift, has said: 'A regulator who takes no account of Government wishes or concerns as to the future of "his" industry is acting irresponsibly. Regulatory independence is not tainted by discussion or consultation with Government: rather it is enhanced through greater knowledge of the concerns of those elected to represent the public' (Swift, 2004).

So the Railways Act does not change the independent status of ORR, and we will continue to play a key role both in providing assurance of value for money to users and funders, assurance to investors in private sector companies about the basis of their returns, and assurance that the interests of different rail operators will be balanced in the public interest.

Even in an industry reliant on public funding, and where the bulk of borrowing is underpinned by a government guarantee rather than being on a proper market basis, independent regulation is necessary if a public and private sector partnership is to be maintained. The regulator has to 'hold the ring' between the different players in this partnership. The White Paper has done little to change the number of different operators in the railway industry, so it will still be necessary to balance the interests of different operators; to balance the interests of operators generally against those of Network Rail; and to balance the interests of different funders where their areas of interest overlap.

So I turn now to the way that ORR will carry out its expanded role in future.

HOW ORR WILL APPROACH ITS EXPANDED RESPONSIBILITIES

In summary, ORR's role following the rail review comprises the following main functions:

- determining Network Rail's allowed revenue to reflect the cost of the outputs specified by Government;
- monitoring and enforcing delivery of those outputs;
- establishing the access and licensing regime (including the Network Code) and approving individual applications;
- enforcing health and safety legislation for railways and developing the safety regulatory framework to promote both increased safety and greater efficiency;
- exercising competition law functions concurrently with the Office of Fair Trading (OFT), where these relate to the railways;
- providing 'information, advice and assistance' to the Secretary of State and Scottish Ministers; and
- developing an 'information network'.

In carrying out these functions, ORR – like other regulators – has to operate in the manner 'best calculated' to achieve a number of duties. These duties have been modified in the Railways Act 2005 to put additional emphasis on matters such as railway performance and value for money (although those objectives were already implicit).

In taking forward these functions, ORR faces a number of challenges.

The first one is how do we bring together our economic regulation functions with our new responsibilities for safety regulation. Our objectives here are clear – to ensure continued effectiveness of the framework of safety regulation through the merger process (which took place in April 2006), but to look for ways to promote better management by companies which lead to all-round improvements in safety, performance and efficiency. Safety and performance could obviously be delivered with further increases in funding, but reducing costs while improving performance and maintaining and improving safety is perhaps a more difficult challenge. Helping the industry to meet this challenge is clearly one of the objectives for the Government in combining economic and safety regulation in the new structure following the Rail Review.

So in our developing strategy for the merged body (see ORR, 2005b) we are looking to ensure that there is continued focus on safe operation of the railway and an effective inspectorate function, but also to establish a strategic safety policy which encourages the industry to review its operation – both on a company-specific basis and collectively – to improve its performance in terms of safety and service to users and remove unnecessary costs. This strategy will apply to all ORR's future safety regulation activities – which includes London Underground, trams and metros and heritage railways – as well as those national rail activities for which it is also the economic regulator.

ORR's role is only to set the framework. Delivery depends on train operators, on Network Rail and on all industry suppliers working together within that clear framework – and with effective dialogue with rail users and other stakeholders – to deliver safety, performance and efficiency.

That gets me to the second issue, which is how competing interests are balanced within this new framework. Although the objective in the White Paper was simplification of the structure, we clearly will have competing interests even in the new framework. To take one example: in London the Mayor, through TfL, will have an increased role in specifying London services, on a rail network already congested in many parts. This could well lead to competing bids for access – with the prospect already of such conflicts on the North London Line.

How to balance the interests of long-distance services with medium-distance commuter services coming in from well outside the Greater London boundary and with short-distance commuter services – and of course with freight services – will present some real problems. So we need clarity both on the rights of different players in the industry, whether it is funders or passenger and freight train operators, and on the obligations of the different players in the industry.

In part this will be achieved through improvements in access agreements and the Network Code, which started before the Rail Review commences and which ORR is continuing to take forward with the industry. Again, though, the Network Code must be seen as the industry's code. It is all about how train operators and Network Rail work together in partnership; it is not about ORR imposing something on the industry. Those who are working together on a day-to-day basis must develop a contractual framework which reflects operational reality and also delivers the right outcomes in terms of the rights, obligations and incentives of different players.

Another development which should help in resolving conflicts is improved longer-term planning. The RUSs previously undertaken by the SRA will in future be the responsibility of Network Rail.[4] To ensure that Network Rail approaches these from a whole industry perspective, and concentrates on the requirements of users and funders, ORR has modified Network Rail's licence, and issued guidelines (see ORR, 2005c). RUSs will play an important role in understanding the options and trade-offs for use and development of the network, which is why they are prepared under regulatory provisions and are not, as hitherto with the SRA RUSs, approved by Ministers.

A third challenge going forward is to ensure that Network Rail does actually deliver both the stewardship of the network and the enhanced performance management and planning role that has been given to it following the Rail Review. So what is the framework of accountability for Network Rail? And does the absence of shareholders make financial incentives less appropriate or less effective, than they might otherwise be?

Network Rail is accountable in a number of different ways. It is accountable through its licence to ORR. It is accountable through access agreements to train operators. It is accountable, less directly but clearly still just as importantly, to funders – the Secretary of State and Scottish Ministers particularly – although there is no direct contractual or licence relationship in this case. It is accountable to its members. It has an accountability, in a sense, to suppliers to make sure that the supply industry is able to deliver effectively what the rail industry needs to do to maintain sustainable assets and sustainable services going forward.

ORR needs to make sure that the different forms of accountability for Network Rail are all pointing in broadly the same direction. If incentives are not aligned, they will be at best ineffective and at worst perverse. There will be some issues where it is more effective for ORR to take responsibility for monitoring and enforcing through the licence, and others where accountability to train operators through access agreements would be more effective.[5] Members have an important role, but they must have the right information to be able to hold the Board to account.

One recent development in this regard has been publication of a quarterly 'Network Rail Monitor', which shows how Network Rail is performing against a broad range of performance and expenditure measures. This has also now been extended to cover Scotland separately, to reflect the separation following the Rail Review of funding for services in Scotland. But to be fully effective, ORR's monitoring framework needs to be able to identify the reasons for variances in expenditure, in particular to identify separately slippage from efficiency, and this is a current priority. A particularly difficult area is where Network Rail claims that some projects reflected in the last charges review are no longer required to deliver planned outputs. The concern is that while short-term outputs might not be prejudiced, longer-term capability is.

So a further current priority is to ensure that Network Rail develops a robust long-term asset management strategy, including their procurement and information strategy, which underpins sensible long-term decisions on the use and development of the network.

If we get all these things right then Network Rail will have a sound basis for planning the use and development of the network – one which meets the reasonable requirements of operators, users and funders – and for carrying this out in an efficient way, and ORR will have a clear and effective basis for monitoring their achievement and enforcement where they have not delivered.

PREPARING FOR THE PERIODIC REVIEW

Sound long-term projections will be key to the next Periodic Review, which takes effect from 1 April 2009. As discussed above, the Railways Act introduces new steps into the periodic review process. In essence, the review will comprise two phases: a 'preparation' phase, leading up to the high-level output specification and statement of funds available; and the formal phase in which ORR establishes regulatory targets for Network Rail and sets its allowed revenue.[6]

The preparation phase for the next review has already started, and runs until mid-2007. It is complicated by two particular factors. The first is the timing of the Comprehensive Spending Review (CSR), which required departmental submissions in the autumn of 2006, but does not reach conclusions until the middle of 2007. DfT will need to be in a position to make well-informed submissions by autumn 2007, and will need to be able to finalise its requirements for the national rail sector very quickly after publication of the CSR conclusions.

So the timescale for starting to understand cost pressures in the next control period is very restricted. That is why ORR published its first assessment of the likely range of expenditure requirements for Network Rail, assuming current service levels, in December 2005, and why it required a developed business plan from Network Rail for the period to 2014 and beyond by June 2006. This plan needs to reflect a robust asset management strategy and take full account of the opportunities to optimise the maintenance and renewal programme to deliver further efficiencies and performance improvements. Although Network Rail has already developed its asset management and business planning considerably, this will be a major challenge.

As an aside, it is worth noting that the London Underground PPP also has a periodic review process, albeit one year later than for Network Rail. But the medium-term requirements for central government grant to TfL will also need to be assessed as part of the 2007 Spending Review.

The formal part of the review process, which will start in autumn 2007 with a revised business plan from Network Rail reflecting what it needs to do to allow delivery of the high-level output specification. The review will then follow the familiar procedure for price reviews in rail and in other sectors, looking at the building blocks which feed into the assessment of required revenue and the opportunities for greater efficiency, aiming to reach decisions in autumn 2008. Assuming that the specification of services required by funders matches the funds they make available, that is the end of the process. But if they do not match, then ORR will have the additional task of reviewing outputs to match funding.

For the 2008 Periodic Review to work as envisaged in the White Paper, national-level strategic issues and options will need to be developed during 2006, with robust analysis and appraisal of those options and effective engagement with stakeholders which enables funders to give clear and consistent advice to ORR in mid-2007. This timing is needed in order for ORR to consult on its final decisions on Network Rail outputs and funding in the summer of 2008.

Ensuring that Network Rail delivers such a plan is one of ORR's priorities, reflected for example in its assessment of Network Rail's 2005 business plan.

LONGER-TERM PROSPECTS AND ISSUES

The next review period is expected to run until 2014. But railway assets have a long life (as well as, in some cases, a long lead time – for example, the Thameslink 2000 project which was part of Railtrack's plans at privatisation has still not started). So decisions taken at the next Periodic Review will have an impact on railway capability, performance and costs over several decades. But to provide clarity for Network Rail – and other long-term investors such as rolling stock companies – may require a development of the regulatory framework to provide more long-term certainty than is possible within a five-year price review framework.

Already, for example, ORR is reviewing Network Rail's signalling programme for the period to 2014, recognising the long lead times in signalling investment, and the need to provide a firm basis for the signalling supply industry if it is to provide innovative and cost-effective solutions. This longer-term horizon for investment may need to be extended to other parts of Network Rail's investment programme. But this in turn would require longer-term commitment by funders and by the regulator.

A longer-term regulatory framework also assumes a clear vision for the future development of the sector. So what might that vision be? And is the current structure of the industry and of the regulatory framework capable of delivering it?

Our vision, which reflects the White Paper's description of the railway as a public and private sector partnership as well as developments in EU policy towards railways, is one where Network Rail and train operators work effectively together to deliver a safe, high-performing, well-maintained and efficient railway which meets the current and future needs and reasonable expectations of passengers and freight users and which offers value for money both to users and taxpayers. This is not a centrally planned railway, although Ministers will clearly need to be closely involved in determining the broad pattern of services which require subsidy. But it does require effective partnership.

In delivering this vision, there could well be evolution of the current industry structure. The proposal in the White Paper for Merseyrail to take responsibility for its infrastructure from Network Rail is one such example. Plans to develop Community Rail Partnerships, where services and standards can be modified to reflect local needs, without compromising safety, is another.

The role of third parties in infrastructure investment is also likely to increase. The extensive use of Special Purpose Vehicles (SPVs) for enhancement investment, as proposed by the late Sir Alastair Morton when Chairman of the SRA, has not progressed as he anticipated. Network Rail is now clearly seen as needing to take responsibility for enhancement schemes as well as for maintenance and renewal, allowing the network to be managed on a consistent basis. But one SPV has been put in place to enhance capacity on the Chiltern Line. Although clearly the financing cost associated with an SPV is higher than Network Rail's financing cost (underpinned as it is by a Government indemnity), the promoters believe that this will be more than offset by more effective specification, design, delivery and operation of the scheme.

The limited use of SPVs to date does not, however, mean that Network Rail should have a monopoly over work on the network. Just as third parties have rights in other sectors to make connections to the network, and extensions can be carried out by third parties, so there should be opportunities for third parties to carry out schemes where these can be managed separately and the risk and assurance issues can be handled effectively. ORR's approach to these issues (ORR, 2005f) envisages these possibilities.

One area where the question of responsibility for investment arises is in respect of stations and depots. Given the passenger-facing nature of stations, is it more effective for Network Rail to be responsible for the station fabric, perhaps achieving economies of scale through use of standard designs and procurement, or for train operators to take responsibility to be more able to respond better to their local customer requirements? And given the important role that maintenance depots play in ensuring the continued availability of rolling stock, would train operators or train manufacturers be better placed to invest in these facilities?

Linked to this is the issue of the extent of commercial freedom open to franchised passenger operators. The model franchise agreement has gone through a number of transformations, and going forward there is a need to consider again how best to promote continuous improvement in railway services for users at affordable cost. It could be argued, for example, that as well as having greater ownership interest in 'customer-facing' assets, they should have greater flexibility to determine what services to offer to meet market demand. This would offer greater prospects of creating an upside for franchise-owning companies, and could bring benefits in terms of greater commitment, willingness to invest and focus on customer relationships.

All of these questions have their parallels in other regulated industries. That comparison also makes it clear that the corporate, financing and ownership structure of Network Rail may not necessarily be the most appropriate one in the longer term. But again these are issues to be considered in the medium term: the short-term priority is to facilitate the industry delivering improved performance and efficiency in the current control period and establishing a robust basis for decisions on outputs and funding in the next period.

SUMMARY AND CONCLUSIONS

The Rail Review White Paper claimed that it provided

> a coherent and effective management structure for the railway [and that] this new structure is robust enough to stand the test of time. [It] will give the industry badly needed stability, but it also allows sufficient flexibility to respond to changing circumstances. It maintains the public and private partnership that is crucial if we are to encourage even more passengers to travel by rail. (DfT, 2004)

So are the changes sufficiently significant to offer a real prospect of improved performance and value for money in the rail industry or – as some have argued – a missed opportunity for more radical change?

Since the White Paper was published, there have been a number of assessments of its proposals, and whether they are sufficient to achieve the aim of improved value for money for rail users and taxpayers. Two in particular are worth highlighting (Wolmar, 2005; Murray, 2005), in that they both criticise the limited scope of changes emerging from the review, but come to (apparently) diametrically opposed conclusions about the way forward.

For Christian Wolmar, the right way forward is clear: 'Any new structure must have at its heart an integrated railway. Decisions over all aspects of the railway must be made by a team of managers sitting at the same table' (2005). In addition, 'the role of the private sector can only be a limited one . . . as a contractor, not to determine how resources should be allocated' (2005).

Iain Murray, too, considers that there is a need for a more vertically integrated railway, but unlike Wolmar believes that the role of the private sector should be increased, not reduced. For him, the main problem is excessive regulation: instead of the invisible hand of the market promoting the interests of rail users, 'a complex and confused regulatory framework placed an invisible foot on the industry's throat, choking off the lifeblood of private sector innovation' (2005).

So the question seems to be whether the White Paper's assertion that 'the involvement of the public and private sectors working together has brought some real benefits for the rail industry and its customers' and that maintaining that partnership 'is crucial if we are to encourage even more passengers to travel by rail' is correct.

Not surprisingly, given my generally positive reaction to the London Underground PPP, I agree with the White Paper's conclusion. Of course, for such a partnership to be successful, roles and responsibilities need to be well defined, and information – particularly on costs and assets – needs to be of sufficiently high quality to support effective decision making. But those requirements apply equally within an integrated organisation. So although the changes are not radical, they do seek to address the concerns expressed in the White Paper.

What certainly is important, whether the relationship is governed by a formal contract, operates through a licence or is informal, is that strategic direction should be clear and incentives should be aligned, and this requires relationships to be effective. That is why, for example, the guidance to the PPP Arbiter from London Underground and the infracos reminds the Arbiter that the parties are

committed to providing the best possible Underground service to the travelling public by:

- working together to improve customer service
- creating an environment based on mutual respect, trust and fairness that promotes open and honest communication at all levels
- solving problems together
- recognising and rewarding those who contribute to the success of the partnership
- working together to achieve our objectives. (PPP Agreement, 2006)

So in the same way, the White Paper sees the new arrangements forming 'the basis of a stable partnership between the public and private sectors, with the Government offering clear strategic direction, a single independent regulator ensuring high levels of safety and protecting the rights of investors, and the private sector supplying the innovation, customer focus and commercial discipline' (DfT, 2004).

Just as private sector involvement has delivered significant efficiency and performance improvements in other sectors, so it can do in rail. The need to operate the system as a network is no different in principle – though certainly more difficult in degree – from operating other networks.

And the benefits of competition in the provision of services are well established.

But equally the existence of public subsidy – a reflection in part of the absence of charging at the point of consumption for travel by road – and the planning and environmental considerations which impinge on transport policy development all point to the continuing need for Government to establish strategy and identify the types of service it is willing to support, and for a regulatory framework to ensure delivery.

ORR, as the independent regulator, has a key role in making this an effective partnership which delivers the public interest. Some of the challenges for ORR are short term and practical, such as integrating economic and safety regulation to promote both safety and efficiency, and establishing a comprehensive framework for setting and monitoring Network Rail's output targets and monitoring asset serviceability. Others will require longer-term development in the regulatory framework, to ensure a robust basis for decisions by funders on outputs and funding and to balance longer-term certainty for service providers with flexibility for funders and users. And all this needs to be done in a way which provides an assurance of value for money without 'second guessing' management.

It is of course too soon to judge how effective the new arrangements are. True, there are encouraging signs of improvements in performance and efficiency, but these owe little to the Rail Review changes. Like other infrastructure networks, investment in the rail network needs long-term horizons, and success can only be judged over the long term. As Hugh Aldous has noted in his comments on the rail review:

> We now have an Office of Rail Regulation with a far more subtle role. The new ORR will have to model and work all the options so as to offer choices: choices about railways that you, the public, could have at different costs to the public and private purse at different outcomes. Praise will go to the secretaries of state who make wise choices – whatever they may be – through an iterative process between department and regulator and the award of wisdom will only be visible in history. (Aldous, 2005)

NOTES

1. Passenger services operated without a franchise agreement (so-called 'open access' services) require only a licence (issued by ORR) and access agreements (which require ORR approval), but do not receive any subsidy.
2. Scottish Ministers have established a new multi-modal agency, 'Transport Scotland', to carry out many of these functions.
3. For example, Wolmar (2005, p. 229), says that 'it is apparent from the legislation that the government has not kept its promise . . . of continuing independent economic regulation'.

4. The first RUS to be prepared by Network Rail, in respect of the South West route from Waterloo, was published for consultation on 3 November 2005.
5. The use of different enforcement mechanisms is considered further in ORR's draft enforcement policy statement (ORR, 2005d).
6. The proposed approach to review is set out in ORR (2005e).

REFERENCES

Aldous, Hugh (2005), 'Rail regulation', in Peter Vass (ed.), *Regulatory Review 2004/2005*, Centre for the Study of Regulated Industries, University of Bath.

Beesley, Michael (1997), 'Rail: the role of subsidy in privatisation', in Michael Beesley (ed.), *Regulating Utilities: Broadening the Debate*, IEA Readings 46.

Better Regulation Task Force (BRTF) (2002), 'Economic regulators: government response', www.brtf.gov.uk/responses_new/regulatorsresponse.asp, February 2002.

Bolt, Chris (2005), 'Regulating London Underground', in Colin Robinson (ed.), *Government, Competition and Utility Regulation*, Cheltenham, UK and Northampton, MA, USA: Edward Elgar, also available at www.ppparbiter.org.uk/documents/Beesleylecture-RegulatingLondonUnderground.PDF.

Department for Transport (DfT) (2004), 'The future of rail', White Paper, www.dft.gov.uk/stellent/groups/dft_railways/documents/pdf/dft_railways_pdf_0 31105.pdf, accessed July 2004.

Helm, Dieter (2005), 'The case for regulatory reform', in Dieter Helm (ed.), *The Future of Infrastructure Regulation*, Oxford: OXERA (Oxford Economic Research Associates).

Murray, Iain (2005), *No Way to Run a Railway*, London: Adam Smith Institute.

Office of Rail Regulation (ORR) (2005a), 'Better information, better decisions: ORRs proposed strategy for developing a rail industry information network', www.rail-reg.gov.uk/upload/pdf/234.pdf, April 2005.

Office of Rail Regulation (ORR) (2005b), 'Updating our corporate strategy: a consultation', www.rail-reg.gov.uk/upload/pdf/263.pdf, December 2005.

Office of Rail Regulation (ORR) (2005c), 'Notice of proposed modifications to Network Rail's network licence: industry performance and planning and route utilisation strategies', www.rail-reg.gov.uk/upload/pdf/235.pdf, April 2005.

Office of Rail Regulation (ORR) (2005d), 'Enforcement policy and penalties statement: draft for consultation', www.rail-reg.gov.uk/upload/pdf/259.pdf, November 2005.

Office of Rail Regulation (ORR) (2005e), 'Periodic review 2008: first consultation document', www.rail-reg.gov.uk/upload/pdf/245.pdf, August 2005.

Office of Rail Regulation (ORR) (2005f), 'Policy framework for investments: conclusions', www.rail-reg.gov.uk/upload/pdf/255.pdf, February 2005.

PPP Agreement (2006), Schedule 1.9, Annex 2, Section 9, available at www.ppparbiter.org.uk/files/uploads/j-PPPAgreementExtracts/200621014240_BCV%20Schedule%201.9%20of%20the%20PPP%20Agreement%20Service%20Contract%20(01_04_03)%20DM11279v1.PDF.

Swift, John (2004), 'Written evidence', in vol. 2, *The Regulatory State: Ensuring its Accountability*, House of Lords Select Committee on the Constitution, London.

Wolmar, Christian (2005), *On the Wrong Line*, London: Aurum Press.

CHAIRMAN'S COMMENTS

Chris Nash

The area I want to concentrate on in my comments is an area that is very important in the White Paper and very important in Chris's chapter, and that is the reallocation of responsibilities, and in particular the allocation of responsibility for strategy versus delivery.

Chris says that experience suggests that responsibility for delivery is not best placed with civil servants. It is clear where large amounts of public money are going into an industry that you would expect ministers, with the advice of civil servants, to be in the lead on strategy, but the whole tendency in 20 years or more has been for delivery to be the responsibility of separate agencies, whether they are public or private. Of course there is a problem about how strategic objectives are conveyed to those agencies. It is not easy.

In October 2005, I chaired a session at a conference where a German urban public transport manager spoke on these things, and he said, 'Well the State is clearly responsible for strategy. I'm responsible for delivery'. I asked him, 'Well, how does the State tell you its strategic objectives?'. He said, 'Well, they give me a map showing the routes I'm to run and the frequencies I'm to run on each route', which was not quite the answer I expected!

It does seem to me that the new arrangements go a little bit in that direction. I suppose, as an economist, I would like to see a situation where governments declared their objectives, told us how to measure them, how to weight them – in other words, set the appraisal framework – and specialist agencies then translated those into the actual services.

In that context, I find some of the new role of the DfT a bit surprising. It does appear that the high-level output specification is going to go into quite a lot of detail about the capability of individual routes, and you cannot do that without giving quite a lot of thought to what timetable you think is going to operate on those routes.

Even more, taking responsibility for the franchising process and for managing the franchises within the DfT gets the Department quite heavily involved in the detail of what services are to be run, even maybe the timetable, and as Chris has already implied, that process on the whole is best kept at arm's length from political involvement. I am not sure whether we are actually going to go back to the days when questions were asked in the House about why the 17:30 from King's Cross does not stop at Grantham – that was always a highly controversial issue in British Rail days. But the degree to which the Department will be involved in the detail of timetabling seems to me much greater than probably ever in British Rail days.

Network Rail, as Chris said, takes responsibility for route utilisation strategies, and maybe they are the people who should know about this. But determination of the level and use of capacity seems a key element in the Government's strategies for the railways, so there must be close links between RUSs, the development of the high-level output specification and the specification of franchises. Likewise, it appears that Network Rail will be even more in the lead on timetabling, which is a little bit odd for an organisation which has no direct relationship either with the fare-paying or freight rate-paying customer or the political customer. Yet there is no direct contractual relationship between the DfT and Network Rail. When I read in the White Paper about a binding arrangement, I thought this meant a contract, but as Chris says, what is actually the situation is that these processes now will be under the supervision of the regulator through the mechanism of a licence condition, and not under political control, as they were with the SRA.

Last but not least, the role of ORR. I admit at first to being a bit surprised to read that ORR would be responsible for advising ministers on the sort of menu of options that they could have for different levels of spending, because this seemed more the role of a consultant than of the regulator, but if the regulator is best placed to do this in terms of knowledge and is ultimately responsible for saying how much revenue Network Rail should be allowed to deliver different levels of service, maybe that is sensible.

I was even more surprised to find in the Act, and I do not remember reading it in the White Paper, the provision that if there was a conflict between the funding available and what ministers said they wanted, then ultimately ORR has to decide which services give the poorest value for money and how the money should be saved. That seems to me to be consistent with my model of ministers setting the criteria and agencies taking the decisions, and maybe we shall get more rational decisions that way, but it is very surprising to me that the government should want franchising in-house and yet leave ORR with this, which is the most politically sensitive of all decisions. I can imagine ORR having a very difficult time if there is a funding gap at the end of the day. Clearly, if the whole procedure works well, then this situation will not arise as consistent high-level output specifications and funding will have been agreed at an earlier stage.

Moreover, I do wonder about whether the whole process of dealing with funding shortfalls really recognises the time lags in cost escapement in the railway. If you really were faced with a position where ORR had to find ways of saving large amounts of money next year, would you not be back to the position British Rail was always in, that you have to cut whatever you can cut quickly rather than what offers the worst value for money? That often means investment and maintenance on the core network, rather than the services that offer the worst value for money.

So as I say, I am rather puzzled by some of the ways in which responsibility for strategy and delivery have been parcelled out in the new system. Chris Bolt at the end declared himself optimistic. I certainly see that the new arrangements provide for the information needed to take rational decisions in a way that was missed before. At the time of privatisation many people had the idea that Government could simply deal with the train operating companies and buy the services it wanted and not worry about how the suppliers to them would perform. That may work in many sectors, but given the time lags in rail infrastructure, and given the indivisibilities involved, the person buying the services has to take an interest in the current capability of the infrastructure and its future developments. SRA never had the information to understand infrastructure costs. It seems that ORR, together with the other players in the industry, is making progress on that. So I can certainly see many improvements in the new structure, but as I say, I still remain somewhat puzzled by the precise split of responsibilities. I look forward very much to learning more about how they will work in practice.

7.   Cost of capital: some current issues
Julian Franks[1]

INTRODUCTION

This chapter has three themes. First, how should regulators approach the issue of leverage? Can and should they intervene to limit a regulated firm's leverage, for example, by restricting it if they can, or incentivising the company to do so, if they cannot, in order to maintain minimum credit ratings. If firms cannot maintain adequate credit ratings, is this a signal of excessive leverage or does it reflect an inadequate price cap and rate of return calculated by the regulator? Second, although the capital asset pricing model (CAPM) has become the favoured model for calculating the cost of capital by regulators, there is considerable doubt about its adequacy among finance scholars. The empirical evidence for the CAPM is far from firm and other models are widely used in empirical studies in the academic field. The question is whether regulators should use these other models as a cross-check, at least on the CAPM. Third, given that the cost of capital of a company is a composite one that reflects a variety of risks within the company, should regulators recognise these differences in risk by applying different costs of capital to separate parts of the business? This issue is particularly important when some parts of the business are regulated and others are not, or when the customers of the regulated businesses and the risks of the assets being used are different.

Finally, the issue of cost of capital is a very controversial one and is likely to remain so. A great deal of money is spent addressing this question and I shall make a proposal that will certainly reduce the expense and I hope take some of the adversarial relationships out of this debate.

SHOULD REGULATORS WORRY ABOUT LEVERAGE?

Current regulatory policy is broadly speaking to allow regulated firms to choose their own capital structures and implicitly their own leverage ratio. This is founded on the principle of leaving as many of the business and financing decisions as possible to the company and its board of directors. It also reflects a perception that although leverage increases the risk of financial distress and failure, the income of utilities is relatively stable and can support significant leverage without unduly increasing the risks of insolvency. Moreover, leverage up to some point reduces the cost of capital and may have the added benefit of increasing the pressure on management to improve efficiency and profitability thereby producing the virtuous circle of improving shareholder returns and lowering prices.

Leverage ratios differ widely among utilities, as illustrated by Figure 7.1, not only across but also within industries.

Using a sample of 16 utility companies in 2000 and 2004, we find that the book–debt ratios range from below 30 per cent to almost 90 per cent. Moreover, the comparison with 2000 suggests that those debt ratios have risen in recent years, a fact better illustrated in Figure 7.2.

Although regulators give much discretion to companies over how much to borrow, it does not mean that they ignore their leverage in setting their price caps. They calculate cost of capital using some estimate of leverage, which has the effect of lowering the weighted average cost of capital. The reduction reflects the tax advantages of debt compared with equity. In setting the weighted average cost of capital (WACC), the regulators will use an actual or target leverage.

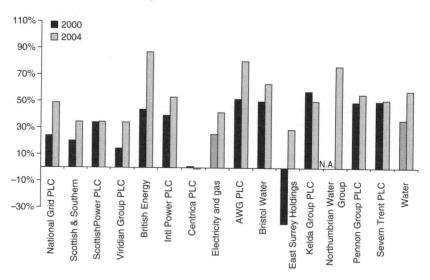

Source: OXERA, 2005, p. 290.

Figure 7.1   Gearing for individual utility companies

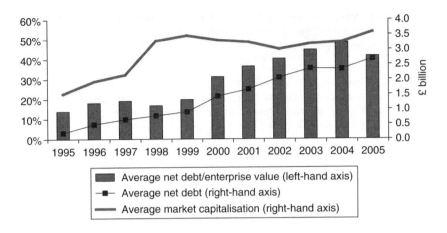

Source: OXERA, 2005.

Figure 7.2   Trends in gearing over time for 15 utilities

In recent years, regulators have become more interested in debt levels for other reasons. There is some concern that particularly high debt ratios may endanger the investment programme of the utility company. Thus, while they do not wish to shield a company from insolvency, they do care if financial distress prevents a company from fulfilling its proposed investment programme.

I would like to express these concerns in a more formal setting. If financial distress does hit a company and it is highly leveraged, the company may find it difficult to raise new equity, even with a profitable investment programme, because of a 'debt overhang problem'. Debt overhang acts as a cost to shareholders in putting up new equity finance because part of the value of the new equity accrues to lenders who find that the equity infusion increases the value of their debt by decreasing the probability of default. The wealth transfers arising from these shareholder–debtholder conflicts can act as a deadweight cost to financing distressed companies and thereby increase the cost of debt capital.

In response, at least in part, to these issues, regulators are using 'a financeability test' to evaluate a firm's ability to finance its investment programme. For example, Ofwat (Office of Water Services) provided additional revenues to water companies to ensure that they could finance their proposed investment programmes. The value of the uplift was £430 million, and by 2009–10 this was equivalent to 0.6 per cent on the post-tax cost of capital. Much of these revenues occurred in the final two years of the price review period. Ofwat described the reasons for this adjustment in their 2004 periodic review:

> A consequence of requiring companies to undertake large capital investment programs is persistent negative cash flow . . . This can lead to a deterioration in credit quality, which could restrict companies' access to capital markets or significantly increase the cost of finance. (p. 41)

> The price limits take account [of the fact that] that companies need to maintain issuer or corporate credit ratings comfortably in the investment grade . . . In a number of cases we have allowed extra revenue to ensure that the level and trend of these indicators will be in line with our target. (p. 230)

> It is not Ofwat's role to ensure a company can finance its functions in any eventuality but to ensure an efficient company can finance its functions given price limits based on reasonable estimates and assumptions. (p. 231)

In another case, Ofgem (Office of Gas and Electricity Markets) (2004) stated that:

> Ofgem . . . indicated that it intends to propose price controls that are consistent with the regulated companies being able to maintain credit ratings that are comfortably within investment grade. (p. 113)

> In the light of discussions with credit rating agencies, Ofgem has concluded that for stand alone distribution companies . . . weaker test ratios than those shown above could still be consistent with ratings comfortably within investment grade. (p. 114)

In both cases, the pronouncements suggest that the regulator considered it within their discretion to place some constraint on a company's leverage, even if this meant adjusting the price cap to preserve investment grade status for its rated debt, and thereby protect the investment programme.

In a third case, that of the Dublin Airports Authority (DAA), The Commission for Aviation Regulation (2005) also concerned itself with the investment grade status of the regulated firm's debt: 'the Commission has concluded that a determination that allows the DAA to maintain an investment grade rating, which includes A as well as BBB, is sufficient for the Commission to achieve its statutory obligation . . . in a sustainable and financially viable manner' (p. 33).

What is the Principle?

If the CAPM is the correct approach for calculating a company's cost of capital then the company should be able to finance its investment programme. If it cannot then either the cost of capital has been incorrectly estimated, possibly because the model is wrong, or the values of the parameters have been wrongly estimated. In this respect, it can be argued that financeability is a cost of capital problem.

A more subtle example is when the investment programme requires new equity. This problem need not be the result of previous high leverage but may simply arise from a large investment programme that requires a significant element of new equity. Why might new equity present problems for a company? First, there may be important imperfections such as information asymmetries between stock markets and managers, where the capital market prices the risks higher than the managers because they do not have or, do not believe management's valuations. This 'lemons problem' may raise significantly the cost of new equity capital. The empirical evidence on new equity issues suggests that markets react negatively to equity issues both in the US and the UK.[2]

How large are these information asymmetries for utilities? It is not easy to answer this question for two reasons. First, there have not been many equity issues. Luis Correia da Silva (2006) describes the average price reaction to six rights offerings by EU utilities as being –1.35 per cent (range of – 4.46 per cent to +1.16 per cent). He also reports the price reaction for two rights issues by UK utilities as being almost 7 per cent for one and –3 per cent for another. Second, it is difficult to predict the source of the price reaction. Is it the lemons problem or bad news that accompanies the rights issue? Irrespectively, regulators will not wish to ignore the consequences of their actions for investors' appetite for new equity, particularly if they wish to constrain the use of debt.

Should the Regulator Worry about High Leverage?

Up to now, financeability has been described as a cost of capital problem or a cost of equity problem. Even so, should the regulator worry about high leverage? The advantage of high leverage is that it reduces the cost of capital (up to some point) and pre-commits management to greater discipline in terms of controlling expenditures and focusing the business on value-creating activities. However, it only achieves the latter objective by increasing the probability of default. I do not believe it is, or should be, the risk of default *per se* that should worry the regulator. The regulator should only be worried if the costs that default gives rise to, are significant. These risks can be particularly complex in utilities because in some cases the product is vital to the everyday life of consumers, and in the end the consumers may themselves pay for these risks.

This issue was highlighted by a DTI–Treasury Report (October 2004): 'Increased risk of failure – if gearing up leads to an increased risk of default, this could potentially transfer risk of cost or revenue shocks onto consumers or potentially even taxpayers' (p. 4). They further warned that 'the effect on the ability of firms to efficiently deliver necessary investment programmes . . . access to capital markets might be restricted for firms with high leverage'.

I suspect that where there is not a large investment programme, guaranteed income for the utility should allow a smooth change in ownership with small costs of distress. However, I think it is different with a large investment programme. Such a programme is accompanied by high leverage and can produce the familiar debt overhang problem, where new equity may not be raised because much of the value seeps through to debt holders.

Then how significant is the debt overhang to future investment? US evidence by Parrino and Weisbach (1999) suggests that it is not very significant. They calculated that for companies with 80 per cent leverage the debt overhang problem adds about 0.55 per cent to the cost of capital for new investment. Unpublished UK evidence by Franks and Sanzhar (2005) suggests that the problem of debt overhang is often resolved by an agreement between banks and companies that will include a write-down of loans in exchange for new equity.

However, this does not mean that in individual cases debt overhang could not harm future investment. The experience with the National Air Traffic Services (NATS) and Railtrack demonstrates the costs to the taxpayer when there is a financial crisis. However, it does suggest that the market in many cases has found a solution to it. Even so the regulator may not be comforted by the fact that only some companies have escaped the debt overhang problem. He or she may be worried about those that have failed to overcome it and as a result faced lower investment.

Possible Solutions to Financeability

What, then, are the solutions to financeability? I suggest three. First, as already argued above, there is a strong incentive for regulators to obtain better estimates of cost of capital so that they can avoid or minimise what appears like *ad hoc* adjustments to their cost of capital estimates.

Second, regulators can better profile the timing of the price cap and cash flows to the regulated company so as to reduce negative free cash flow arising from a large investment programme. The objective would be to better profile the cash flows, and make it as close to net present value neutral as possible. If this means giving commitments beyond the usual 4- or 5-year regulatory period, then so much the better. Five-year price reviews for investments which have cash flows stretching over 20 or 30 years, lack regulatory commitment.

Third, regulators should promote appropriate low-cost mechanisms for transferring licences in the event of failures. Lowering the costs of transferring licences will help to mitigate concerns that regulators have about financial failure. In some cases it is uncertain how effective they would be in mitigating the underinvestment problem. For example, should the regulator intervene when distress starts to affect the investment programme or wait for the company to default? The case of Railtrack will be a reminder of how easy it is to get this wrong. As a result, I do not believe that regulators will be able to entirely sleep soundly at night when a utility has high leverage and a large capital expenditure programme.

This contrasts with one approach that seems to have been taken by Ofwat which is to link financial ratios (and credit ratings) to adjustments to the price cap. This approach carries risks. First, there is no easy relationship between financial ratios and cost of capital. Second, linking financing constraints to the price cap directly risks producing an interaction between investment and financing decisions which will affect the value of investments and even their choice. On the whole this is undesirable. It could even lead to gaming by the regulated companies where they deliberately lever up or move projects around through time in order to obtain a higher price cap by producing an apparent financeability problem. These risks are particularly acute if the regulator confines itself to fairly short-term horizons such as a single regulatory review, when the investment returns are spread over three or even four price reviews.

OTHER MODELS OF COST OF CAPITAL

The second theme of the chapter is that regulators should consider using other models of cost of capital, at least as a cross-check on the CAPM calculated cost of capital. It is not a sweeping generalisation to say that most finance scholars would not use the CAPM on its own as a benchmark of performance. There is a general acceptance that market movements are not the only source of risk. The most popular alternative model is Fama and French's (1997) three-factor model. This model uses three different proxies for risk in the economy to estimate the cost of equity capital for a company: market movements (as in the CAPM), small minus big firm returns and high minus low book-to-market firms' returns. Thus, for a particular company Fama and French estimate three coefficients, measuring the sensitivity of the company's returns (that is, the betas) to each of these proxies for aggregate sources of risk.

This three-factor model seems to do better at explaining returns than the CAPM, which relies on only one factor, excess returns on the market. John Cochrane, in his book, *Asset Pricing* (2001), argues:

Book-market sorted portfolios show a large variation in average returns that is unrelated to market betas. The Fama–French three-factor model successfully explains the average returns of the 25 size and book-to-market sorted portfolios with a three-factor model. (p. 237)

James Davies, VP Dimensional Trust (2001) says:

For investors, there are two crucial points to remember. First, factors based on value and size have explained much of the common variation in US stock returns for the past three quarters of a century. Second, value and size premiums have been observed in several other countries, with the value premium being observed in nearly every country that has been studied. While these observations are consistent with a risk-based story, they do not prove anything. (Section IX, Conclusions)

Table 7.1 reproduces US industry costs of equity data provided by Fama and French (1997) using both the CAPM and the three-factor model described above. The costs of equity are very different in some cases. For example, in the case of utilities the cost of equity is 5.41 per cent using the three-factor model compared with only 3.39 per cent using the CAPM.

Table 7.2 provides estimates of cost of equity for a sample of UK utility companies, using data provided by Gregory et al. (2003). The data are for 13 utility companies. To avoid controversy I have omitted the names of the companies and simply identified them by a number. For 11 of these companies, the cost of equity using the three-factor model is higher than that using the CAPM; for the remaining two it is lower. The average cost of

Table 7.1   Estimates of US industry costs of equity using the three-factor model

Industry	CAPM	FF 3-factor
Aircraft	6.43	7.54
Banks	5.55	8.08
Chemicals	5.57	6.58
Computers	5.29	2.49
Construction	6.52	6.42
Food	4.44	4.09
Petroleum & Gas	4.32	4.93
Pharmaceuticals	4.71	0.09
Tabacco	4.08	5.56
Utilities	3.39	5.41

Source: Fama and French (1997).

Table 7.2   Cost of equity using CAPM and the three-factor model for 13 UK utilities, 1993–2003

Stock	CAPM	FF 3-factor
1	6.36	8.91
2	7.30	9.83
3	11.84	13.67
4	9.26	6.97
5	6.72	8.02
6	6.22	8.20
7	6.58	6.88
8	5.52	8.01
9	6.10	7.33
10	6.08	8.14
11	7.88	10.32
12	6.37	7.82
13	6.08	4.52
EW portfolio	7.14	8.38

Note: EW = equally weighted.

Source: Gregory et al. (2003) and own calculations.

equity for all 13 companies is 8.38 per cent compared with only 7.14 per cent using the CAPM.

Table 7.3 replicates the results in Table 7.2, except that I fix the one factor, the market excess returns (that is, the equity premium) at 4 per cent, in order to capture what regulators actually use for the equity risk premium. The numbers do not change very much; the average cost of equity is higher for both models but the cost of equity remains higher for the three-factor model than for the CAPM in 11 of the 13 cases, as in Table 7.2.

My own view is that regulators should use the three-factor model as a cross-check on the CAPM, particularly as an independent dataset is now available. The CAPM is from the evidence clearly not 'the holy grail'. Other models are widely used and these should inform regulatory decisions. This is particularly so in recent years when the CAPM numbers for utility companies has proved less than robust. Estimates of beta, for example, can provide very different answers using daily, weekly or monthly price data, while there is considerable variation in estimates over time. Are these differences the results of statistical artifacts or changes in real underlying risks? We do not know for sure. However, the use of other reputable models will provide important supplementary evidence.

*Table 7.3   Cost of equity using CAPM and the three-factor model for 13
             UK utilities, with 4 per cent market equity premium
             (1993–2003)*

Stock	CAPM	FF 3-factor
1	6.60	8.53
2	7.69	9.85
3	13.01	15.48
4	9.99	7.75
5	7.01	8.55
6	6.43	8.01
7	6.85	6.60
8	5.61	7.79
9	6.29	7.21
10	6.27	7.98
11	8.38	11.52
12	6.61	7.77
13	6.26	4.63
EW portfolio	7.51	8.62

Note: EW = equally weighted.

SETTING COSTS OF CAPITAL FOR DIFFERENT PARTS OF THE BUSINESS

In the third theme of this chapter, I shall address an issue that regulators must often consider but usually shy away from, and that is whether to impose differential costs of capital for different parts of a utility company's business.

As a matter of principle it should be generally accepted that a company's cost of capital should not be used for all new investments. Risks differ and the risk-adjusted costs of capital will also differ. We have been teaching our students for 30 years or more that it is likely that differences in risk will justify the use of different costs of capital. For example, would we expect the cost of capital to be the same for a new investment compared with an existing one? Compare a new drug with an existing one, a developed oilfield with an undeveloped one, a regulated business with an unregulated one.

In our first-year finance class we illustrate these principles using Figure 7.3. There we show that a single cost of capital used for investments of different risks will lead to the rejection of low-risk profitable projects and the acceptance of high-risk unprofitable ones. On average these mistakes do not average out.

Required return

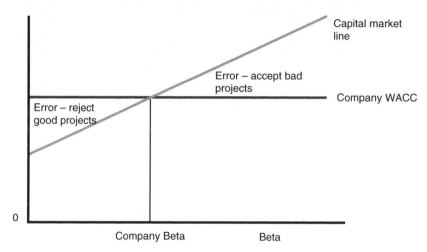

Figure 7.3   Mistakes in investment appraisal when using a single-company WACC

Ofcom has recently set different costs of capital for different parts of BT's business. I should say that I advised Ofcom on this matter so you may regard me as prejudiced or informed, or indeed both. It was stated that: 'Ofcom's view is that a more robust approach to modeling the relationship between risk and return will bring about significant improvements in welfare' (Ofcom, June, 2005). Ofcom set different WACCs for the copper access business and for the rest of BT, 10 per cent for the former and 11.4 per cent for the latter (Ofcom, August 2005, p. 4). In another change that recognised that different risks deserved different costs of capital, Ofcom proposed 'to assess the value of real options on a case-by-case basis . . . [where] wait and see options have a significant value' (ibid., p. 5).

In a robust response, BT responded by not disagreeing with the principle but rather arguing:

> The strongest argument cited by stakeholders against estimating an equity beta for BT's copper access business was that, in the absence of pure play compara-tors (i.e. companies that offered only copper access services), a beta for BT's copper access business could not be estimated with any reliability. (ibid., p. 4)

My own view is that this is too high a hurdle. Moreover, it is wise to recognise that pure plays are rarely 'pure', particularly where an indus-try benchmark is used. The benchmarking of a business against other companies primarily or solely in the same industry ignores the issues of size and book-to-market, precisely the issues I raised earlier when I discussed the Fama–French three-factor model. There have been other cases where pure plays were not available but some judgement was made on differential risks. For example, The Competition Authority agreed to raise the British Airports Authority's cost of capital by between 0.25 and 0.5 per cent because of its proposed investment in Terminal 5; in my view they used two costs of capital in everything but name. In a Treasury-sponsored study of rates of return in Private Finance Initiative (PFI) projects, Pricewaterhouse Coopers used utility betas as benchmarks for PFI projects that were not in the same industries. Instead judgements were made on the basis of a rough similarity of regulation and the relative certainty of income streams.

This issue will arise again in other regulated industries, gas and electricity. Indeed, Ofgem has already stated that 'there may be differences in the risk profiles of NGET and the distribution companies, so that this does not necessarily mean that the allowed rate of return for NGET will be the same as for electricity distribution' (Ofgem, 2004).

Under what circumstances might we go along with disaggregation? There are three guides: the businesses must be identifiable, there must be prima facie differences in risk, and the differences must be significant. I mention all of these because there is a danger that regulators will take a chance and try to use differences in risk to reduce the profits of utilities without due cause.

HOW CAN WE REDUCE THE CONFLICTS ARISING FROM COST OF CAPITAL ESTIMATION?

I believe that the cost of capital debate among utility companies and regulators has advanced our knowledge. However, the adversarial nature of that debate and the fact that a great deal of money is spent can colour our judgement of the issues. As a result, I would like to resurrect a proposal that Colin Mayer and I made informally to regulators some years ago. We suggested then that a standing committee of economists be appointed that would review new evidence for cost of capital estimation and provide regular updates both on existing and new models, and on estimation of the relevant variables. The committee's proposals would initially at least not be binding but I would guess that if such proposals were well constituted, both regulators and companies would use them. I believe that such a proposal would not only save money, but much more than that, bring much greater independence into the decision-making process.

NOTES

1. I wish to thank Pedro Saffi for excellent research assistance. I am grateful to Colin Mayer and Colin Robinson for comments on an earlier draft, and to Tim Jenkinson and Dieter Helm for helpful discussions. I am solely responsible for the views expressed in this chapter.
2. See a summary of the evidence by Eckbo et al. (2005).

REFERENCES

Cochrane, John (2001), *Asset Pricing*, Princeton, NJ: Princeton University Press.

Commission for Aviation Regulation (2005), 'Commission Paper CP3/2005: Determination on maximum levels of airport charges', Dublin, September.

Da Silva, Luis Correia (2006), 'Choosing between debt and equity: at what cost?', presentation to Water UK City Conference, April.

Davies, James (2001), 'Explaining stock returns: a literature survey', December, http://library.dfaus.com/articles/explaining_stock_returns/.

Department of Trade and Industry (DTI) (2004), 'The drivers and public policy consequences of increased gearing', DTI, London, October.

Eckbo, E., R.W. Masulis and O. Norl (2005), 'Security offerings: a survey', Working Paper No. 2005–08, Tuck School of Business, November.

Fama, Eugene and Kenneth French (1997), 'Industry costs of equity', *Journal of Financial Economics*, February, 153–93.

Franks, Julian and Sergey Sanzhar (2005), 'Evidence of debt overhang from distressed equity issues', working paper, London Business School, February.

Gregory, Alan, Richard Harris and Maria Michou (2003), 'Contrarian investment and macroeconomic risk', *Journal of Business Finance and Accounting*, January–March, 213–55.

Ofcom (2005), 'Ofcom's approach to risk in the assessment of the cost of capital and second consultation in relation to BT's equity beta', 23 June 2005.

Ofcom (2005), 'Ofcom's approach to risk in the assessment of the cost of capital', Executive Summary, August 2005.

Ofgem (2004), 'Electricity distribution price control review: Final proposals', London, November.

Ofwat (2004), 'Future water and sewerage charges 2005–10: Final determinations', Birmingham, December.

OXERA (Oxford Economic Research Associates) (2005), 'Utility financing', Report prepared for Utility Finance Group, Oxford, 19 September.

Parrino, Robert and Michael Wiesbach (1999), 'Measuring investment distortions arising from stockholder–bondholder conflicts', *Journal of Financial Economics*, **53**, 3–42.

CHAIRMAN'S COMMENTS

Philip Fletcher

I agree with a great deal of what Julian says. What I want to do is to offer some thoughts, sticking to my own last, and offer a few examples and expansions on some of the points that he makes.

Some of the issues faced by Ofwat are, to a greater or lesser extent, relevant also in other parts of the utility regulation field. We can all agree, to start with, that setting the cost of capital for regulated industries is not, at least any longer, a precise science. CAPM does not provide the firm foundation which regulators would like to see. It compares with Winston Churchill's view of democracy: the worst form of government except for all the others. We do not have a magic wand, Holy Grail Julian called it, to look to. It is extremely helpful to have the developing work around Fama–French, and a series of other issues. I agree with Julian that no regulator should rely on one approach, certainly not the CAPM on recent evidence. But the track record of the other possible models is still relatively short, and therefore I go with him completely in saying you should look across the board at various different approaches.

So where does that leave an unfortunate regulator? For Ofwat in 2004, it left us facing the need to enable water companies to finance another very large capital programme – another, that is after £50 billion spent up to 2005 since privatisation. Negative cash flow has applied for all companies since 1989, and there is no prospect that these very large programmes are going to fall away, at least with any certainty, even from 2010. Looking ahead there is the continuing capital maintenance need, which accounts for about half the overall programme up to 2010, security of supply issues – and possibly a very large further environmental programme in prospect, under the Water Framework Directive. At the same time, it is incumbent on a regulator to set a cost of capital that does not featherbed the companies, does not make life too easy for them, but requires them to search for greater efficiency, whether it is in financing or any other part of their functions. But it must also ensure, as long as the companies are efficient, continuing access to the markets. So back to the pragmatic approach, which is how we arrived at the financeability element on top of a 5.1 per cent post-tax, real terms, weighted average cost of capital.

Why did we come up with this financeability element? Simply because, as Julian has quite correctly described, it was a pragmatic approach to the need, as we saw it, to ensure that companies could finance their functions. We did not use their individual financial structures, but used a consistent structure applied across the board, and thereby reduced any temptation to gamble on a particular high-risk structure. Using this common, reasonably cautious financial structure, we looked at a basket of financial ratios, incorporating within it all the main parameters favoured by the credit rating agencies. We do not say that each company must hit each ratio each year for the five-year period, far from it. But we asked ourselves how each company looked pragmatically against this basket. Incidentally we have also, much to the companies' chagrin, taken away the benefits of the tax shield, where that was available to them. This was for the benefit of customers, who were given the tax shield by the chancellor in the first place. But that perhaps is material for another time.

Hence financeability, a pragmatic approach, looking at the City's attitude to risk. We used a similar approach, at less cost, in 1999. Our aim was to avoid deterioration in the balance sheets, and that of course requires of the companies that they should not overdistribute. Were they to do so, then Ofwat, even under its new authority from April 2006, is unlikely to look sympathetically at any company that got into trouble effectively at its customers' expense. So it would be wrong to assume, for Ofwat or any other regulator, that the approach taken last time applies at the next review. Again, gamers beware.

Now, Julian has correctly suggested that regulators ought to be working together on some of these issues, and we are. Taking account of the very real differences in characteristics of the various sectors that we regulate, we are thinking together around cost of capital issues, and we are approaching the stage where Ofgem and Ofwat, which have been doing a particular piece of work around financeability, are going to publish a study. It has been subject to proper scrutiny before it comes out, because we do not want to make fools of ourselves. But it will be published for an open consultation early in the New Year 2006.[1]

As we move forward towards the next water review in 2009, elements of financeability may become increasingly unnecessary, as confidence in companies' performance, in the approach taken by the regulator improves, and as the City itself develops and the pattern of very low debt rates becomes, if it does become, more firmly established. All those factors will be taken into account before the cost of capital is established at the next review.

Meanwhile, company failure has so far been avoided. For all the main sectors, provisions for coping with company failure do exist, but apart from the rather specialist case of Railtrack, they have not so far had to be used seriously and in earnest. They are, however, tested from time to time behind closed doors to make sure that they are robust should they ever need to be used. I share Julian's view that the system could cope perfectly well if it absolutely had to with one or two companies going to the wall. It would obviously be more difficult if the whole sector got into trouble. That would be a regulatory nightmare, and is one of the reasons that I am reasonably comfortable with the variety of financial structures in the water sector. There is strength in the various different structures going forward.

Many other interesting questions arise from Julian's chapter – for example, there is his suggestion that the Competition Commission should have a standing expert committee looking at these issues. It is noticeable that there has not been a very recent reference from at least my part of the regulated sector, or on large areas of Ofgem's work. That means one area of uncertainty is what the Competition Commission would do if it had to deal with a real case. There are interesting questions about how that might be addressed.

NOTE

1. The Ofwat/Ofgem consultation paper 'Financing Networks' was published in February 2006 and is available on the website www.ofwat.gov.uk. A response to the consultation was published in Ofwat/Ofgem, 'Financing Networks: Summary of Responses', August 2006, available on the Ofwat website www.ofwat.gov.uk.

8. A strategic approach to the economic regulation of spectrum, telecoms and broadcasting

Ed Richards

PART I

INTRODUCTION

In talking about our strategic approach to regulation of spectrum, telecoms and broadcasting, I shall cover four main areas:

- consider Ofcom's general approach to economic regulation;[1]
- review some of our key regulatory actions from an economic perspective;
- set these in the context of an underlying approach to economic regulation; and
- conclude by identifying some challenges which still remain and which we shall have to address in consultation with others in the near future.

OFCOM'S GENERAL APPROACH

In an article written by Michael Beesley, who gave his name to this important annual series of lectures on regulation,[2] I came across a succinct and valuable summary of the core tasks of regulation as Michael saw them. With his co-author, Stephen Littlechild, he placed promoting competition at the heart of a regulators' purpose:

> Promoting competition involves facilitating the entry of new competitors, including the entry of existing competitors into new parts of the market. To do this effectively involves three main steps.
> The first is to assess the likely pattern of entry over the foreseeable future. This will require a prediction of likely changes in technological and market conditions, since these will often provide the necessary opportunities for market entry.

The second step is to identify decisions that the regulator himself can make in order to change the regulatory framework and to assess the likely impact of these changes on the future pattern of entry. Examples of these regulatory decisions (in the British system) are the licensing of new entrants, identification and prohibition of anti-competitive practices, determination of interconnect or common carrier (use of system charges), collection and publication of relevant information, and so on.

The third step is to choose which regulatory changes to make. Other things being equal, the preferred changes are those likely to have the greatest positive impact on entry. (p. 466)

This seems to me to be a very good place to begin. It is an encapsulation which has a strong sense of regulatory *strategy* at the heart of its message:

● understand the context in which you work;
● identify all the levers at your disposal and their relative efficacy; and
● make choices between competing approaches which in sum amount to a strategic approach.

Ofcom was conceived many years ago, but born only on 29 December 2003. As the newest of the sectoral regulators, our job was indeed to consider exactly what approach to regulation we were going to take – interestingly, not with a single chief executive or director general, but as a board of nine people.

For Ofcom of course, there is a significant additional dimension to those objectives that I described above. We are *not* purely an economic regulator of the kind that Beesley had in mind. Our duties require us to be concerned with both the citizen and the consumer. Our task is to navigate a path between these sometimes complementary but occasionally competing conceptions of the purposes and ends of regulatory activity.

Our approach can be characterised as seeking to apply economic principles wherever we can, even to the darker recesses of the cultural pole of our twin duties. This is not to stage a 'takeover of the economists' but rather the more limited objective of illuminating complex problems using the tools of economics, as a means of making a rounded, informed judgement.

We begin always by seeking to embed our approach in sound general principles of regulation; evidence based, transparent, consultative, proportionate and as predictable as possible.

In developing our regulatory strategy we have sought:

● to be engaged with consumers and industry to understand these changes and developments, thereby avoiding the role of passive observer;

- to reflect the highly dynamic nature of industry and technological evolution, remaining therefore at all times cautious of an excessively static view of markets;
- to take a broad view, seeking to look at the connections and similarities between obstacles to competition across a range of markets rather than to focus exclusively on each economic market in isolation; and
- to make choices between competing approaches, based on evidence and analysis and thorough review.

In a sense we have no option but to take this approach. Media and communications markets are highly dynamic, more so today than arguably at any time in their history. They are driven by great technological change and a speed of change which means that decisions made on the basis of static analysis, assessing a narrow set of evidence, will be overtaken by events.

We are in a period of unprecedented change. From analogue to digital, from narrowband to broadband, from passive to interactive services, from circuit switched to packet switched internet provider (IP) networks and many more rapid technological changes. It is precisely for these reasons, for the tumultuous change that these developments represent, that one further principle is at the heart of our approach. That is the wise counsel which advises that regulatory intervention needs to be weighed against the option of doing nothing or at least doing less.

There are at least two cases where this holds: first, where market failure may exist in some form, but where the costs of regulatory intervention outweigh any benefits from taking action; and second, where the risk is specifically to nascent competition, and the cost of regulatory intervention is to inhibit the development of that competition by creating new or higher costs of doing business.

As ever with strategy, an organisation's approach is defined as much by what it does *not* do as by what it does do. Our approach is *not*:

- a process by which we try and determine which products, technologies and firms should succeed, as was the case for so much of the history of spectrum management, for example;
- nor is it a process which looks to create specific market outcomes, with predetermined market shares, levels of switching or quantities of investment.

It *is* a structured approach that seeks to be anticipatory, informed and analytical:

- we try to take account of the trade-offs inherent in regulation. For example, the problems faced by market entrants against the legitimate rights of incumbents;
- we try to consider regulatory activity in the round, identifying options as part of an overall set of policies influencing an industry and group of markets in ways that serve the interests of consumers, recognising that changes in one place may give rise to consequences in another; and
- we try to identify clear aims, such as focusing regulation at the real economic bottlenecks, targeting action on these root causes and ensuring that this is coupled with deregulation in areas where effective competition can be established.

I shall now turn to how this approach has manifested itself in some key areas of policy. However, before doing so, I should acknowledge Ofcom's other important role as a national competition authority. I shall focus on *ex ante* economic regulation, but we should not forget Ofcom's ability to deal with competition concerns through the application *ex post* of competition law – something that we always consider before embarking on *ex ante* regulation.

PART II

REVIEW OF KEY ECONOMIC REGULATION BY OFCOM

I shall begin with fixed link telecommunications. In fixed telecoms we have had to address the combination of economic bottlenecks and vertical integration.

Unlike traditional utilities, much of the fixed telecoms network is potentially competitive. There are plenty of long-distance networks in the UK. But many customers only have access to one supplier for the line into their house. Cable covers around 50 per cent of homes, and there are other operators in some dense urban areas, especially for business consumers. But anyone wanting to offer anything close to a national service faces this bottleneck: no-one other than BT (British Telecommunications plc) can viably supply the line between the customer and the exchange, and in many cases from the exchange further back in the network, too.

Anyone wanting to compete with BT in the parts of the network that are competitive needs access to this bottleneck. Yet BT is a vertically integrated company. Its wholesale customers, to whom it sells access to this bottle-neck, are also its retail competitors. So the combination of vertical integration and market power in this bottleneck part of the network gives BT an incentive to discriminate against its wholesale customers.

The traditional remedy to this was to require BT to provide open access to these bottleneck facilities, and to do so on cost-based terms. That was combined with further general requirements not to discriminate, and not to engage in margin squeezing.

These remedies do not take away the incentive on BT to discriminate. They restrict its *ability* to discriminate – but only to the extent that such discrimination can be detected, and demonstrated. As a regulator, we can fairly easily prove price discrimination when it happens. But non-price discrimination is a different story. Interconnection of networks requires agreement at a very detailed level to ensure that services work smoothly. Local loop unbundling, for example requires rules about issues such as where competitors' equipment can be located in an exchange, who can have access to the key to the exchange, what power supply is available, and a host of other matters.

All of these are real barriers to competition, but if everyone had an incentive to solve them, they could be solved pretty quickly. That alignment of incentives did not exist and the outcome was endless disputes and allegations of discrimination. The problem is not confined to local loop unbundling. It applies also to a whole range of other wholesale products, such as line rental, carrier pre-selection, partial private circuits and leased lines.

To avoid regulatory micro management, one obvious solution would be structural separation: the separation of ownership of the bottleneck access network from the competitive parts of the network. In our telecoms review, we looked closely at whether this was the right answer.

This solution has arguably worked in other regulated network industries. But there are more difficulties with structural separation in telecoms than in other network industries – and let me remind you at this point of the earlier injunction to ensure that the benefits of regulatory action are indeed higher than the costs of that intervention.

There are two main problems. One is that telecoms is so fast-moving. The dividing line between the bottleneck and the competitive part of the network might be in one place today, but in a completely different place tomorrow. If you had a fibre network for example, you might not even bother with local exchanges at all. If you break up the network for good, it cannot adapt; you fossilise your break point in one place for ever.

Second, the bottleneck is not at the same level in the network everywhere. In the City of London, for large business customers, some would argue that there may not be a bottleneck at all. But for a small telephone exchange in Cornwall, the bottleneck is unlikely to be limited to just the line between the customer and the exchange; it includes all the equipment in the exchange, plus the line from the exchange 50 miles back to the nearest big town.

So our review settled on a concept that has not been used in telecoms networks anywhere else in the world: what we call 'equality of access' (Figure 8.1). This involves two things. First, equivalence of input on a product-by-product basis. If BT uses the bottleneck part of its network, it must make *exactly the same* wholesale product available to its wholesale customers, on *exactly the same* terms, and using *exactly the same* systems and processes, as it supplies it to itself. Not a similar product, *the same* product. The reason for this is the incentive that it gives BT. If a wholesale product or system is not up to scratch, then its own downstream business suffers too.

The second aspect of equality of access is organisational change within BT. It is no good BT's wholesale customers sharing their commercial plans with BT – which they have to, if they want to buy its bottleneck assets – only to see these plans gradually leak out to the parts of BT that are their direct competitors. So the organisational change in BT has set up a new, ring-fenced division called Openreach, which controls the bottleneck asset. Openreach is independent in many respects: it has its own brand; significant discretionary capital expenditure and its staff bonuses are based on Openreach's performance, not BT's.

To reinforce these changes, BT has established the Equality of Access Board which will monitor, report and advise the BT Group plc board on

Equivalence at product level

* Access to same or similar set of regulated wholesale products as BT

* Same product, price, systems, product development processes

* Incentive compatible

Operational separation

* Operational separation of unit providing bottleneck products

* To address incentives and ability for unfair treatment

Source: Ofcom (2005).

Figure 8.1   Equality of access

BT's provision of products on an equivalence of input basis and on the operation of Openreach.

All of this sounds like a lot of regulation, but our aim is that this should permit significant *deregulation* in time. This is for two reasons.

First, by focusing regulation on the bottleneck part of the network (Figure 8.2) we expect to be able to deregulate elsewhere. You can already see examples of this: we are deregulating aspects of retail business telecoms services and examining the possibilities for deregulation of large business markets and relaxation in the retail line rental price cap and the case for changes in leased line regulation in major urban areas. We will also look at the potential for deregulation in areas including wholesale international calls, wholesale broadband access and interconnection services and the need for a residential price cap at all – all assuming that the necessary competition concerns can be met.

Second, if you can give BT the incentive to build fit for purpose wholesale products first time around, then you have a good chance of avoiding being drawn into detailed product design – an area unequivocally best left to companies rather than regulators if at all possible.

A key feature of this approach is that it was not a market review, but a strategic review of what we wanted our overarching policy approach to be. We looked at a series of markets together not in isolation and tried to establish an approach that would be effective in general as well as in specific cases. We were able to do this by accepting undertakings from BT under the Enterprise Act – the key part of our competition law framework which enables us to deal not just with specific instances but

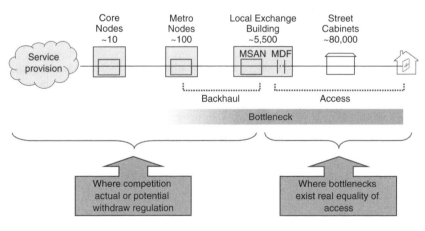

Source: Ofcom (2005).

Figure 8.2   Focus regulation on bottlenecks

where features of a market are preventing, restricting or distorting competition.

BROADCASTING

I want to describe three areas which come together as the components of what we are trying to achieve in broadcasting. The first is the move towards digital switchover, second is the range of measures that are deployed to support competition in broadcasting and third, the case for continuing market intervention in the form of public service broadcasting.

The broadcasting market is becoming more competitive and open. One of the key changes taking place in broadcasting is the rise of digital television driven through satellite, cable and terrestrial platforms. This process, which brings dozens or hundreds of channels to viewers, will become universal as a result of switchover.

At present this is market driven, as consumers choose to adopt digital TV to take advantage of the great increase in choice offered by the multi-channel environment. But in due course it will involve some compulsion (at least for those who wish to continue watching television).

We have supported this approach:

- it offers the prospect of a far more efficient use of the spectrum;
- it hastens the development of a well-functioning broadcast market by eliminating many of the barriers to entry that characterised the analogue age; and
- it offers a significant increase in choice to viewers and listeners which would otherwise not be available.

Alongside this we also have a range of measures which support competition in the broadcasting market. These cover two broad areas: access to distribution and access to content or the commissioning of content. Our work in this area is very much work in progress but the approach includes:

- cross-promotion rules intended to prevent the leveraging of a position in one market into a separate one;
- intervention to address the imbalance in the negotiating positions between independent producers and vertically integrated broadcasters; and
- a regulatory regime for electronic programme guides, conditional access and access services to ensure that provision is made on fair, reasonable and non-discriminatory terms.

I might also mention work on premium rights, Digital Terrestrial Television (DTT) capacity and minimum carriage requirements.

Finally, we have made no secret of the fact that we believe that a fair system should be applied to all broadcasters, which means including the BBC under the regime of *ex ante* powers in the broadcasting area. Competition in broadcasting and the evolution towards a more open market is of course part of a wider debate. We must also consider the role of public service broadcasting, (PSB).

The origins of PSB of course lie very much in the analogue age. A key economic feature of broadcasting in the analogue world is its public good characteristics. Broadcasts in this world are both non-excludable and non-rival: when a programme is broadcast to enable one person to receive it, it is available to all who have a TV set in the broadcast area (that is, it is non-excludable), and consumption by one person does not lead to a reduction in the amount available to others (that is, it is non-rival in consumption). This leads to a situation where the market would underprovide, because there is no means to charge viewers for what they watch. Advertising funded channels are to some extent an answer to this problem, but under those arrangements there is no direct way in which viewers can express their preferences.

In the age of satellite and cable this has changed. While broadcasts are non-rival in consumption, there is the scope for excluding non-payers and for the market to reflect viewers' preferences. This means that it is possible for a market to operate, with suppliers charging consumers according to their level of consumption. The non-rival characteristic remains, which is essentially the same as there being a zero marginal cost. This potentially leads to inefficiency, as the costs of making programmes need to be recovered. Prices need to be significantly above marginal cost to recover these costs, and this leads to the exclusion of some viewers whose valuation exceeds the marginal cost of supply. Pricing strategies of bundling and discounting ameliorate this inefficiency but it remains to some degree.

While prices which depart from marginal cost are common and are not usually regarded as a reason for intervention, more weight might be given to this issue in broadcasting. This is for two reasons: first the inefficiency is potentially large, as it is equal to the total valuation of the programmes of all excluded viewers; but second, and I think more importantly, because the inefficiency arises in the form of exclusion, this might be regarded as a socially, as well as an economically, undesirable outcome.

This concern is underlined by a second feature of broadcasting – the presence of externalities in the form of benefits accruing to, or costs being borne by parties other than the producer or the consumer involved in the market transaction. To take one very obvious example, broadcasting often has an educational dimension, and this may generate benefits to parties other than the viewer of the broadcast. There are also broader benefits to society which can be generated by programmes with a strong element of information – news, current affairs and documentaries being obvious cases. Content which makes people aware of wider issues in society, the way in which a healthy democracy works and so on may lead to our society generally being one in which people prefer to live, compared with an alternative where there is no, or less, broadcasting of this type.

Quantifying this type of effect or value is no easy task and it is not one that I would claim we or anyone else has run to ground. However, there is some interesting evidence. Research carried out by the BBC and Human Capital in 2004 asked people how much they would be willing to pay to avoid being excluded from watching BBC programmes, and then how much they would be willing to pay to avoid the BBC being closed down. The first of these values is an indicator of their private valuation of BBC programmes that they watch themselves, while the second includes also a broader benefit to society – how much they believe we benefit from the BBC being available to others. In the survey, the second valuation was significantly greater than the first – by 10 to 20 per cent. So there appears to be a significant difference in private and social valuations in this area.

Does this matter, in the sense of there being a reason for intervention? Well, individuals, when they decide what to purchase and at what price, will reflect only the first of these values in their decisions. They will not reflect the broader social value because they will believe that they will receive these benefits whether they make that additional payment or not. This is similar to the free-rider problem with public goods. Thus, a subscription-type service would not fully reflect the benefits generated, and there would be too little PSB-type content produced. So while it is difficult to quantify the relevant factors accurately, it is clear that such effects do exist.

High-quality broadcasting is also sometimes argued to be a merit good, whose value exceeds that which an individual consumer would place on it. This leads to an underprovision by the market left to its own devices and this underprovision justifies intervention to raise the level of provision of this type of programming. This type of intervention is more likely to be more effective in achieving its aim of promoting the viewing of high-quality programming where viewers have restricted choice over what they view. This was the situation in the old analogue five-channel world, but the situation is very different in a multi-channel world. Of course, this is a challenge for the externalities argument as well.

There is one further argument that warrants consideration. This is that the underlying economics of broadcasting might tend to lead to a concentrated industry structure in which consumer preferences are not always fully reflected in the operation of the market. In particular, in an oligopolistic broadcasting market, the most likely detrimental consequence is that producers would attempt to improve profitability by reducing costs through offering low-quality but cheap to produce programmes.

Oligopolistic market structures are not easily dealt with under competition law and, in an area as important to people and society as broadcasting, there is a case for addressing this quality issue by ensuring the existence of broadcasters operating on a not-for-profit basis to set quality standards. This is an argument which is likely to become less persuasive as the market functions more effectively, with reductions in barriers to entry and the ability to offer a range of different products and services reflecting different viewer preferences.

So the arguments for public service broadcasting intervention from an economic perspective are many and varied. Our own view is that there remains an enduring case for public service broadcasting into the digital age but that, in the future, the case will rest more on the broader citizenship benefits than the conventional consumer market failure arguments of the analogue age, see Table 8.1.

How do these three strands – digital switchover, the range of competition policy and the case for PSB – come together? Well, we can observe that one major consequence of the move to digital broadcasting and a more

Table 8.1   Relevance of market failure in broadcasting

	Pre-digital	Digital
Public goods Non-excludable, non-rival: welfare losses from charging	****	**
Market power Consumers' choices are not fully reflected in programming	****	**
Externalities Private preferences do not yield optimum outcome	****	****
Merit goods Consumer does not recognise full value of good/service	***	**
Information problems Consumers cannot make fully informed choices	***	*

Source: Internally prepared by Ofcom (2005) for this chapter.

open market is that the historic model of commercial PSB is being irreversibly undermined.

The historic model in television has been to trade PSB obligations (such as news, regional news, children's programming and so on) in return for access to scarce analogue spectrum rights at below full market value. As the value of these analogue rights declines to zero with digital switchover, so the ability to extract PSB obligations that carry a significant opportunity cost declines.

This requires us to reconcile the features of the preceding arguments. First, there is an enduring (if hard to quantify) case for public service broadcasting even in a fully digital age, but at the same time, we wish to see the market develop in the direction of more competition and more choice for viewers and listeners.

This combination is likely to lead us towards greater transparency in the economic support for PSB and some fundamental questions and almost certainly revisions to the model of how PSB is delivered, under what funding arrangements, and to what scale.

We have made a contribution to that debate – arguing that if PSB is to be maintained and strengthened (the remit we were given by parliament) then overall funding levels should be broadly in line with today's levels and that we need to consider whether a new form of intervention (a public service publisher) might be part of a revised set of institutional arrangements for delivering the aims and purposes of PSB in the post-switchover world. We look forward to a new phase of that debate in the future.

SPECTRUM

Finally, I turn to spectrum. I have left it until last in this particular triumvirate because it is typically underestimated on a number of fronts:

- it is a crucial raw material for both telecoms and broadcasting; and
- it is arguably subject to the greatest change in the direction of policy.

These changes to spectrum policy have the scope to influence profoundly and irreversibly both telecoms and broadcasting markets.

In thinking about spectrum, it is helpful to keep in mind that its two key economic characteristics are similar to those of land. First, like land, spectrum varies in quality and for high-value types of spectrum, there is scarcity and so a key question for economic efficiency is how the asset is to be allocated among competing uses and users. Second, again as in the case of land, unlimited access to it can lead to excessively intensive usage. In the case of land this leads to the well-known phenomenon of the tragedy of the commons, whereby individuals having free access to the land seek to maximise the value of *their* output, but in doing so fail to maximise the *overall* value of output.

In the case of spectrum the users interfere with each other, so attempts to increase output by one individual reduce the value derived by others. That is, there are externalities in the use of spectrum which have to be managed to allow it to be used efficiently.

In the past the problem of scarcity has been dealt with by a process in which spectrum has been assigned to users and uses on the basis of administrative judgement. Negative externalities have been dealt with by granting exclusive rights of use for particular blocks of spectrum.

Over time some economic principles have been introduced – for example, cost–benefit analysis is often used to inform the assignment process, and auctions have increasingly been used to release spectrum into the market. In addition, forms of administrative incentive pricing (AIP) have been used to confront spectrum users with the opportunity costs of the spectrum they use.

But the reach of these market mechanisms has been limited until very recently. Ofcom is committed to changing this and putting market-based measures at the heart of the spectrum allocation process. This has the potential to yield very large benefits by promoting more efficient use of spectrum. Many studies have shown that the potential benefits of allocating spectrum efficiently could be very large, running into tens of billions of pounds (see Chapter 2 by Tom Hazlett).

The measures introduced and proposed by Ofcom include:

- removal of unnecessary restrictions on type of use – or spectrum liberalisation;
- allowing free trade in rights of spectrum use;
- the use of auctions to release new spectrum into the market – a raft of which are planned for the coming months and years; and
- the use of AIP to create incentives for more efficient use in cases where public policy dictates an administrative rather than market allocation (for example, defence).

In combination these measures should result in the allocation of spectrum to its most productive use and this is the heart of our approach.

However, we also recognise that the problem of the tragedy of the commons does not apply to all parts and uses of the spectrum, and that a commons approach, rather than the granting of individual rights of use might be suitable in some circumstances. For example, the explosive growth of Wi-Fi technology, which operates in the unlicensed commons of 2.4 Ghz.

Essentially, the question of whether a commons model or an individual rights of use model should be preferred comes down to the relative sizes of the negative externality of interference and the transactions costs associated with an individual rights regime. High interference externalities favours an individual rights approach, whereas high transactions costs tends to favour a commons approach.

Indeed, an individual rights approach can bring its own problems. One example is the risk of hold-up – where multiple ownership of a piece of spectrum required for a particular enterprise confers on some owners the ability to delay or prevent the venture from going ahead unless they are to receive a large share of the benefits. This outcome has been referred to as the 'tragedy of the anti-commons'. Another potential problem is the issue of anti-competitive hoarding which also may not be straightforward to deal with.

Thus, while the individual rights approach is suitable in most cases and is certainly at the heart of our strategy, there should not be a presumption that it is always superior to a commons approach.

Nor indeed should it be assumed that there are no circumstances in which broader public policy concerns will have a bearing upon a particular spectrum decision. We have already proposed that spectrum in VHF Band III be used to allow further Digital Audio Broadcasting (DAB) compatible Broadcasting Act licences to be awarded in the interests of completing the public policy objectives associated with digital audio broadcasting, better known as digital radio. Similar debates will rage in relation to the spectrum released as a result of digital switchover.

So while our view is that markets are generally superior to regulation, our twin duties mean that we must always weigh both the interests of the consumer and those of the citizen. Equally, in those cases where administrative non-market assignments have been made, it is likely to be appropriate to apply AIP to the spectrum to encourage efficient use.

Finally, technology may well begin to allow us to have our cake and eat it. It might be possible to use some parts of spectrum for both licensed and commons applications simultaneously. This might be possible where an alternative spectrum commons use does not affect the technical use of the licensed holder and yet generates consumer value.

Accordingly, we are proposing that certain types of very low power use, such as ultra wide broadband (UWB) should be allowed to use spectrum on an unlicensed (that is, commons) basis, subject to their staying within a specified emissions limit. This type of hybrid approach to spectrum licensing – an individual rights-based approach running side by side with an unlicensed approach – has the potential to unlock large amounts of currently unrealised economic value in the way we use the spectrum. It is also a source of enormous potential innovation.

Table 8.2   Spectrum award programme

Auction/award	Bandwidth
Auction planned by March 2006	1781–1785 MHz/1876–1880 MHz (DECT Guard Band)
Auction planned Q2 2006	412–414 MHz/422–424 MHz
Awards planned for 2006/7	1785–1805 MHz (in Northern Ireland) 872–876 MHz/917–921 MHz 10, 28, 32, 40 GHz 1452–1492 MHz (L-Band)
Further awards – date to be set	2010–2025 MHz 2290–2302 MHz 2500–2690 MHz (3G Expansion Band)

Source: Internally prepared by Ofcom (2005) for this chapter.

Let me conclude this part by trying to bring a little of this to life. Over the next year or so Ofcom aims to release to the market spectrum in a variety of bands, notably the GSM–DECT Guard Bands and part of the L-Band (Table 8.2). We expect a number of exciting new technologies to compete for these bands, including those for broadband wireless access and mobile multimedia as well as new applications like GSM services for a campus or business premises.

In the slightly longer term there is a large block of spectrum – 190 MHz – which will be available for new uses across the EU from 2008. We have argued that this spectrum – the so-called 3G expansion band – should be allocated on a basis that is as technologically neutral as possible. We have also recently announced the start of our work on allocating the spectrum released from switchover – again very valuable spectrum that could be used for mobile video, high-definition television (HDTV), or 3G services for rural areas to name but a few.

PART III

UNDERLYING APPROACH AND COMMON THEMES

So is there anything that ties all this activity together?

In a sense we start with a range of market structures that many would argue are inherent to the nature of the industries in which we work – industries which exhibit network effects, increasing returns to scale, economies of density and so on.

Equally, we have the legacy of historic policy making and technological limitations which in their own way have tended to underpin the monopolistic or oligopolistic characteristics of many of these markets. Anything to do with the historic approach to spectrum illustrates this point – from the allocation of mobile licences and scarce broadcasting rights – and of course in fixed telecoms the incumbent was originally created by the state.

Our fundamental aim in relation to competition is to make more and more of these markets either contestable or, better still, subject to effective competition. The nature of our intervention is guided by two principles: first, remedies should be concerned with making markets work more effectively; and second, market failures should be tackled at their root cause – in other words as far upstream as possible, since this allows other regulation to be removed and for innovation and competition to flourish downstream.

So in spectrum the approach to assignment is market based and the approach to correcting for externalities is to define individual usage rights. This approach reduces the intervention to a minimum and targeted level and allows markets to allocate resources.

In broadcasting it involves encouraging the development of competition in the market for content – a situation in which many organisations may test their ability to create attractive services in the market rather than just a handful approved by the regulator. It means backing this increase in competition by appropriate access requirements in the distribution of such services.

In telecoms, the key market failure is the existence of enduring market power caused by barriers to entry combined with vertical integration. I have explained how we are seeking to address this problem.

In a market such as fixed telecoms and indeed many communications markets, the realistic goal is not perfect competition, but contestability or better still, effective competition. Contestability does not strictly require there to be any actual competition: the threat of entry if customers are not properly served is sufficient to discipline firms. Perfect contestability is a rare thing in real life – perhaps as rare as perfect competition – but there is no doubt that making entry easier and less costly can have a beneficial effect, both through the effect of actual entry and through the threat of entry.

Effective competitive is the idea that might best be described as a state of rivalry among firms, striving to win customers. It does not require the large numbers of small, price-taking competitors as in the perfect competition model, but it requires competitors to behave in an active, rivalrous, customer-seeking way. Effective competition and contestability therefore both describe market conditions which serve the interests of consumers, and which are realistic goals in many of the markets in which we regulate, even those which appear relatively intractable.

Our task remains to make markets more competitive and to increase the degree of contestability and effective competition by reducing barriers to entry and focusing regulation on the root causes of bottleneck power. It is this pursuit of effective competition in communications markets which characterises our overall approach to economic regulation (which must, of course, co-exist with our broader regulatory remit, that goes well beyond economic regulation). Are there any fundamental tensions in our approach? There is certainly one which we are alive to and reflects a core judgement that we have made.

A more pure Schumpeterian approach might suggest that the bottle-necks themselves could be susceptible to the forces of creative destruction, with high economic rents attracting technological development and competitive challenge. In this analysis cost-based access would of course undermine such forces.

Our judgement has been that for the fixed link access network in telecoms this is highly unlikely within a credible planning horizon. There is little if any evidence around the world to support the alternative proposition. Competing technologies may offer genuine multi-player inter-platform competition for some well-established markets but fixed link access will retain a structural advantage for the foreseeable future, particularly in markets requiring higher bandwidths. So on balance, we have taken the view that consumers are better served by a tough regime for fixed access regulation which enables downstream competition, innovation, and where possible deregulation.

That is not to say that for lower bandwidth markets we do not see significant scope for the development of inter-platform competition. Freeing up key input markets such as spectrum are crucial to such developments and are illustrated already by the potential for fixed/mobile voice call substitution and also for lower bit rate broadband. Nor does it mean that we are pessimistic about the contribution from existing high bandwidth inter-platform competition, notably cable. Look to the US to see what a healthy rivalry between DSL (digital subscriber line) and cable can deliver. And, of course, the success of a policy to increase competition in the provision of DSL, alongside cable, will itself introduce an interesting dynamic in the distribution of television and radio content.

Convergence – written off as a fad a few years ago – is an important part of the argument. Convergence allows many types of delivery systems to convey services that were previously deliverable only by a single-access technology.

So now voice, data and video can all be carried over a cable, satellite or various broadband networks – or a mixture of such networks. The multi-product network is gradually becoming a reality and will in due course begin to change the boundaries of market definition. This is shown in Figure 8.3, which was prepared by Dr Robert Pepper. While this has not happened yet, the signs are that it will be a major influence in the years to come. Technology has enabled us to begin to think of a wide variety of broadband platforms – mobile, Wi-Fi, WiMAX, DSL, cable – all capable of distributing the same or similar voice, data, video using common TCP/IP protocols.

Mobile operators are already offering video services, Sky has entered the DSL market through its purchase of Easynet, subject to regulatory clearance, BT has entered the television market and will offer on-demand video and of course cable has long provided a triple play service.

These developments sit alongside and not in opposition to our attempt to open up enduring bottlenecks to give multiple players the opportunity to provide the triple or even quadruple play services that are likely to become the focus of consumer demand in the years ahead.

This is likely to raise a number of complex but important issues in applying the regulatory and competition rules in the communications sector. There is the prospect of large players from one market exploiting technological convergence to enter adjacent markets and offer multi-play services to consumers leading to a greater number of players in the provision of each service and an increase in competition.

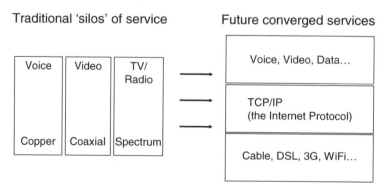

Source: Ofcom (2005). With thanks to Dr Robert Pepper.

Figure 8.3   Implication of IP: no longer one network/one service

The prospect of large players competing aggressively is an attractive one, and one that should be encouraged – it certainly sounds like effective competition. But there is a word of caution to note at the same time: large players providing bundled services might make life very difficult for providers of a single service. The test of whether this is a concern will rest with the consumer. If consumers generally want to buy services as a bundle, it will be difficult to argue that suppliers should not sell bundles. But if consumers continue to want to buy significantly on a separate basis, the question arises of whether bundling strategies by large players have an exclusionary motive.

Taken in the round we see this as an opportunity for more competition that should benefit consumers, but equally we must be alive to the potential for abusive behaviour.

PART IV

SOME ISSUES FOR THE FUTURE

Let me conclude by raising some of the issues that will require some close attention in the coming months and which I hope may spark a little debate.

The first is the interplay between competition policy and consumer policy. In many ways, a lot of what I have discussed has focused on structural rather than behavioural issues of regulation. But behavioural issues are becoming more not less prevalent as we see the development of more competitive markets and as technology opens up radical new opportunities for commercial exploitation. This is common to other sectoral experience too.

In the textbook, competition delivers the right outcomes for consumers. We never get textbook competition, especially in the communications markets. Where the consumer is ill-informed about choices available the otherwise smooth mechanisms of the market fail to deliver optimal outcomes. Equally, where consumers do not feel protected against scams and exploitation they may face direct harm and, even where a consumer is not a direct victim, the perception of an unreliable, exploitative market may itself threaten to undermine the benefits that flow from healthy competition.

This suggests that we need to consider competition policy as a set of tools that go hand in hand with consumer policy. Successful consumer policy will need to consider explicitly the effect on competition, and the potentially longer-term effect on consumer benefit. Equally, we need to make sure that competition policy initiatives are carried out in the context of an explicitly defined consumer interest, and delivery against that interest. Indeed, if we cannot define the consumer interest in any particular policy we should consider carefully the reasons for carrying through that initiative.

Second is the issue of new bottlenecks or what we might call risky bottlenecks. There is a lot of literature on how to identify and deal with long-established bottlenecks – it has been the stuff of the Beesley lectures over many years. But we also know that in general regulators should not interfere with risky investments.

But how do we proceed when both these elements are present together, as they are likely to be in the next generation of broadband access networks? The question of rewards for investment mattered much less when telecoms was a utility business with a low risk premium but telcos are now facing a very different set of challenges, with the transition of plain old telephone system (PSTN) to IP. This presents the cost of upgrading networks when there is uncertainty about the level of demand for the new services which would justify the upgrade – in other words, a major investment which by its nature carries substantial risks. This problem is increasingly recognised but there is less agreement at present on how regulators should respond.

Finally, challenges in the international arena. I have said little so far about policy developments at international, and specifically EU level. The latter in particular is of critical importance. The broad thrust of EU activity in communications is largely consistent with the approach I have outlined in this chapter. In communications policy, we do not recognise the ideological divide that is often said to characterise our relationship with Europe. In telecoms, broadcasting and spectrum management the trend in recent years in Europe has been towards much greater liberalisation and a break from the old models of industrial and cultural policy.

There are, however, one or two concerns worth noting. The first is that as we review the framework directives we need to look at their effectiveness not only in terms of a harmonised approach to the process leading up to regulatory outcomes but also perhaps in relation to the effectiveness and timeliness of remedies. In the absence of a debate of this kind, the process will remain an easy target for those who say that regulation in some member states is still being used to inhibit competition, particularly from other member states or from beyond Europe.

A second international issue ripe for debate is the issue of the role of harmonisation of spectrum use. The debate about how spectrum should be allocated could sometimes be characterised as one between 'liberalisers' on one side and 'harmonisers' on the other. The former group emphasises the role of the market in achieving an efficient allocation, the latter argues that there are benefits from ensuring a common international approach. These benefits comprise the lower equipment costs that result from the exploitation of economies of scale and the user benefits of interoperability across countries.

We remain of the view that flexible deployment of spectrum according to market needs is the best approach to unlock its true economic potential but recognise that harmonisation arguments have some merit. We would like to explore whether a market-based approach might actually produce the kind of harmonised outcome that some of our colleagues in Europe value or whether, with a proportionate level of intervention, it could be made to do so.

CLOSING REMARKS

I have set out in this chapter how I believe Ofcom's approach to economic regulation seeks to be engaged, informed and attempts to take a broad view of the industries and markets in which we work.

I have summarised our approach in key areas of fixed telecoms, broadcasting and spectrum. This has been by no means exhaustive (I have not really mentioned mobile at all and have said little about radio) but has tried to illustrate our focus on developing effective competition throughout the value chain, or at least downstream from enduring economic bottlenecks. I have highlighted the scope for convergence and the evolution of communications networks to increase competition and deliver benefits for consumers. Finally, I have noted three issues which will certainly concern us in the future.

NOTES

1. This chapter, like others in the book, focuses on economic regulation. Ofcom's (Office of Communications) remit is much broader than this. The range of Ofcom's overall duties is reflected in the twin duties to serve the interests of both consumers and citizens.
2. M.E. Beesley and S.C. Littlechild, 'The regulation of privatised monopolies in the United Kingdom', *Rand Journal of Economics*, **20**(3), Autumn 1989.

CHAIRMAN'S COMMENTS

Richard Feasey

Ed gives a characteristically fluent and persuasive account of Ofcom's activities to date and their approach to this formidable set of issues. It occurs to me that if you were to do a scorecard on Ofcom and the management approach that has been described, at least so far, as an interim scorecard, then you might make a couple of points. I have seven I want to run through very briefly on reflections on Ofcom and what is different.

The first is just the calibre of senior management in regulators, and particularly in Ofcom, sets the benchmark and demonstrates that you really get what you pay for in regulation, and given the formidable set of challenges that Ofcom faces as an institution, certainly for companies like mine, complaints about the direct costs of regulation are pretty trivial and trivial in comparison with the indirect costs of people getting it wrong.

The second thing that strikes me in observing Ofcom is that the relationship between the regulator and the various regulated groups is a bit less cosy, and there are fewer favoured constituents than there were in the past when we had vertically organised regulation between the radio communications agency, the Independent Television Commission (ITC), and the other regulators and their various constituencies. In general a degree of distancing between the regulator and regulatees as we move towards more horizontal markets is a welcome development, and we see that reflected, for example, in particular in the way in which Ofcom has gone around its approach to spectrum, in a form which would have been pretty inconceivable in the days of the radio communications agency. This is in part enabled by the changing view of the regulator of its relationship with its constituent bodies.

The third thing that strikes me at the moment is that Ofcom has managed to avoid, by and large, litigation. Litigation as a feature of regulation in the UK thus far seems to have largely disappeared from view, and we may come back to a question about whether that is a good or a bad thing, a sign of success or otherwise, but my impression, and the evidence would back it up, is that Ofcom, by and large, has managed to secure agreements of the kind we heard described with BT. Perhaps the litigation in future will be private enforcement by companies against each other rather than people suing the regulator, but there is a marked absence of litigation in the transition from Oftel to Ofcom.

The jury is out on the next three points. The first is the BT settlement on the telecoms side, and I think Ed has described the principles around that. The issue that my American friends outline is effectively a model in which – Ed said it very strikingly – we have effectively concluded that at least a certain part of the local loop is fundamentally uncontestable, at least in the foreseeable future. Previous regulators have not said that in such stark terms, but the consequence is that essentially the UK will have a copper network, which will have varying degrees of technology overlaid on the underlying copper network. My American friends say, well that is fine, but actually in the United States, where you have platform competition between cable companies and telephone companies, the telephone companies are being forced to take out their copper and replace it with fibre all the way to the home. In the long term, there is a question of whether Ofcom's model of essentially regulating the copper assets of BT is sufficient to deliver to the UK the kind of underlying local access infrastructure that in the long term we need.

The other unresolved issue is the whole question about pay TV, and Ed referred to that as work in progress. As somebody who started my initial experiences with Oftel in the cable industry nearly 15 years ago now, the cable industry seems to have rather disappeared off the map as a part of the future vision of competitive broadband infrastructure in the UK, and those of us who spend a fair bit of time in the United States would contrast that with the central role of re-emerging cable companies in the United States at the moment as major players, both in the public policy debate and in the commercial environment that we see emerging in the United States at the moment. Curiously silent and curiously absent in the UK it seems, despite the UK, at least 15 years ago, championing itself as a leader in attracting inward investment into the UK. The cable industry seems a very long time ago now.

As regards the final two challenges, one that is still open is where the beginning of Oftel's international charm offensive began – that a lot of people, at least in the telecoms industry, said essentially that we still have an irrational market structure, we have too many players in these markets, and markets need to concentrate. It is very easy for regulators to encourage and to support people venturing into new markets, so venturing across market boundaries is all fine and we are all in favour of that, but there is another question sitting in the background in the UK, that Ofcom has yet to be asked properly, which is how far are you prepared to go in your capacity as a competition authority in allowing market concentration, if that proves to be necessary or is expected by the capital markets in order to fund the kind of investments that the UK will need to upgrade infrastructure, high-risk infrastructure going forward?

The final point that Ed mentioned at the end and I would also underline is that Ofcom has undersold itself internationally, given the amount of thought and the formidable capabilities that we have seen on display. As somebody who operates in an international environment, the UK historically, in part because of people like Michael Beesley many years ago, has been regarded as a thought leader in areas of regulation. Ofcom have been understandably concerned to get their own thoughts in order before going out and persuading the rest of the world of their case, and now we see some evidence that Ofcom is going to engage in that, and that will be a thoroughly welcome development.

The final thought is that Ed still ends with a question that says where is the consumer voice and how strong is it? The great challenge for regulators is how do you stop being somebody who just shifts rents around the industry between one player and another? One of the remaining challenges and observations that I would make is that I am not sure where the consumer voice is. We have heard a lot about producers' access to inputs, to spectrum, to unbundled facilities, to production facilities, to programming guides and so on and so forth, but articulating how all this complicated jargon-ridden stuff translates into something meaningful for consumers remains a challenge, not only for Ofcom but probably for everybody engaged in this sort of activity.

Index